Practical
Group Therapy

Practical
Group Therapy

William H. Friedman

Practical
Group Therapy

A Guide for Clinicians

Jossey-Bass Publishers

San Francisco • London • 1989

PRACTICAL GROUP THERAPY
A Guide for Clinicians
   by William H. Friedman

Copyright © 1989 by: Jossey-Bass Inc., Publishers
                       350 Sansome Street
                       San Francisco, California 94104
                              &
                       Jossey-Bass Limited
                       28 Banner Street
                       London EC1Y 8QE

Library of Congress Cataloging-in-Publication Data

Friedman, William H.
   Practical group therapy.

   (Jossey-Bass social and behavioral science series)
   Bibliography: p.
   Includes index.
   1. Group psychotherapy.   I. Title.   II. Series.
RC488.F76 1989   616.89′152   88-46082
ISBN 1-55542-139-3

Manufactured in the United States of America

The paper in this book meets the guidelines for
permanence and durability of the Committee on
Production Guidelines for Book Longevity of the
Council on Library Resources.

JACKET DESIGN BY WILLI BAUM

FIRST EDITION

Code 8912

The Jossey-Bass
Social and Behavioral Science Series

Contents

Preface

Group therapy is an increasingly important context for the treatment of interpersonal problems and intrapsychic conflict. In these days of soaring medical costs and shrinking health care resources, it has become an attractive option. Group therapy allows mental health facilities to provide relatively low-cost therapy to larger numbers of people, and at greater length, than would otherwise be possible.

Group therapy is also important for reasons other than financial ones. For clinicians, it provides an opportunity to work in a setting characterized by complex interactions and high stimulus intensity. It also allows them to work more directly with interpersonal problems than is usually possible in individual therapy. For clients, group therapy provides the opportunity to modify in the microcosm of the group the maladaptive patterns that brought them into therapy.

Unfortunately, clinicians who lead groups in mental health settings are seldom adequately prepared for the task. Frequently, they are asked to do group work with little training or preparation for the difficult conditions they confront. Training workshops lasting a day or two may be available in some settings from time to time and may be helpful in developing techniques. But frequently practitioners do not have a ready resource to turn to.

The literature has paid scant attention to the problems practitioners face daily. Most books on theory and techniques in group therapy tend to portray the ideal; that is, they present an endless supply of good group referrals, talkative group members, skilled and compassionate therapists, and comfortable and well-appointed group rooms. But much group therapy is done under difficult conditions: few referrals, taciturn and sometimes involuntary group members, clinic procedures that impede rather than facilitate the group therapy program.

Practical Group Therapy is intended to fill these gaps. It is a resource in which busy clinicians will find solutions that make sense to them and that have applicability to their settings. This book provides answers to the questions therapists commonly encounter when they begin leading groups, including some questions that beginning group therapists might not think to ask. Its particular strength is that it describes real-world, rather than ideal, situations. The reader is taken along the path followed by the client—from referral and screening, to the group sessions, and ultimately to termination. The clinician will find guidelines for what to do when referring therapists do not make good group referrals, when clients are inarticulate, and when supervision is not available. Research has shown what works in group therapy and what does not; the reader is shown how to best use the demonstrably effective therapeutic factors. The more traditional impassive-group-leader stance is contrasted with an initially active and structuring group leader. There are specific directions for implementing structure, which the new group leader will find helpful. More experienced group leaders will find the discussion of responses to client comments useful, as well as the chapters on advanced techniques.

Intended Audience

The primary audience for *Practical Group Therapy* is group therapists in clinical settings who have completed their classroom course work and training in individual therapy or counseling. Therefore, I have referred to—but not described—

such things as establishing rapport and conducting diagnostic interviews. At the same time, I have not assumed that the reader is already well-versed in some of the fundamentals of group therapy, such as how to conduct a screening interview, how to start the group session, or how therapist interventions in group therapy differ from therapist interventions in individual therapy.

While the practicing clinician will find *Practical Group Therapy* especially pertinent, the book is also useful to clinical psychology interns, psychiatric residents, social work students on clinical placements, and counseling trainees. Although oriented primarily toward various types of outpatient groups, much of the material—with the exception of the chapters on referral and screening—applies as well to inpatient groups. The psychiatric nurse and the occupational or recreational therapist with group skills will find the strongly practical orientation here especially helpful.

Overview of the Contents

In Chapters One and Two I discuss what takes place before the client enters a therapy group. Chapter One shows how to work with referring therapists in order to maintain a good flow of referrals for screening and how to assemble a mix of people that is likely to work well together. Chapter One concludes with a discussion of the training and supervisory arrangements a therapist should have completed before leading a therapy group. Chapter Two takes the reader step-by-step through a screening interview; discusses policies related to fees, absences, and group starting times; tells what to do with clients who are screened but not accepted into the group; and outlines how to introduce new group members.

Chapter Three discusses theory. My purpose is to provide an orientation to some of the major theories of group therapy and to delineate the theoretical framework that underlies most of the technical issues addressed in the rest of the book.

In Chapter Four I detail the factors that research on therapeutic efficacy has shown to enhance the probability of successful outcomes. I also discuss what the group therapist can do to facilitate operation of those factors.

Chapter Five tells how to start a group session and how to determine what to do after the session gets started. It describes an active therapist role and a structured opening procedure. Long, uncomfortable silences are neither necessary nor helpful at the beginning of a therapy group, and this chapter enables the therapist to avoid or shorten them. I include information here on how to start the first few sessions of a new group and how to begin a session of a group that has been meeting for some time.

Chapter Six puts the reader in the group room where a client has just said something about her relationship with her husband. What should the therapist do? This chapter takes the reader through some alternatives, discussing possible therapist responses to the client's comment and showing where each of those responses might lead.

Chapters Seven, Eight, and Nine are devoted to problems: Chapter Seven to problem behaviors, such as clients who talk too much and groups that are silent; Chapter Eight to clients with a diagnosis of borderline personality disorder; and Chapter Nine to problems having to do with the framework or context in which the group therapy service is delivered. Here I show how to handle issues such as sexual attraction/involvement, as well as the special problems posed by working with involuntary clients.

In Chapter Ten I discuss termination. I describe the work necessary to bring about successful termination of both the individual client and, in a time-limited group, an entire group.

The next two chapters provide techniques that allow the reader to go beyond the basics covered in the first ten chapters. Chapter Eleven discusses specific guidelines for introducing and managing role-play techniques. Chapter Twelve provides the clinician with three ways of dealing with dreams in the context of group therapy.

The concluding chapter discusses some issues implicit in the preceding chapters: group development, trusting one's judgment, tolerance of differing theoretical approaches to group therapy, and the politics of the group therapy program in the clinical setting.

Deciding what to include and what to exclude in a book involves arbitrary and sometimes frustrating choices. I have not included discussions of ethical issues. Short-term time-limited groups (for example, assertiveness training, grief, or hospital discharge planning) are not specifically discussed. *Practical Group Therapy* provides information about issues most relevant to clinicians in mental health clinics and hospitals.

The principles described here are applicable to therapy groups conducted in solo private practice settings. However, the problems posed by private clients and by the private setting may be somewhat different, more closely approximating ideal conditions. In addition, there are some issues unique to the private practice setting, ranging from marketing strategies and practice management concerns to sibling rivalry within the group, which occur when clients who have been seeing a therapist individually must now share the therapist's attention with other group members. Such topics are not discussed here.

Acknowledgments

I owe a special thanks to Jay Ritzer for arranging a number of the training workshops on which *Practical Group Therapy* is based, for his requests for readings relevant to his clinical setting and experience, and for his enthusiasm for group therapy as an effective treatment modality in rural outpatient mental health clinics. It was his energy that gave initial impetus to the present work. John Gladfelter, Stephen Shuchter, and Richard Hayes read an early version of the manuscript. I am particularly indebted to Richard Hayes for his many comments and suggestions.

My children were tolerant and understanding of my absences and preoccupation during the months I worked on the manuscript. My wife, Liz, in addition, offered encouragement and support and kept me from straying into irrelevancies like reading office supply catalogues cover to cover. She also read the manuscript and made many valuable suggestions for improvement. However, the responsibility for any remaining obscurities is mine alone.

Chapel Hill, North Carolina   William H. Friedman
December 1988

The Author

William H. Friedman is clinical associate professor and head of the group therapy program in the Department of Psychiatry, School of Medicine, University of North Carolina, Chapel Hill. He is also on the psychology faculty of the Fielding Institute and maintains a private practice in Chapel Hill.

Friedman was awarded his B.A. degree (1958) with honors in psychology from the University of Kansas and his M.A. (1960) and Ph.D. (1964) degrees in psychology from the University of Connecticut.

Friedman has been doing group therapy for thirty years and has been involved in the training and supervision of group therapists for over twenty years. He presents training workshops in group therapy around the country and has been an instructor at the annual Institutes of the American Group Psychotherapy Association. He has published numerous articles on both group and individual psychotherapy training and technique. He is the author of *How to Do Groups* (1979).

In addition to being a Fellow of the American Group Psychotherapy Association, Friedman is a member of the American Psychological Association, the North Carolina Psychological Association, and the Carolinas Group Psychotherapy Association. He is licensed as a practicing psycholo-

gist and as a marital and family therapist in North Carolina.
Friedman is a listed member in the National Register of
Health Care Providers in Psychology.

1

Criteria for
Selecting Group Members

In this first chapter, I describe the purposes of groups, the criteria for selection of group members, the principles of group composition, and the factors affecting the decision to admit a client into a therapy group. I also describe the types of information you should provide to staff therapists who refer clients to your group. And, finally, I discuss the important roles of therapist training and supervision in the development of clinical skills for the group context.

Purposes of Groups

There are many ways to conceptualize the purpose of psychotherapy (individual, group, or family). How you look at it depends on your training, your theoretical preference, and your experience. Theories of psychotherapy can be complex, but most have in common the concept of change—change in attitude, change in life circumstances, change in behavior.

Although individual therapy is an interpersonal context (there are, after all, two people involved), the focus is on one person and on what is going on inside that person's head. Even in the interpersonally oriented individual therapies, the focus is frequently limited to what transpires between client

1

and therapist, and there is much that the therapist might think but cannot say in the context of the one-to-one relationship.

Group therapy (often referred to simply as "group") is considerably broader than individual therapy as an interpersonal context. The purpose of group therapy is to facilitate change in interpersonal behavior—change in attitudes or beliefs about other people and about how one relates to them. Group is an interpersonal context for the resolution of interpersonal problems.

In many clinics, however, activities labelled group therapy often are not oriented toward change. Day hospital (post-hospitalization) programs, for example, are oriented, in practice, toward maintenance rather than change. These programs are designed to help people maintain a fragile and precarious status quo outside the hospital. This is sometimes called supportive psychotherapy, which sounds to me like the kind of approach you take when you have lost hope that things can be any better for the people who have come to you for help.

Still, there are times when, because of limited resources or limited time, or for other practical reasons, you have to focus on the prevention of something bad, such as deterioration or rehospitalization, rather than on the reaching for something better. A group geared toward maintenance and support is in some ways very different from one geared toward change. If you are responsible for such a group, it is important to keep in mind that what you should be trying to do is different from the approaches described in most textbooks on group therapy—books more oriented toward change than support.

Another purpose of group therapy is to meet the mandate requiring clinics to provide this type of service. In clinics which provide training for group therapists, an important purpose of group is to provide that training. And still another purpose of group therapy is simply to relieve staff therapists overburdened with individual clients while at the same time delivering some therapy services to people in need. In many clinics, the measuring unit of therapist performance is the number of clients seen, so group therapy is an obvious method to improve the numbers.[1]

Clearly, the group therapy enterprise serves a multiplicity of purposes. In conducting screening interviews, it is important, indeed vital, to be clear about the purposes your group is serving. It is essential that the selection criteria for admission to a group be developed in such a way as to ensure a group that can fulfill the intended purposes. The secret of having a successful group—one in which the clients report benefit and the therapists experience themselves as competent—lies in appropriate selection of individual candidates during the screening interview and in careful attention to principles of group composition.

The screening interview determines whether the client should be invited to join your group, and it provides an opportunity to identify the goals of therapy in terms of benefit or change. These issues are discussed in Chapter Two. To facilitate efficient screening, you should have selection criteria clearly in mind when you talk with therapists who refer clients to you for screening. By communicating clear criteria, you increase the probability that the referring therapists will send clients you are likely to accept.

Selection Criteria

You can choose from among several approaches to developing selection criteria. Kaplan and Sadock (1972) suggest criteria oriented toward symptom, diagnosis, and structural issues such as the size of the group. However, most writers do not favor using diagnosis alone as a selection criterion; see Kellerman (1979) for a brief but thoughtful discussion of this issue. Brook (1980) suggests three issues to consider in the selection process: what is best for the client, what is best for the group, and countertransference issues.

Deciding on what is best can be a tricky task. Hawkins and White (1978) offer guidance for this task in their discussion of both general and specific indications for group therapy. The general indications they present form a rationale for group therapy. One rationale is that the group is a microcosm in which the client's interpersonal behavior patterns resemble those in his or her relationships outside the group. The therapist, the client, and the other group members are thus able to see directly and to monitor changes in the client's maladaptive behaviors. A second rationale is economy: one or two therapists are able to see up to eight clients in ninety minutes, thus lowering the cost to the unit—and to the client—of service delivery. A third rationale is that the group offers clients the opportunity to see that others have similar experiences or problems.

The specific indications Hawkins and White suggest are confrontation needs, discussed in terms of character neurosis, characterological problems, and provision of social input. Rosenbaum (1978), discussing suitability for psychoanalytic group psychotherapy, suggests evaluation of each client's early life experiences and of "the desire to engage in the mutualism of a psychotherapeutic group"—a reference to client motivation for this form of therapy.

Rutan and Stone (1984), in a thoughtful and practical chapter in their slim volume on psychodynamic group therapy, suggest criteria including (1) the client's ability to experience and reflect upon his or her interactions as an indicator of ego capacity, (2) the client's ability to take on a variety of roles (for example, leader and follower), (3) the client's capacity to acknowledge his or her need for others, (4) the client's ability to give and receive feedback appropriately, and (5) the client's capacity for empathy.

This is a good and potentially useful set of criteria because of its emphasis on interactions. The criteria I use are in many ways similar, but are somewhat more interpersonal and less intrapsychic in orientation than Rutan and Stone's list.

In my experience, the ideal clients are those who

- Define their problems as interpersonal
- Are committed to change in interpersonal behaviors
- Are willing to be influenced by the group

- Engage readily but not inappropriately in self-disclosure
- Are willing to be of help to others in the group

Such clients may be rare in some clinic settings.

The question you are likely to be faced with in the screening interview, then, is, how much deviation from the ideal are you willing to tolerate in deciding whether or not to admit the client to group? The further you deviate from the ideal, the harder you will have to work to make the group a success. Some deviation from the ideal may be necessary in order to have enough people to keep the group going.

As a group therapist, you have a great deal of latitude in choosing the clients you will accept into your group. Group therapy has been tried with just about every type of client. It has been tried with psychotic patients (see, for example, Yalom, 1983; Battegay and von Marschall, 1978), and it has been tried with a vast range of people with other characteristics or problems, as evidenced by the extensive literature on the subject. (Bond and Lieberman [1978] review examples of this literature in their article, "Selection Criteria for Group Therapy.") Indeed, if you consider any characteristic such as depth of pathology, type of pathology, intelligence level, age, sex, or sexual orientation, you can be sure that someone has tried group therapy with clients having that characteristic.

The success of this range of selection strategies, however, has not been clearly demonstrated. The clinical and research literature on selection for group treatment has been reviewed recently by Toseland and Siporin (1986), who conclude that the research literature "did not yield a clear pattern regarding the types of problems most effectively treated in groups" (p. 171). That being the case, it may initially seem workable to have fairly lax standards and to admit clients to group unless it is clearly inappropriate to do so. In a similar vein, Yalom (1985) and Power (1985) suggest that it is better to be inclusive rather than exclusive, and to admit people to group unless there are clear contraindications.

My own experience over the years, however, both in groups I have led and in those I have supervised, strongly suggests that inclusivity generates problems leading to a less therapeutic experience than is the case for groups in which some prudent exclusivity is practiced.

The people who do best in group are those who are psychologically and interpersonally oriented. The converse is also true: the people who do least well in group are those who are neither psychologically nor interpersonally oriented. Exclusion from group should be considered, before or during the screening interview, for clients who

- Have significant organic mental deficit, unless such a deficit is a criterion for group composition
- Have an impairment of consciousness, such as that seen in floridly psychotic inpatients or in heavily medicated outpatients
- Give indications that they will be impervious to interpersonal influence—as in statements such as "I don't care what anyone says" made in a context of self-absorption
- Have impaired capacity for empathy, as might be found in some individuals with personality disorders
- Meet the behavioral criteria for paranoid personality disorder

If you admit an individual to your group who has one or more of the above characteristics, the probability that the client will benefit from group is small and the probability that the therapeutic efficacy of the group will be impaired is high.

Other clients may have characteristics which make therapeutic success difficult but still probable; this type of client is discussed in Chapters Seven and Eight.

To this point in our discussion of selection criteria, we have considered client characteristics independent of group composition. However, the decision to admit or exclude a client from group cannot be made independently from consideration of the salient characteristics of those clients already in the group.

Group Composition

One of the questions you will have to resolve during the screening interview is, how well is this candidate likely to fit into this group? Should you consider the client's symptomatology, level of pathology, diagnosis, and the like? Or should you look at characteristics such as common interests and background, potential for activity or silence in group sessions, or compatibility with the other human beings in the group—independent of their diagnostic labels and independent of the problems that brought them to group?

Diagnosis is an important consideration because it helps you know what to expect from the client and because it helps you predict at least some aspects of his or her interpersonal behavior with some degree of accuracy. However, this is not to suggest that groups should be homogeneous with regard to diagnosis. A group made up only of depressed patients or of schizophrenic patients, for example, poses formidable challenges to the therapist while offering minimal resources to the group members.

Some therapists believe that heterogeneity with respect to level of pathology is helpful. That is, you should put people who are minimally disturbed into groups with high-functioning clients. The high-functioning clients are supposed to serve as models for the more disturbed ones and to pull them toward more adequate interpersonal adjustment. It is a nice theory, but it does not work. Generally, a group will move as fast as its sickest member will permit. Hence, it is important to have as much homogeneity as possible with respect to level of pathology.

One important advantage of single-diagnosis groups is that group members can readily see that they are not alone and that others have similar problems. Such perceptions are therapeutic, as we shall see in Chapter Three. Moreover, the increased potential for empathy, understanding, and acceptance among group members who share a common diagnosis can enhance the therapeutic effectiveness of the group.

When it comes to type of pathology included in a group, however, heterogeneity is probably better. If you have a group of withdrawn, depressed clients, the characteristic they are most likely to have in common, besides diagnosis, is silence. Similarly, a group of schizophrenic clients is a group of people who have difficulty relating. In such groups, the therapists must provide the heterogeneity that, in mixed groups, would come from other group members. For outpatient work, another disadvantage of homogeneous groupings is the difficulty of assembling a sufficient number of clients with the same diagnosis.

Usually when you begin screening for group therapy, you already have an ongoing group, and the question you will have to ask is, how well does this particular client fit in with the group that is already there? The clients in that group will have been selected by others, and, as noted above, this may be a less than optimal situation for you. (On the other hand, client selection may have been done by group therapists more experienced than you, and you may get off to a better start than if you had done the selection yourself.) Your task, then, is to figure out how this client whom you are selecting will fit in with this group of people selected by others. This task may be difficult at first, but it will become easier as you become more familiar both with the people already in the group and with the screening process.

Principles of Group Composition

Use of common sense is the most important principle when deciding on the composition of a group. You naturally have some skill to figure out how people will fit together in social situations, as, for instance, when you consider whom to invite for a party or for membership in a fraternity or sorority. Use that skill here, bearing in mind that the prime consideration is not how well people will like each other (which might be a consideration in a social group) but how well they will interact. Generally, you will have to look at three dimensions: how verbally active or passive a person is, whether his or her perceived locus of control is internal or external, and whether he or she tends to intellectualize about emotion or to display it in interactions.

Verbal Activity or Verbal Passivity. If you have several people in your group who tend to be quiet, adding a quiet candidate (who would otherwise be appropriate) is likely to make matters worse. Groups need at least one, and preferably two, members to be interpersonally lively during the group sessions. A frequent concern of therapists is that the more verbally active group members will overshadow the quieter ones. That is certainly a possibility, and one you have to guard against. But the fact is that the world consists of people who are verbally active and people who are quieter. Sometimes those characteristics don't go well together, and such different people may have difficulty getting along. But group is a good place for them to learn the skills that will allow them to interact more effectively with the world's wide variety of people.

On the other hand, if you have five or six highly verbal group members, and a verbally passive candidate comes along, it may be very difficult for you to get the verbal members to make room (verbally) for him or her over any period of time. If the candidate's intellectual level is roughly similar to that of the group, it may be worth the effort, and the more active group members may come eventually to listen carefully and to respect the few words that the quieter person utters. However, if there is a significant disparity along intellectual (and, occasionally, educational or social class) lines, then putting a more quiet person into a verbally active group is likely to reinforce feelings of inferiority and inadequacy in him or her and perhaps opposite feelings in the other group members. This is one of the points at which common sense should prevail if it is in conflict with clinical issues.

External or Internal Locus of Control. Some people perceive themselves as controlled by external forces over which they have little influence. Others assume personal responsibility for whatever happens and tend to blame themselves whenever anything goes wrong. (However, when things go well, they tend to attribute good outcomes to external forces.) Another way of putting it is that some people are extrapunitive, blaming others, and some people are intropunitive, blaming themselves. There is a third group, people who are impunitive, blaming impersonal chance forces rather than people. The verbal formulations might be (1) it's your fault, (2) it's my fault, (3) it's nobody's fault.

Ideally, group membership should be split equally between intropunitive and extrapunitive clients, but the ideal is seldom available. Groups that are all one way or the other, external/extrapunitive or internal/intropunitive, are viable, though somewhat more difficult for the group therapist than groups that are heterogeneous along this dimension. The thing to watch out for is having four or five people who are, say, external/extrapunitive and then adding one who is internal/intropunitive—or the other way around. It is important to have at least two people on each side of the fence. If, as sometimes happens, there is only one group member on one side of the fence or the other, you have to be very sensitive to the possibilities for scapegoating and of the group situation reinforcing feelings of differentness and alienation.

Intellectualizing Feelings. Some people talk about feelings; others express them. Clients who talk rather than express are frequently called *intellectualizers.* The diagnostic categories into which they are placed (based in large part on the symptoms associated with intellectualization of emotion) include obsessive-compulsive behaviors or one of the schizophrenic disturbances. Such clients may need to work on expression rather than discussion of emotion.

Clients who express emotions rather than discuss them are frequently placed in diagnostic categories denoting a borderline or histrionic personality disorder. Such clients may need to work on developing verbal (and, preferably, cognitive) mediators of emotional expression, so that they begin to think before (but not instead of) emoting.

It is possible to have a viable group that is homogeneous with respect to this intellectualization/emoting dimension. A group of intellectualizers will work, and its members will likely benefit. (Such a group might be found in university mental health clinics.) A group of emoters will work too, though here it is important to distinguish diagnostically between histrionic and borderline clients. Ideally, groups should be as heterogeneous as possible along these lines, that is, a fifty-fifty split between intellectualizers and emoters. As with the other dimensions, you should guard against having one emoter or one intellectualizer in a group where everyone else is way over on the other side of the fence.

These three dimensions of (1) verbal activity/passivity, (2) internal/external locus of control, and (3) intellectualization/emoting are the most salient but there are some others to consider. For example, groups will work better if they are relatively homogeneous with respect to intelligence, education, social class, and, to some extent, age. With age, however, some heterogeneity is tolerable along generational lines; if there are one or two people in the group who differ in age by twenty or more years (and some whose ages are between those two), there may be an opportunity for the younger person to work out some parental issues and for the older one to work out some parenting ones. But if you have a group consisting of three or four people in their twenties, someone in his or her forties or older probably will not benefit much from membership in that group.

Groups that are homogeneous with respect to sex have become increasingly popular in recent years. In my experience, if there is this kind of segregation, a clinic is more likely to have a women's group than it is to have a men's group. But this may be changing. If you are coming into a group which is already segregated on the basis of sex, it is probably better not to try to change it, since the clinic's contracts with the group members probably is that they will have such a group. Whether to continue that group as members withdraw or whether to plan to offer other groups segregated by sex are separate issues, which depend largely on the personal preferences of the group therapists.

When Clients Know Each Other. A group characteristic you should consider when screening a candidate for membership is acquaintanceship between a group member and the candidate. Usually, you won't find out whether clients know each other until the new member walks into group for the first time. The likelihood of this happening depends on the size of the clinic's catchment area. In a clinic serving a university with twenty thousand undergraduates, it might happen occasionally; in a town with twenty thousand inhabitants, it will occur more frequently. In towns smaller than that, everyone usually knows everyone else, and in some communities it seems that most people are related to one another. These situations can cause some special problems having to do with confidentiality. If you are new to the town and the clinic, the older hands will acquaint you with the way the clinic handles such problems.

In clinics serving smaller communities, you often will know by the time of the screening interview whether the candidate knows someone in the group, and, if so, who and what the relationship is or was. The question then is whether that knowledge immediately disqualifies the applicant from consideration for that particular group. The issue becomes salient when there is only one group available and group is the only psychotherapeutic treatment the candidate is likely to be offered. In this situation, you should evaluate, as much as possible, the closeness of the relationship. In smaller towns, many people have at least nodding acquaintances, but that should not rule out comembership. Nor should an applicant necessarily be denied membership because he or she grew up and went to school years ago with a current group member. If there is a current or recent relationship, however, and you know about it beforehand, it would be better not to schedule the screening interview, but to take up the matter with the referring therapist.

It is a different matter if you (and the client) do not realize, until the first meeting, that he or she already knows someone in the group. In this situation, you can surmise the relationship is not close, since otherwise the candidate would have known that his or her friend/relative was coming regularly to the clinic at the time the group meets. However, you need to determine, either in the group session or in individual meetings with each person, the extent to which the clients feel the relationship might inhibit their participation in the group. If they are comfortable, go ahead and let the new member in for the usual trial period, and reevaluate at the end of that time.

In small towns or clinics with small catchment areas, it may be necessary to admit new clients who already know one or more group members if you are to have a group at all. In larger catchment areas, or where there are suitable alternatives to your group (such as another group that meets at the same time), you can be more selective about letting the new client in. If it looks as though the clients know each other well and would use the group to work on their relationship, the new client should be transferred. Otherwise the group will, sooner or later, spend considerable time on the relationship. The process of working out a previously existing relationship is seldom in the therapeutic contracts of the group members and is likely to be of little interest to the rest of the group.

Admissions issues are quite straightforward in special purpose groups. Such groups usually focus on a specific status (like parenthood) or a specific problem (like bulimia). Criteria for both referral and admission to these groups may be little more than the client's manifesting the target characteristic and being able to come to the clinic at the time the group meets. In such instances, the screening interview can be devoted largely to preparation of the client for the group experience. Less time and energy need be devoted to questions of whether to admit the client to group.

Factors Affecting Admission Criteria

Pressures Toward Accepting the Client. By the time a client arrives for the screening interview, you, he or she, and probably the referring therapist have some investment in the client's being admitted to group. For the client, the process usually has involved at least two visits to the clinic (intake and group screening). Such visits are seldom convenient, and the fact that the client comes at all is an indication of his or her interest in obtaining mental health services. The referral itself indicates the referring therapist's belief that this client will benefit from group. Making the appointment and meeting with the client represents your own investment of time and the various energies required to conduct a group screening interview. These are all pressures toward accepting the client into group unless it is impossible to do so. That is, there are some pressures to be inclusive rather than exclusive. These pressures influence the application of admission criteria.

The need for additional group members is a second source of pressure to bend admission criteria. If you already have five people and are looking at a possible sixth, you are likely to be more picky than if you have three people and are looking at a possible fourth. In the former instance, it is possible to have a clear idea of the kind of personal characteristics a prospective group member needs in order to fit in well with the group. If the person you are interviewing does not have those characteristics, you can turn him or her down and still have a viable group. But if you have only three group members, refusing admission to a prospective fourth is likely to mean that you won't have a group. Depending on your needs, and those of the clinic, that can be formidable pressure indeed.

A low rate of referral can be a third source of pressure to lower admission criteria and to accept a marginal candidate. If a referral for group comes along every couple of months, it may seem a virtual necessity to take whoever comes along—if it is important to maintain a group. If referrals are plentiful, the consequences of being picky will not be so negative.

Other sources of pressure to modify admission standards may include your cotherapist, the clinic administrator, or therapists in other components of the clinic programs who might like to see a particularly troublesome client parked somewhere else for an hour and a half. Of these people, the most important person to reach an understanding with is your cotherapist. None of the others will have to deal with the client during group sessions.

Pressures Toward Rejecting the Client. On the other side of the coin are those pressures that both raise admission criteria and encourage exclusivity rather than inclusivity. These pressures are most likely to come from you (and your cotherapist) and from your knowledge of the current group members. It is natural to want the best possible group experience, one with group members who are attractive, verbal, intelligent, and psychologically sophisticated. The pressure to have the best possible group is pressure to exclude candidates unless they are clearly suitable for your group. So what you end up with in the screening interview is a kind of balancing act. You have to consider the best interests of the group—the people who are already group members—and you have to consider the best interests of the candidate.

The ideal situation is one in which group is clearly the treatment of choice for the candidate and your group is in need of a member with just this candidate's characteristics. Sometimes, however, a candidate needs group but would fit poorly into your group. On occasion, a group needs a person for whom group is not the treatment of choice but who might reasonably be expected to benefit from the experience. In other words, it won't hurt, it might do some good, and the client's presence would help several other clients. The balancing act you have to perform in deciding whether to admit such a candidate to group has ethical or moral as well as practical implications.

Both kinds of admissions pressure—the pressure to lower standards in order to admit someone to group and the pressure to keep standards high to exclude people—should be resisted. Letting people into group who really should not be there and who are unlikely to benefit is a waste of time—yours, theirs, and the other group members'. Excluding people who might benefit in order to maintain a "high-functioning" group may deprive both the candidate and the incumbent group members of experiences that would be helpful to them and to which they may be entitled.

Yet it is not easy to steer such a middle course, especially when you do not yet have a great deal of experience observing how people you have screened have fared in group. Generally, if you are relatively new to the group therapy technique, you probably should be doing screening interviews along with a more experienced therapist or with your supervisor. When that is not possible, consider the following questions during the screening interview:

- Can the client come to the group meeting at the scheduled time?
- Can I work with this person?
- How much work is it going to be to integrate this person into my group; is it likely to be worth the effort; and will the net result be beneficial to both the individual and the group?

Of these three, the first two are likely to be most important initially, because if the answer to either of them is negative, the client is not likely to benefit from group.

Training and Supervision

The success of any therapy group depends to a great extent on the therapist's competence—competence in the conduct of groups and, as we have seen, competence in the process of screening potential group members. Training in group under the supervision of experienced professionals is essential for the new clinician, as well as for the fully credentialled, experienced therapist whose only clinical background has been in individual therapy.

Training. The purpose of therapist training is the development of clinical skills. The American Group Psychotherapy Association (AGPA) offers a training program having four components: ninety hours of didactic instruction, sixty hours of experience as a group member, sixty hours of group leadership, and at least twenty-five hours of supervision. Prerequisites for training include graduate courses in normal growth and development, personality theory and psychodynamics, psychopathology, clinical diagnosis, principles of individual psychotherapy, and "social and cultural factors" (AGPA, 1978). (In order to qualify for associate membership in AGPA, candidates must, in addition, hold a doctorate in medicine or psychology or a master's degree in social work, nursing, or some other mental health professions, and have 1,140 hours of psychotherapy experience plus 25 more hours of supervision.)

Many group therapists do not have such extensive training. Some have not done graduate work or have not taken the suggested courses. In my experience, only a minority of group therapists have taken as many as ninety hours of didactic instruction in group therapy, though experience as a group member is somewhat more common. Supervision, outside of group therapy training centers, is sometimes problematical.

Training for group therapists, in many clinical settings, is informal and unsystematic, consisting of attendance at one- or two-day workshops and cotherapy with a more experienced group therapist. Occasionally, clinic administrators are reluctant to make training workshops available to the group therapy staff, in part for financial and staffing reasons and in part because of the mistaken assumption that there is considerable transfer of individual therapy skills to the group setting.

Dies (1980) surveyed 100 supervisors of group therapists. These supervisors reported a strong tendency among beginning group therapists to conduct individual therapy in the group context. Yalom (1985) reports a study (Ebersole, Leiderman, and Yalom, 1969) of twelve beginning group therapists. Half received training and supervision and half did not. Ratings by observers six months later suggested that the trained group therapists improved but that the untrained therapists were less effective than at the beginning. As Yalom notes, experience alone does not develop competence. Results of this study suggest persuasively that skills in individual psychotherapy are not transferable to the group modality. Specific training in group therapy techniques is necessary to enable the therapist to shift from an individual psychotherapy orientation to a group therapy orientation, which is quite different, and to shift from a focus on the intrapsychic to a focus on the interpersonal.

As a practical matter, clinicians skilled in individual therapy who are beginning to do group therapy often find they are expected to determine for themselves the minimum level of training and experience that will allow them to colead therapy groups. Their ability to develop minimum competency depends on the availability of training workshops, experienced cotherapists, and skilled supervision. These three components balance one another. Strength of one component can compensate for weakness of another. If good training workshops are readily available, it is less important (though not less desirable) to have an experienced cotherapist. If your cotherapist has enough experience, training, and background to do supervision, a skilled supervisor is less important, and you can make do with fewer training workshops.

In many clinics and hospitals, completion of a single one-day training workshop is the only requirement for clinicians to begin coleading therapy groups. Such a workshop can provide little more than an orientation to group work. This is not really enough training, but if it is all you can get, you must be sure that your cotherapist knows what he or she is doing and is someone you are willing to learn from.

If you have skills in individual therapy and are in a setting where you are expected to start doing groups, it is important to participate as a member of a group for at least twelve hours—a two-day experiential training workshop or an eight-week training group. You do not have to be a member of a therapy group in order to be a good group therapist, but you do have to be a member of an experiential group, or training experience, where you can learn about how you function in group, how you come across to a group of people, and how you can reduce anxiety (your own and others'). Above all, you have to have direct experience, as a group member, with group function and with group influence, and you have to learn to appreciate the considerable difference between group and individual therapy.

If you do not have experience as a group member, a one-day training workshop is not likely to be sufficient to orient you toward group therapy. You will have to rely on your cotherapist and on the post-group discussions and supervisory sessions. It may be a month or more before you say very much in group sessions and longer than that before you are really helpful either to your cotherapist or to the group members.

Students in designated training programs can begin to

function as cotherapists with less preparation than even a one-day training workshop, but in such cases the cotherapist and supervisor should be expert. Fully credentialled clinicians who begin on-the-job training in group therapy may be neophyte students of group therapy, but even so they must meet professional standards of practice and ethics expected of credentialled therapists. Consequently, a professional therapist may be required to obtain more training than a noncredentialled student prior to functioning as a junior cotherapist.

A social work student on field placement, a clinical psychology intern, or a psychiatric resident may begin to colead a group before having done much observation or participation as a group member. In those circumstances, they are not delivering services to the public as independent, qualified professionals, but as apprentices under supervision. But a clinician who is just beginning to do groups comes into the group room as a fully credentialled professional and does not leave that status and its responsibilities outside just because he or she is new at this particular therapeutic modality.

While most licenses permit you to do anything that anyone in your profession is competent to do (a psychiatrist can legally perform surgery under his or her medical license), codes of ethics prohibit the delivery of services for which you lack adequate preparation. It is probably unethical for a fully credentialled professional to function even as a junior cotherapist without having seen group therapy done as observer or participant or both. It is certainly unethical for a fully credentialled professional to begin on-the-job training in group therapy without competent, ongoing supervision in that modality.

Supervision. The purposes of supervision are to help group therapists improve group skills, enhance therapeutic effectiveness, and facilitate desirable change in clients who are members of therapy groups. There are several ways that group therapy supervision is done. The best way, in my opinion, is when the supervisor watches the entire group session through a two-way mirror and then meets with the cotherapists immediately afterward. The experience is fresh in everyone's mind, and the discussions have an immediacy and thoroughness difficult to achieve in any other way. Such supervision is not usually available outside of training facilities.

The second best method of supervision involves the supervisor's seeing some portion of the group session, either directly or via videotape. The less-desirable alternative of audiotape does not convey sufficient information about the nonverbal component of the interactions, but is better than simply trying to recall, during supervisory sessions, who said what during the group sessions. The essential component of supervision is that the supervisor, rather than the therapist, is able to choose which portions of the tape to review.

A more common supervisory model, outside of training settings, calls for the cotherapists to meet with the group supervisor and to recall events either from memory or from notes made immediately after the group session. Ideally, the group leaders meet with their supervisors weekly; but, in many clinics, such a standard is difficult to attain.

Another model entails the supervisor's meeting jointly with three or four cotherapist pairs. This model works well with an experienced group therapy staff. The group of group leaders can, to some extent, re-create and explore clinical problems arising in any of the groups, thus arriving at enhanced understanding and, frequently, alternative solutions.

Supervision should begin before you have your first screening interview for group therapy. As this chapter has shown, the criteria for group therapy differ from the criteria for individual therapy, and the screening processes for the two therapies also differ. In group therapy screening, you spend more time explaining group functions and procedures and negotiating for specific change. Getting supervision prior to your first screening interview will help you avoid doing a screening interview that is more appropriate for individual than for group therapy.

Finally, you should note that supervision is not always provided by outpatient clinics, so the clinician must pay for the supervisor's services. In rural areas, supervision may be difficult to find, and clinics may be unable to afford both fees and travel costs for experienced group supervisors. In these instances, group therapists sometimes join together to share the costs of supervision and to persuade clinic administrators to grant time off for supervisory sessions. In my experience, inpatient psychiatric facilities, both public and private, invariably provide supervision for group therapy.

Notes

1. Occasionally, clinic administrators will claim that if you are spending an hour and a half in group, that should count as one or one and a half patients, instead of the eight, for example, who were actually in attendance. Such an approach, which may best be characterized as naive, actually penalizes the group therapist, who must still find time to meet with his or her cotherapist and to do the additional charting.

2

Referral, Screening, and Entry into the Group

The referral process brings the client to the screening interview. In the screening interview, both client and therapist reach some decision as to whether this client should be invited into the specific group led by that therapist. The process begins with the client's application to the clinic for services, which usually results in an appointment for an intake interview.

While intake procedures differ in their particulars from clinic to clinic, the general outline is probably similar. There is an initial interview or screening, some kind of evaluative or diagnostic procedure, and then a referral for therapy. The initial screening is done by an intake worker who may be a member of the therapist staff rotating through the intake assignment or who may be permanently assigned such duties. The task of the intake worker is to match the client's needs with the clinic's resources.

In my experience, direct referrals from intake workers for group therapy are rare. People coming to a mental health clinic are usually seeking individual therapy and are usually resistant to the suggestion that they reveal their problems and fears to nonprofessional strangers. If such a referral is made by an intake worker, it is likely to be rejected by the client. Clients who have been in group before may be more willing to accept such a referral, but if their previous group experience was poor, they tend to be more resistant. Clients who are more psychologically sophisticated and clients, such as adolescents, for whom peer group issues are centrally important may be more willing to accept referral to group therapy from an intake worker.

For the most part, referrals for group therapy come from the therapist staff. Individual therapists refer clients for group for many reasons. Seldom, it seems, is a referral made because group therapy is the treatment of choice. (The adolescent programs, where group therapy is almost always the treatment of choice, may be an exception here.) More frequently, referrals are made in an effort to reduce the therapist's individual therapy case load, or for similar reasons having to do with the conservation of scarce resources. Other reasons for referral may include countertransference issues or the clinic's need to provide a group therapy program. So, groups are likely to be some mix of individuals who were referred primarily for the benefit of the clinic or the therapist and those for whom group therapy is actually the treatment of choice.

It is important to know why the referral was made. It is not unusual for clients who have been seeing an individual therapist for some time to feel rejected when they are referred for group. The screening interview and subsequent group therapy will proceed more smoothly if you are prepared to deal at the outset with the client's feelings of rejection by his or her individual therapist.

Sometimes clients are puzzled by referral for group therapy, and they may show up for the screening interview primarily in an effort to be compliant with clinic procedures they regard as mysterious but beneficial. And in many clinics there is a more or less surreptitious competition among therapists for clients who are regarded as high functioning. Unless the clinic has a tradition of referring high-functioning clients for group, it is particularly important for you to find out the reasons, both explicit and implicit, for the referral. Therapists sometimes refer clients for group because of conflict or other countertransference issues. When that happens, the client may arrive at the screening interview hurt, angry, and wary. It is important to know whether those feelings stem from the client's pathology or from the individual therapy relationship.

If you are dependent on the therapist staff for referrals for group therapy, it is prudent to provide them with feedback about the screening interview and with progress reports from time to time. Such feedback serves a dual purpose. It reminds therapists (or intake workers, if they refer directly into the group) of group activities, and it is a form of thanks. In addition, feedback helps train the referral sources to make appropriate referrals. Informal reports of client progress provide information about the accuracy of the referring therapist's guess about how the client would fare in group.

Informal is a key word here. In most mental health clinics, therapists (both individual and group) must spend a large fraction of their time documenting what they do. Charting treatment or progress notes for a group is a formidable task—more so if your clinic administrator, medical records committee, or quality control committee will not allow the placement of an identical standard paragraph in each group member's chart. Staff therapists, who must keep up their own chart work, usually do not read chart notes made by other therapists on clients whom they are no longer seeing. Thus, your informal feedback to referring therapists is the only information they are likely to get about clients they've referred into your group.

The staff therapists may not seem interested in your feedback, and certainly life can go on without it. However, the occasional informal contact with referring therapists, in most instances, facilitates the referral process and helps maintain a steady flow of clients into your groups.

In the preceding discussion, I have assumed that the intake workers and staff therapists know how to refer clients for group. Whether or not that is the case will depend on their training and background as well as on their experience in this particular clinic. If you are going into a clinic where there is an active group program and everyone has been doing it for years, it is safe to assume initially that people know what they are doing and that they are reasonably good at it. If that is not the case, you will find out soon enough. But it is better to go in with the assumption of competence.

You may find that you are dealing with a new intake worker or staff therapist who does not know how to refer for group. Or you may be in a situation where there has not been much referral for group, and now you are trying to get something going. Even when there is a good referral flow and people have been doing groups there for years, if you are new to the clinic, the clinicians will not know how to refer for your group.

That being so, you may find it a very good investment of your time to meet with the intake workers and staff therapists to talk about group, and about whom to refer for your groups. If the clinic staff is large, it may take some time to meet with all the therapists who are potential referral sources, but the effort is likely to be worth it.

In talking with referral sources, you should emphasize two points. One is that the referral is not directly for admission into a group, but rather for screening for group therapy. Thus, making the referral does not mean that the client will automatically get into a group, and acceptance of the referral by the client is nothing more than agreeing to meet with the group therapists one time. Hence, acceptance of a referral for screening involves no obligation on the part of the clinic to offer or on the part of the client to attend group therapy sessions.

The second point to emphasize is that, when in doubt, it is better to refer than not to refer for screening. The intake worker or staff therapist cannot know all the details involved in the decision to admit or not admit a client into a therapy group. That is the group therapist's job, and you cannot evaluate clients for your group unless they are referred for screening. So it is important for staff therapists to know that referring a client for group does not mean that the client will certainly get into a group.

Screening Interviews

Screening interviews serve two functions. The first is to enable the therapist to decide whether to admit the client to group therapy, and to enable the client to decide whether to attend. The second function is contractual, between client and therapist. The contract defines the specific content issues with which the client wants help initially, and it describes the ways the therapist and the group are most likely to offer help. In the contract, the therapist also may offer help on some content issues not necessarily perceived as problems by the client at the outset. As the client makes progress in group, other issues, usually more central, may emerge, and the initial contract may change—though not always explicitly. And, as we shall see in Chapter Ten, the initial contract serves as a reference point for estimating client progress and readiness for termination from group therapy.

In some clinics, screening interviews for group are not routine. The referring therapist assigns the client to group and provides information about the time and place of the group meeting. The client simply appears at the appointed time. The group leaders may or may not have met the client, conferred with the referral source, or read the client's chart. Such an entry into a group creates difficulties for the client, for the therapists, and for the other group members.

Screening interviews are less likely to be done when status referrals are made—when the clients are assigned to group on the basis of what they are rather than who they are. For example, a client assigned to a day hospital program is assigned to group because all day hospital clients are in group. There seems little point in doing screening interviews. Similarly, in programs for alcoholics or other substance abusers, where group is an intrinsic and required part of the program, screening specifically for group therapy seems pointless since everyone admitted to the program will be in a group.

Screening interviews are more common in the adult outpatient programs of mental health clinics, though even here some therapists simply accept all referrals and admit unscreened patients into group with no preparation.

Studies show, however, that screening interviews make for better groups (Friedman, Jelly, and Jelly, 1978; Power, 1985). By better groups I mean groups that have enhanced potential for therapeutic efficacy and a focus on treatment issues. When clients are screened for admission to group therapy, therapists do not sit in group wondering why they are there, wishing they were not, and feeling some combination of boredom and ineptness. If you screen clients well, you will not have such a difficult time in group and your clients are more likely to improve.

But, realistically, you sometimes will not be able to do your own screening. If you are responsible for one of the day-long treatment programs, it may be difficult or impossible to get free (because of coverage problems) long enough to devote even ten minutes to a single client. If you are a staff therapist, there may be other severe time constraints. In addition, there may be political constraints. It is not unknown for referring therapists to be defensive, viewing the screening interview as a test of their own abilities to make appropriate referrals, and therefore of their overall competence. In such a politically sensitive setting, screening interviews can be very costly in terms of your energy and time.

Structure of the Screening Interview

In this section, I assume you already know how to do interviews in general. So I will not describe in detail how to start the interview, establish rapport, and orient the client toward the interview's purposes and goals. I will instead describe a way of structuring the screening interview.

At the beginning, you should determine (1) client expectations for the interview, and (2) the client's understanding of why he or she is there. If there are any serious misconceptions, they can sometimes be spotted and dealt with at the outset.

Next, find out from the client what he or she (not you)

sees as the precipitant for coming to the clinic. You might ask, for example, what was the event that finally led to the client's decision to seek an appointment. This information will be in the chart, or course, but what is in the chart will have been filtered through another person (the intake worker). You need to hear the reasons directly and in the client's own language. This statement is termed the *client's presenting complaint.*

The next step is to come to a diagnostic formulation. There may be diagnostic information in the chart. But how good is it? Do you trust the diagnostician? Does the client act like someone with that diagnosis? Is there any point to diagnosing, or is it just something that is done in your clinic because you have to fill in the blank on the forms?

In my experience, mental health workers seeking training in group therapy frequently do not seem particularly interested in the diagnostic labelling of their clients. The prevalent feeling among staff therapists seems to be that labelling a person diagnostically increases the danger of relating to and treating the label rather than the individual. The label *schizophrenia,* however, is a frequent exception, but even here the concern of the therapists is with schizophrenic behaviors— how to handle the patient whose hallucinations disrupt the group, how to reach the withdrawn schizophrenic—rather than with more abstract theoretical concepts of schizophrenia.

Diagnostic labels serve an important predictive function. They tell us what behaviors to expect and what types of client response have a high probability of appearing. The predictive function of diagnostic labelling can generate therapist expectations of client behavior. Whether such expectations may become self-fulfilling prophecies is not at issue here. Therapists form expectations of behavior based on observations made and information gathered in screening interviews and elsewhere. You will form some expectations of the client in any event, and such expectations can become self-fulfilling prophecies whether or not you explicitly link them to some diagnostic labelling scheme. The important point is that diagnostic labelling helps guide your expectations. It allows you to anticipate client behaviors whether or not there is any hint of them in the screening interview.

Knowledge of the kinds of behaviors to expect from clients gives you some idea of how they might relate in a therapy group, how they might fit into your group, and whether the ambience and the content issues of your group make it likely that they can benefit from membership. This knowledge, in sum, makes it easier for you to decide whether to admit the clients to your group. That is why it is important to make at least a tentative diagnostic formulation during the screening interview.

I am assuming that you know how to do a diagnostic interview. If you do not, you should not be doing a screening interview alone. Ideally, there will be a good diagnostic work-up in the chart done by people you know and whose clinical judgment you trust. With this information, and your own interview skills, it should be possible to come to some tentative diagnostic formulation during the course of a single interview. Once you have gotten that far, the next step is to consider treatment strategies.

You are now at the point in the interview where you have some idea of what the client's problems and issues are, of the assets and liabilities that he or she brings to bear on those problems, and of how he or she is likely to relate, at least initially, to other group members. That is enough information to come to a tentative decision about whether to admit the client to group. Whether you do so depends on the admission criteria you use and how you use them. We discussed those criteria in Chapter One.

Contracting for Change

Assuming you have decided to admit the client to your group and have ascertained that he or she can actually come to the clinic at the time the group meets, the remaining tasks in the screening interview are to identify specific problems or problem areas to work on initially and to provide some orientation to the group. Research (see, for example, Yalom, 1985) has shown that clients who come to group to work on specific problems or issues will report, at termination, greater benefit and satisfaction than those who come to group with a generalized expectation of change. Accordingly, the more specific you can be during the screening interview about what problems to work on, the greater the probability of client benefit.

The client's presenting complaint, which we discussed back on page 28, ideally would identify a specific interpersonal problem, such as difficulty engaging in self-disclosure sufficient to maintain an intimate relationship. That seldom happens. Much of the time the client will arrive at the screening interview with, at best, a generalized expectation of benefit. Sometimes clients come only because they are compliant with authority, and referring therapists are seen as authority figures. Thus, if you ask most clients what they want to work on in group therapy, the answer you get is not likely to be very helpful to you or to them.

Your task, then, is to help the client identify a problem or two that can be worked on—that is, discussed—early in his or her experience with the group. For the hypothetical client who comes to the clinic seeking medication for "bad nerves," group therapy offers the opportunity to talk with other people whose nerves are bad too. For clients who are quite strongly focused on somatic complaints, like bad nerves, a suggestion that "you will feel better when you talk with other people who have bad nerves" may be a sufficient initial set of goals. (In this instance, there are two goals: (1) talking with other people, and (2) feeling better. The behavioral referents of feeling better are not specified.) Later on, after the client reports that he or she is feeling better, it may be possible to negotiate other behavioral changes, such as increased interaction with other family members, getting out of the house more, and so on.

Thus, the initial problems that you suggest the client work on in group therapy should be as close to the client's presenting complaint as possible, as specific as possible, and reachable within a few months at most.

Take for example a client, a woman in her late twenties, who came to the clinic with presenting complaints of anxiety and depression. While these symptoms had been present for several years, they became much worse when she separated from her husband. She experienced significant weight loss and had difficulty sleeping. However, she lost little time from work and continued to care quite adequately for her three-year-old son.

Within a few months, this client had responded well to a combination of medication and individual psychotherapy. She was significantly less anxious and depressed and had gained back about half the weight she had lost; there was some improvement in her sleep pattern, and she had found a better job. But she began to express feelings of isolation and loneliness. She had a few brief relationships with men who were far beneath her in terms of intelligence, education, ambition, and coping skills. When she attempted relationships with men who were more her peers, she had a succession of one-night stands with no intimacy—a pattern that had prevailed during much of her adolescence up to the time she met the man she eventually married.

It was clear to her individual therapist that this young woman sexualized all of her relationships, particularly with men. She was seductive even with her individual therapist. She presented herself as a sexual object while complaining that men seemed interested only in going to bed with her. Her therapist referred her for group therapy, suggesting that she could get feedback from other people about how she was perceived, and about what she was doing to generate such perceptions.

In the screening interview, the group therapists discussed what had brought her to the clinic initially, and asked what she would like from the group. The client replied that she was not sure that group therapy could help her because what she wanted was a more satisfying relationship with a man, and she doubted that she would find a good candidate among the group members. The therapists talked about her anxiety in social situations, and how she sought to reduce it. They agreed that the group would help her find out what she needed to know about other people (such as their motivation for being interested in her) and that this knowledge would help reduce her anxiety in social situations.

Clearly, in the above case, there is much more the therapists could have gone into. But not everything that can be explored need be explored. In the screening interview, your objective is a contract for some finite and readily attainable goal that both you and the client can agree on. Such a contract will almost certainly be modified as the client becomes better acquainted with the group and with his or her own interpersonal needs.

Preparation of the Client for Entry into the Group

In this discussion I am assuming that the client will be joining an ongoing group—the most common situation. If you are screening clients for a new group, initial preparation is somewhat different.

Toward the end of the screening interview, if it has not come up earlier, it will be helpful to the client for you to talk about what to do during the group session, and how other clients are likely to act. The more clients know about what to expect, the more rapidly their anxiety about being in a group is likely to diminish. Your purpose here is simply to let the client know a little about what it will be like. Here's an example:

> When the group session starts, we all go into the group room and sit down anywhere. I will introduce you to the other group members by telling them your first name. They will then tell you their names, and they might ask you some questions. You can answer them or not, depending on how you feel. Particularly if someone asks you a question you don't want to answer, all you have to say is that you don't want to answer that. They've all been in this same spot and they all understand how you feel. They might ask if you have any questions about them, or I might ask

you that. If you do, go ahead and ask. Same thing applies to them—if they don't want to answer you they'll tell you so.

Then we'll go on. I will ask people how they've been doing, and what they want to talk about today. People will usually pick up from where they left off last week, and it might take you a while to figure out what's going on—sort of like coming into a movie in the middle, after it's already started.

What I'd like to emphasize is that you don't have to talk at all if you don't want to. After you've been coming for a while, you'll begin to feel more comfortable there and then you can decide if you want to talk about yourself, and, if so, how much.

There's one other point, and I'll remind you of this again when we get to the group meeting. That is that we don't talk about the group outside the group. What people say in there is private, and you have to respect their privacy— just as they will respect yours. Do you have any questions?

For some clients, it is important to use as few words as possible; lengthy explanations such as the one above tend to either confuse them or increase anxiety, or both. Here's a shorter example:

When group starts, I'll introduce you. The other people will tell you their names. You don't have to talk after that. Watch and listen. When you're ready to talk in group, you'll know. Take your time. Remember that we don't talk outside of the group session about what people say in there. Do you have any questions?

Clients rarely have questions at this point. When they do, the questions are usually sufficiently general—what are the other people like, how old are they, how many are there altogether?—that you can answer them readily without breaching confidentiality.

This type of introduction may seem insufficient, so some therapists present new clients with written materials about how groups work in general and about how their particular group functions in terms of meeting times, fees, missed sessions, and the like. One therapist I met some years ago presented his new group clients with eleven typed, single-spaced pages of rules and procedures. That seems a bit much. Some therapists meet individually with new group members two or more times, essentially training them in the role of group member, prior to admission to group. And there are a number of other schemes (showing videotapes to new group members, for instance) that help to prepare the new client for entry into group.

In most clinic settings, however, resources are sparse and time is limited. One screening interview is all that is practical. Two screening interviews represent a significant investment of clinic resources (therapist time), as well as expense and delay for the client. A second interview should be regarded as desirable but not necessary.

If you are doing group with a cotherapist, both of you should attend the screening interview. By the end of the interview you each will have reached some decision about whether to invite the client to join your group. The question then is how to communicate your opinion to your cotherapist. One possibility is to agree on some nonverbal signals, and, if you both are in favor of acceptance, to tell the client then and there. A second possibility is to ask the client to withdraw to the waiting room while you both confer, and then to call him or her back into the interview room to hear your decision. A third possibility is to remain noncommittal and to tell the client that you will be in touch with him or her in the near future. Of these, the first method, employing nonverbal signals, is probably best; it conserves time and avoids having the client sit and wait while judgments about him or her are being made. But the choice is yours. You should use the method that fits your style and on which you and your co-therapist agree.

Screening interviews, which will be discussed more fully below, perform an instructional function for the client. If you are unable to do the screening yourself, the intake workers can provide the client with some information and orientation at the time of intake into the clinic program—for example, in day hospital or substance abuse settings where group is usually required of everyone. While less desirable than a more structured or formal screening interview, such orientation nonetheless helps clients prepare for group; and the better prepared the clients are, the more likely they are to benefit (Truax and Wargo, 1969), and the less disruptive they are likely to be.

This approach requires that intake workers, or the people introducing and orienting new clients to the clinic's programs, be trained to do screening for group, or at least to orient prospective group members. Such training need not be formal or extensive; indeed, it can be brief. Ideally, the training should be in-service, under the continuing education or staff development programs. But in some clinics, the only available training might consist of the group therapists talking with the intake or orientation worker about what to tell clients.

Some therapists routinely ask current group members to orient new members to the group during the group session. Presumably this is a way of integrating the new member and facilitating interaction. But this practice involves abdication of the therapists' responsibility to the client and to the group; it deprives the new member of the therapists' expertise at a crucial time; and it increases rather than decreases anxiety and discomfort within the group. The procedure also increases the risk that the new member's initial information about the group will be strongly biased by the idiosyncratic perceptions of some group members. Asking group members to orient new clients may be better than no orientation at all, but in some cases, it may not be.

Of course, it is possible that group member orientation of new clients might be accurate and empathic, and it could serve as a kind of welcome to the new member. But, while the procedure of asking group members to orient new members may be justifiable at times—particularly when most of the other group members have been attending for a long time and are well socialized into the group culture—its routine use is not recommended.

Fees, Absences, and Group Starting Time

Before the screening interview ends, it is prudent to at least mention your policies concerning fees, the handling of arrears, whether or not the client is obligated to pay for missed sessions, and what happens if the client cannot get to the group session on time.

Fees. If the client is going to be responsible for some or all of the fee for group therapy, it is important to discuss fees during the screening interview. Discussion of the fee for group therapy should be handled in the same way that discussion of fees for individual therapy or other clinic services are handled. Many clinics have a set fee for group therapy, and the therapists are free to negotiate a reduced fee with the client, depending on ability to pay and other factors. And in some clinics, therapists are fortunate in not having to be involved in fee negotiations with clients.

Issues related to fees include the amount, if any, of reduction of the standard fee, late payment policies, and policy regarding discussion of fee issues during the group sessions.

Yalom (1985) says very little about fees, referring to them as secret. Mullan and Rosenbaum (1978) recommend that all group members pay the same fee, and suggest analyzing, in the group, "the peculiar ways in which patients pay" (p. 87). Rutan and Stone (1984) regard fee issues as group issues, and hand out statements to members during the group session. Kadis and Winick (1968) discuss the importance of the fee issue to therapists as well as to patients.

A discussion of fees might go something like this:

Therapist: The clinic fee for group therapy is $65.00 per session.

Patient: I can't afford that.

Therapist: How much can you afford?

Patient: Five dollars.

Therapist: OK.

Frequently there are other factors, such as insurance coverage, which could lengthen the negotiation. In clinics where the therapists are required to generate fees sufficient to cover their salaries, fee negotiations may require additional time.

Some clients are expert in negotiating reduced fees for both individual and group therapy. If you are on salary and are not required to generate revenue for the clinic, it is difficult to resist making the lowest possible fees available to these clients, sometimes in violation of clinic fee guidelines. The challenge comes later on, when the client does not pay his or her bill. Given the amount of energy that has gone into negotiating a reduced fee, it is frequently surprising to therapists when the clients fall in arrears. The quandary for the therapists is how to call attention to the situation effectively, and whether to do so in the group, as a group issue, or outside of group sessions, as a private issue. This quandary can be avoided or reduced if you mention to the client during the screening interview how arrears are handled.

Whether to discuss nonpayment during the group session should depend on the precedents already set by the group and its coleaders. If such discussions have already been taking place, there is no particular reason to discontinue them and move the battleground about fees into a private (and special) arena. If you are starting a new group, you and your cotherapist can decide before the first screening interview whether fees and arrears are something you want to make public. Since there is no clear evidence that it makes much difference one way or the other, you are probably on safe ground to follow your own preferences in this matter. It is important to ensure in the screening interview that the client knows and understands how fees and arrears will be handled.

Absences. There are two issues related to absences from group. One is prior notification of the group, or of the therapists, that a group member will be absent. The other is whether to charge fees for missed group sessions. Most therapists (and clinics) ask for prior notification, usually twenty-four hours, if a client will miss a session. Occasionally, clients will ask to take leaves from the group—not to attend for a span of some months, not to pay the fee, and then to return. Reasons for the request are varied: a temporary work assignment in another town, a scheduling change on the job, going home for the summer, pregnancy, illness of a relative, and so on. While these circumstances can come up with people of varying diagnoses, they seem to occur with more regularity among group members who have borderline disorders.

Generally, such requests should be honored; however, absences of more than three months, even in a group with relatively stable membership, should be allowed with the understanding that readmission to the group will not be automatic but will depend on its composition and structure at the time the client wishes to return. Usually that will mean allowing the client back into group, unless you want to take that opportunity to exclude him or her.

Your clinic may already have a policy about charging for missed sessions, or the group, if it is a continuing one, may have its own procedures. Generally, those policies should be followed. In regard to group therapy, the two most common arrangements are (1) to pay for every group session whether or not the client is actually there, and (2) to not be charged for missed sessions when sufficient prior notification is given. The most difficult circumstances are a variant of (2) in which there is an agreement that the therapists will decide whether the reason for missing the group is of sufficient importance to warrant waiving the fee for that session.

If at all possible, use (1); it leads to much less controversy than (2), and option (2) may require you to sit in judgment on ambiguous issues.

Group Session Starting Time. It is prudent to ask early in the screening interview if the client will be able to arrive on time for the group sessions. If you fail to ask, you run the risk of going through the whole interview and deciding to accept the client only to find that he or she cannot get to the clinic at the time the group meets. If the client cannot change his or her schedule, he or she will not be attending that group.

The situation is less clear-cut when it turns out that the client can arrive ten or fifteen or twenty minutes late and is even more difficult when the client's tardiness will occur only infrequently—every month or two. The reasons are usually good: "I can't get off work earlier than this," "The bus doesn't get here until 5:15," "The meeting I have to go to doesn't end until after the scheduled group time," and so on. Decision in such matters is difficult. Do you hold the line and risk losing the client? Do you bend and say OK, you can come in late? Or do you try to renegotiate the group time— say, get everyone's agreement to meet fifteen or thirty minutes later in order to accommodate the tardy client?

The surest guide here is some combination of your own feelings (and your cotherapist's) and your sense of what the group is willing to tolerate. Some groups are loose, and their actual starting times indefinite. Agreeing that a client can come in late is therefore not a big deal. Some groups are more tightly organized and punctual, so coming in fifteen minutes late is regarded as a major disruption. Some therapists are simply indifferent to timeliness, while others are more rigid. Negotiating an agreement to tolerate a client's tardiness is probably the most efficient way to handle the issue. Shifting the group starting time in order to accommodate a client, especially one with a borderline personality disorder, usually buys time of the sort that Neville Chamberlain bought in Munich in 1938. Chamberlain, you may recall, was the British prime minister who agreed to Hitler's occupation of northern Czechoslovakia in exchange for a promise of "peace in our time." World War II began the following year.

Rejected Clients

Clients may be rejected because they are inappropriate for any group, or for your group in particular, or perhaps for other reasons. Usually if a client is going to be rejected, it will be clear to both you and your cotherapist by the time the interview is half over. You can then begin to talk with the client about alternative sources of help. However, it may be necessary to schedule a second interview in order to work through, as much and as gently as possible, the client's feelings about the rejection. Even if the client would not have wanted to join the group, rejection is frequently painful, especially when it comes from professional helpers. Fortunately, such situations seldom arise, and most often it is clear to both you and the client when admission to group would not be in the client's best interests.

If a client is rejected, it is prudent to meet with the referring therapist to discuss reasons for referral and reasons for rejection. If the therapist meant well but didn't know how to refer for your group or didn't know some things about the client that emerged during the screening interview, a meeting between you and the therapist will be especially helpful—both for that therapist and for the client's further individual therapy. The individual therapist can then work more effectively with the client on the issues that emerged during the screening interview, as well as working through any possible feelings of rejection. On the other hand, if the referral represented the therapist's effort to transfer a difficult client out of his or her caseload and into yours, such a meeting may decrease the probability that similar efforts will be made in the future.

Preparation of the Group for the Client

Once the client has accepted your invitation to join the group, it is necessary to say something to the group prior to the new member's entry. An informal discussion among group therapists at a recent meeting of the American Group Psychotherapy Association suggested that most therapists tell the group that a new member is coming on a certain date (usually two weeks in advance), and nothing more. But practices vary widely. Some therapists tell the new member's age (or age range) and sex; others tell the new member's name as well. One psychoanalytically oriented group therapist, after announcing a new member would be coming, would invite the group to speculate about what the new member would be like. Most therapists admit new members singly; a few said that they prefer to wait until two can join at the same time.

Regardless of the specific practice, it is important to say something to your group prior to the arrival of a new member. My own practice has been to give the client's age range and sex, nothing more. Most group members understand, implicitly, that new members will be coming in after old ones leave, in order to maintain the size of the group. Unless the group is large (more than eight members), the addition of a new member is rarely an issue.

Some group therapists ask the group's permission to add a new member. Their rationale is that seeking permission in this way is an attempt to encourage the group to take responsibility for its own behavior. Such a stance may stem from a theoretical framework which regards the group as an egalitarian enterprise and the therapist as facilitator rather than leader. In the context of a health care delivery system, however, the contracts, whether implicit or explicit, between client and therapist are asymmetrical rather than egalitarian. Clients and therapists are not coming together for common and similar benefit. In the clinic also, therapists have more power than clients. In such an asymmetrical context, for which the present volume is intended, the group therapist functions as a leader rather than a colleague. Asking the group's permission to add new members is therefore an attempt at abrogation of the leader's gatekeeping function, and is not recommended.

3

Understanding Major
Approaches to Group Therapy

It is possible but imprudent to conduct group therapy without an explicit theory. Your theory of individual therapy can be adapted to the group situation, but if you do that, you will be minimizing the potential impact of group therapy. Most clinicians who begin to learn group therapy after having been trained in individual therapy find it difficult to shift from the dyadic orientation of individual therapy to the multipersonal orientation of group therapy. Failure to understand group process and the use of group dynamics to effect individual change is one of the most common limitations of group therapists (Dies, 1983). A different theory—a group theory—is required. The purposes of this chapter are to provide the clinician with an orientation to the major theories of group psychotherapy, to discuss the implications of these theories for therapist technique, and to provide a theoretical rationale for the therapist interventions described in the rest of this book.

Overview

There are many theories of group therapy. Some are based primarily on the clinical experience of the theorist; some have an empirical base. Some theories appear to be minor variations of a central theme, and can be grouped together. There are four major clusters or families of theories of group therapy. These are referred to as (1) psychoanalytic or psychodynamic, (2) group dynamic, (3) interpersonal, and (4) behavioral or cognitive-behavioral. Two minor clusters of theories round out the picture. One includes group theories that have persisted for some time but which have very small followings. An example is the psychomotor theory of Albert Pesso (1973), which is deserving of more attention than it has so far received, and Gestalt group therapy, which enjoyed considerable popularity in the 1960s and 1970s but has waned recently. The other group of theories is more of a category than a cluster, consisting of theories and techniques that are, at best, on the margin of acceptability. Membership in this category changes from time to time, and includes group theories that advocate screaming (Janov, 1970) and vomiting (Lowen, 1958).

Of course, the theories of group therapy could be categorized differently than I have done here; any classification scheme is largely arbitrary. The present grouping is sufficient for my purpose, which is orientation rather than explication.

Psychoanalytic Theories

There are two subgroups under this heading: psychoanalytic theories proper and psychodynamic group theories (not to be confused with group dynamic theories). Under the general heading of psychoanalytic group therapy there is psychoanalysis in groups (Wolf and Schwartz, 1962, 1971), group analysis (Foulkes and Anthony, 1965), and psychoanalytic group therapy (Ezriel, 1973). These theorists share psychoanalytic terminology such as *transference* and *resistance,* and emphasize the primacy of historical and intrapsychic factors like unconscious motivation. They differ in emphasis on group versus individual focus, on attending to the interaction between the individual and the group or between the therapist and the group, and in the level of activity or impassivity to be adopted by the therapist.

The analytic group therapist begins the task of understanding and interpreting what is going on in the group in terms of the hypothesis that things are not what they seem. For Wolf and Schwartz, observable behaviors and interactions in the group are manifestations of transference, involving unconscious motivations and historical determinants. The group members do not know why they interact with other group members in particular ways. The therapists, because they are analytically trained, can discern these motives and can help the group members to perceive them. There is much exploration of events in the distant past of each individual.

Foulkes (Foulkes and Anthony, 1965) understands observable behaviors in the group in terms of underlying group themes, as do Wolf and Schwartz. However, Foulkes places more emphasis on the common group theme and on the transference relationship between the group and the therapist. The therapist avoids facilitating transference by remaining silent. By avoiding even the semblance of exercising power, the therapist encourages the group to assume responsibility for itself. The result is a therapist who says little, who seldom addresses any individual group member, and who responds more frequently to what he or she perceives as the group theme than to anything that the group members may have been discussing.

Like Foulkes, Ezriel (1973) emphasizes the importance of the underlying common group theme rather than observable behavior. The task of the therapist is to detect the common group theme, to present it to the group, and to clarify the idiosyncratic reaction of each individual in relation to the group theme. The therapist is not supposed to respond in group until he or she knows what the theme is and has carefully formulated an intervention. The result is a therapist who is rather peculiarly unresponsive to whatever else is going on in the room at the time.

Techniques based on any of these three theories are difficult to learn and to apply correctly. Wolf and Schwartz (1971) seem to assume that practitioners using their theory will be trained in classical psychoanalysis. The application, if not the comprehension, of the approaches advocated by Foulkes and Ezriel seem to require an intimate knowledge of psychoanalytic theory and practice. It seems likely that these analytic group techniques would benefit the same clients who would benefit from classical psychoanalysis.

Groups based on these theories are probably rare in clinic settings, except for psychoanalytic training institutes. However, like psychoanalysis itself, psychoanalytic theories of group psychotherapy have had an influence far beyond the circle of analytic practitioners.

Psychodynamic Theories

Concern with unconscious dynamics and concepts like *regression* and *ego defenses* places psychodynamic theories within the psychoanalytic family of theories. The psycho-dynamic approaches differ from the psychoanalytic theories in their focus on interpersonal as well as intrapsychic and group issues. Historically, the psychodynamic theories also have a somewhat different background from the more ortho-dox psychoanalytic theories in that they are strongly influenced by Slavson (1950), who (as all of the psychoanalytic writers who mention him never fail to point out) was not analytically trained. Rutan and Stone (1984) provide an excellent description of current psychodynamic theory and technique.

Another variation on the general psychoanalytic theme, a little further from orthodoxy than the psychodynamic theories, is the contribution of Wilfred Bion (1961). He says little about transference, regression, or unconscious dynamics and resistance in the psychoanalytic sense. However, he sub-scribes strongly to the basic psychoanalytic tenet that things are not what they seem. Bion describes the underlying, or latent, group themes largely in terms of the group's need to depend on the leader—a need which he regards as both insatiable and unhealthy. Bion's theory is somewhat difficult to classify. A psychoanalyst himself, he became interested in how groups work, which is different from how groups heal, and is sometimes classified as a group dynamicist (Shaffer and Galinsky, 1974).

Group Dynamics Theories

This set of theories stems from a tradition quite different from the psychoanalytic/psychodynamic theories discussed above. The origins of the latter are psychotherapeutic and stem from therapists' efforts to understand and modify psychopathology. The origins of group dynamics are largely in social and industrial psychology and stem from the efforts of experts in these fields to understand group influence on individual behavior and on productivity in the workplace and in other human groups. In their classic work, *Group Dynamics*, Cartwright and Zander (1968, p. 19) define group dynamics as "a field of inquiry dedicated to advancing knowledge about the nature of groups, the laws of their development, and their interrelations with individuals, other groups, and larger institutions."

This is a focus very different from that of the therapists concerned, ultimately, with healing. In group dynamics, the focus is on learning about group process and, almost incidentally, about one's own impact on others. Through the process of feedback from others in the group, one learns about one's own relationship to the group process. The history of how group dynamicists and group therapists got together is an interesting story which would take us too far afield here but has been well documented by Shaffer and Galinsky (1974) and in a book of readings assembled by Kissen (1976). The classic work integrating the two fields is *Psychotherapy Through the Group Process* by Whitaker and Lieberman (1964). More recently, Lakin (1985) has discussed, from a group dynamics standpoint, therapeutic principles in what he calls "helping groups."

It is interesting to note that Freud's own theory of groups (Freud, [1922] 1949) is more closely related to the group dynamics position than to the psychoanalytic. His is indeed a book on group psychology rather than group therapy. Freud discusses the psychology of mobs, armies, and the church, seeking to account for an individual's willingness to follow a leader while subsuming his own interests under those of the leader or the group, and to account for the intensity of emotions sometimes experienced during group actions. The fundamental mechanism, for Freud, is identification rather than transference. Since identification is a normal developmental phenomenon, Freud is able to account for group psychology, the interpersonal power attributed to the group leader, the intensification of emotion, and other factors as normal group phenomena rather than as manifestations of neurotic need or unresolved transference issues. Freud's theory of groups is readily understood and applicable to nonanalytically oriented therapy groups. I strongly recommend his slim volume.

Interpersonal Theories

This group of theories focuses on here-and-now relationships among group members and on observable interpersonal behaviors in the group. These theories also focus on group issues and, to some extent, on underlying group themes. By far the most well-known and influential of these theorists is Irvin Yalom (1985). A psychiatrist, he has consistently produced scholarly work based on empirical data (1985; see also Lieberman, Yalom, and Miles, 1973). Yalom's emphasis on interpersonal learning as a therapeutic factor in group psychotherapy is similar to the group dynamics concept of interpersonal feedback. However, Yalom's position is explicitly Sullivanian, which would place him more in the category of neo-Freudian theorists. He is one of the few theorists who have attempted to identify the curative or therapeutic factors in group psychotherapy. These are discussed in Chapter Four.

Yalom regards the therapeutic factors as core mechanisms of change, independent of theory and intrinsic to the therapeutic process. His description of the therapeutic factors is based on research that Yalom and his associates have carried out over a period of many years. However, it has been noted that the questionnaires and research methods used by this group are biased toward interpersonal theory (Weiner, 1974). It is not surprising, therefore, that the data collected and cited by Yalom support his interpersonalist position. Yalom's claim to be dealing with universal and theory-free factors is not supported by examination of his research methodology. While his findings and conclusions deserve careful consideration within the context of interpersonal theory, his contention that it is the only show in town should be regarded with caution.

Behavioral Theories

This is a set of theories that apply the principles of learning, derived from the experimental psychology laboratory, to the modification of dysfunctional or deviant behavior (psychopathology). The basic approach involves identifying, one at a time, behavior patterns that client and therapist agree need modification. Together they evaluate client resources for dealing with the problem behavior and devise, implement, and assess modification strategies. Therapist interventions are based on the intelligent and sensitive application of research findings to the individual case. (It should be noted that behavior therapists would hesitate to use words like *intelligent* and *sensitive* because they refer to intrapsychic, unobservable phenomena. These therapists emphasize observable behavior.) Once the client is emitting the desired behaviors with the desired frequency, or sometimes before that, the therapist introduces strategies for maintaining the new behavioral patterns.

In addition to general outpatient and inpatient groups, behavior therapy techniques are used in short-term, single-topic groups, such as assertiveness training and social skills.

Just as psychoanalytic training would be helpful to therapists leading psychoanalytic groups, familiarity with and training in the principles of learning and reinforcement would be helpful to therapists leading behavior therapy groups. Such training is most readily found in graduate level courses in learning theory and behavior modification in academic departments of psychology.

Shaffer and Galinsky (1974) provide an overview of behavioral therapy in groups. Behavioral approaches to group therapy have been nicely described by Rose (1977) and by Heckel and Salzberg (1976).

Group Cognitive Behavioral Therapy

This therapy is a recent development based in part on the cognitive theories of Aaron Beck (1976), Albert Ellis (1962), and Donald Meichenbaum (1977). The major difference between the behavioral and the cognitive theories is in the willingness of the latter to deal with what people are thinking, and to seek to modify maladaptive or disturbed thoughts and thought patterns. Merging of the two types of theory is relatively new, and it is still too early to determine whether individual and group therapy techniques based on these theories represent the next fad in psychotherapies or a natural evolutionary step in a more enduring process. Given the solid research base on which these theories and techniques rest, the interest they are currently arousing among clinicians seems more likely to grow than to fade.

Techniques used in group cognitive behavioral therapy are similar to those employed in group behavior therapy in that they are highly structured, and they involve homework, the keeping of copious records by group members, and role play (behavior rehearsal). They differ from the pure behavior groups in their attention to cognitive restructuring and similar techniques that do not directly involve change in client behavior. Because the groups are highly structured, they may resemble classes or workshops rather than traditional therapy groups. The techniques lend themselves readily to what has been called a cookbook approach, with the group leader following an instructional recipe for conducting a series of group sessions. A good example of this kind of approach is *A Therapist's Manual for Cognitive Behavior Therapy in Groups* by Sank and Shaffer (1984). An important contribution to the literature on the treatment of older adults is *Group Cognitive Therapy: A Treatment Approach for Depressed Older Adults* by Yost, Beutler, Corbishley, and Allender (1986).

Other Theories

Gestalt therapy was originated by F. S. Perls shortly after World War II (Perls, Hefferline, and Goodman, 1951; Perls, 1969). It gained considerable popularity in the 1960s and 1970s before beginning to wane. Many therapists trained during that time are still practicing, and excellent training in these techniques is still available at facilities like the Gestalt Institute of Cleveland.

Most Gestalt (the word, a German noun meaning pattern, is always capitalized) therapists focus exclusively on the individual, with very little attention to group or relationship issues. Some, however, are more group oriented. One basic Gestalt technique is *counterphobic*. That is, the therapist helps the client to face whatever the client fears and helps him or her to accept (integrate) the feared action as well as the fear itself. For example, clients who are afraid to cry because they fear they would never stop or would lose control are encouraged to go ahead and cry. Eventually, and usually in a surprisingly short time, the clients stop crying.

Another Gestalt technique involves a kind of role play. If a client talks about a relationship with another person not physically present, an empty chair may be placed opposite the client, who is asked to imagine that the other person is in the chair. The client talks to the imagined person, and then is asked to move over to the empty chair and talk back as though the client were now the other person, talking to the client. For example, a client may want to talk about his or her relationship with his or her mother. He or she would (usually with some encouragement by the therapist) engage in an imaginary conversation with his or her mother, and then move over to the other chair. The client would then respond as the mother would have responded to the client. This switching back and forth between the two chairs continues until some sort of conclusion (called "closure") is reached.

It can be seen from these examples that the Gestalt technique is primarily intrapsychic rather than interpersonal. The therapist usually works with one client at a time in front of the rest of the group. Occasionally the therapist will draw in the other group members in order to facilitate what the therapist is doing with the client who is working; but even when the entire group is involved, the primary focus is on the therapist-client interaction, and the group is ancillary.

There are many Gestalt techniques. Indeed, some Gestalt practitioners would argue that Gestalt is more an attitude, a frame of mind, than a set of technques. Erving and Miriam Polster have described the Gestalt approach quite well (Polster and Polster, 1973). Zinker (1977) emphasizes Gestalt therapists' innovative attitude. A Gestalt approach to dream interpretation is presented in Chapter Twelve.

Psychomotor Therapy

This therapy was originated by Albert and Dianne Pesso (Pesso, 1973). A brilliant theorist and innovator, Albert Pesso offers training and certification in his techniques to mental health professionals. However, he has published little and has not set up the kind of organization that readily permits others to teach his theory and technique.

Pesso's theory may be classified as neoanalytic since he uses concepts like *ego, repression,* and *instinct,* attends to *psychic energy,* and emphasizes the historical antecedents of present behavior. The psychomotor techniques based on Pesso's theory are in a sense cognitive in that they involve recreating, in the group, the individual's intrapsychic, cognitive experiences, both verbal and nonverbal. For example, if a client describes feeling pressured or burdened, Pesso might ask where in his or her body the feeling is located, and then arrange for other clients to press inward on the client until the external feeling of pressure matches the client's internal experience.

Thus, the focus of psychomotor theory and therapy is intrapsychic. However, Pesso assumes that the goal of instinctual drives is interaction with other human beings. Intrapsychic dialogues, which may be metaphoric or symbolic, are translated into interaction with real human beings who temporarily, during group sessions, assume metaphoric or symbolic roles—as, for instance, the role of one's internal critical parental voice. An adaptation of Pesso's technique for working with internalized critical voices is described in Chapter Eleven.

Therapist Activity Level

The three traditional types of theory of group psychotherapy (psychoanalytic, psychodynamic, and group dynamic) require therapists to be passive or impassive, rarely intervening in whatever is going on in the group, initiating few or no interactions, and responding minimally or not at all when addressed by group members. The theories differ in their rationales for this therapist stance. For the psychoanalytic theorists (Wolf and Schwartz, 1962, 1971; Foulkes and Anthony, 1965; Ezriel, 1973), the impassivity of the group therapist is analogous to the impassive attentiveness of the classical psychoanalyst.

Bion's position (1961) is in many ways similar. Bion understands the group's initial cue dependency on the leader in terms of the group's assumption that it is ignorant and powerless. The leader, according to Bion, is imbued with godlike omniscience and omnipotence. If the leader responds to the group's dependency needs and basic assumptions about itself, he or she will inevitably fail since no one can meet the group's expectations, based as they are on neurotic need. The leader then suffers the same fate as any failed god. Impassivity and refusal to meet the group's needs is therefore appropriate.

Whitaker and Lieberman, representing the group dynamics position, take a similar stance, referring to the omniscience with which the leader is endowed and assuming that the group will misunderstand the character of the leader's expert knowledge. They refer to the group's "magical belief that the therapist can understand and fix everything" (1964, p. 196). Whitaker and Lieberman advocate that the therapist maintain an aloof position, which in practice translates into appearing distant and uninvolved.

Other theories requiring therapist impassivity have a different origin, in social and industrial psychology rather than in psychopathology. The connotations of impassivity are different, pertaining to the leader's role as facilitator of group process, and therapist comments tend to have a contemporary focus. Kissen's (1976) collection of readings provides a good overview of group dynamics from the standpoint of group therapy, and Lakin (1985) addresses issues of helping groups in general from this frame of reference.

All of these theories have in common the advocacy of therapist behavior that involves a good deal of waiting and very little leading. In these theories, and in others like them, therapist impassivity is advocated because it is believed to avoid undesirable results, such as the transient satisfaction of neurotic need. On the other hand, impassivity is thought to facilitate the occurrence of desired results, such as the acceptance by the group of increased responsibility for itself. The frequent result of this therapist inactivity is a lot of silence and initial group interactions characterized by hostility. The following assumptions appear to be implicit in theories that advocate therapist impassivity:

- The expectation by group members that the therapist will provide leadership is based on a neurotic need or trait and not on a reasonable assessment of ambiguous reality.
- Since neurotic needs cannot be satisfied, therapist efforts to meet such needs are doomed to failure, and making such an effort is a technical error.
- The frustration experienced by group members because of the therapist's refusal to attempt to meet the group's neurotic needs is inevitable and desirable. It mirrors the frustration experienced by group members outside the group when their neurotic needs are, inevitably, not met. The group thus becomes a microcosm in which members can work out their reactions to frustration in more adaptive ways.

All of these theories assume that the initial stages of group are inevitably characterized by conflict. Whitaker and

Lieberman (1964) describe their theory of group development in terms of focal conflict points that arise and are resolved as the group matures.

The cognitive-behavioral group of theories, in contrast, require an active therapist stance. Indeed, the therapist fills a role similar to that of teacher or consultant to the group. This high activity level is also found in Gestalt groups, encounter groups (Lieberman, Yalom, and Miles, 1973), and in some special topic, time-limited groups such as assertiveness training, where the differences between doing therapy and teaching become a matter of definition. In these groups, interactions are typically between a single client and the group leader, and group dynamics issues tend to be ignored. What is regarded as therapeutic in these groups is leader application of theoretical principles and techniques. The group itself is not regarded as a therapeutic agent except perhaps to the extent that it is ancillary to and facilitative of what the leader is trying to do.

Yalom's interpersonal theory occupies a midpoint between these two poles of therapist activity. For Yalom (1985), the therapist is sometimes active, as a gatekeeper, manager, and producer. At other times the therapist functions like an expert consultant, helping to keep the group on track. Thus, therapist activity level varies from time to time. While Yalom does not directly discuss therapist activity level, a careful reading of his work suggests that he is far closer to the less active or reactive therapist stance than to the active, directive approach required by behavioral and Gestalt theories.

There are data that address the issue of therapist activity level. Dies (1983) reviews research carried out between 1970 and 1979. On the basis of the data, he defines three major tasks for the therapist: (1) providing therapeutic structure, (2) developing a meaningful learning environment, and (3) building a supportive environment for learning. In terms of therapist activity, Dies suggests that the therapist should be more active and structuring early in treatment, and less directive later on. More structuring and greater activity are necessary "with patients whose psychopathology restricts their capacity to interact in socially competent ways" (p. 61). Even advice giving, a clear technical error for therapists adopting an impassive stance, has been shown to be effective under certain conditions. In general the research reviewed by Dies supports an active but not domineering therapist role early in the life of the group, to be gradually relinquished as anxiety decreases and as cohesiveness and supportiveness increase. The data Dies reviews are not generally supportive of the passive therapist stance nor of the group-as-a-whole approaches stemming from either the psychoanalytic or the group dynamics theories.

In my experience, clinicians advocating a passive or impassive therapist stance, whether from the standpoint of psychoanalytic or of group dynamics approaches, have difficulty understanding and tolerating clinicians advocating a more active role; and the converse is equally true. Both tend to ignore the middle ground typified by Yalom, who in turn is critical of both extremes. The vehemence with which these various positions are held by practicing clinicians, and the genuine antipathy experienced by the antagonists, suggest that the issue is not likely to be easily resolved.

It is possible that underlying the controversy is a difference in the way clinicians view interpersonal reality and emotional growth. Some people, clinicians and others, assume that because emotional supplies are limited, the need for those supplies cannot be met, and that frustration is therefore inevitable. Growth comes from transcending that frustration based on emotional deprivation. Freud's theory of emotional development may be regarded as based on such an assumption. But others seem to assume that emotional supplies are plentiful and that growth comes from gratification rather than frustration. The so-called Third Force theories, exemplified by Maslow (1968) and nicely summarized by Robinson (1979) in his book on systems of psychology, seem to take the latter position.

The position I take in the present volume is generally in the middle ground, which is where most of the research

data seem to be. I advocate an active therapist role early
in the life of a therapy group, and I encourage the therapist to actively facilitate the entry of new members into
ongoing groups.

Psychotherapy involves learning, and learning seldom
takes place under conditions of high anxiety. The position
I take in this book is that therapists generally should intervene actively to reduce group anxiety and to keep it at as
low a level as possible in order to facilitate learning. There
are, however, a few situations in which it is necessary to
allow group anxiety to rise. They occur when the group has
fallen silent because the group members are reluctant to
initiate discussion of some feared topic. The conditions under
which this silence is likely to occur, and suggested therapist
responses to it, are described in a later chapter.

Fulfilling Group Needs

The issue of whether frustration or fulfillment of group
needs best facilitates learning and growth has not yet been
empirically determined. It seems likely that both are effective
at different times, depending on situational determinants in
the group. The position taken here is that in general fulfillment and gratification of needs are preferable to deprivation
and frustration.

A therapy group is a multilevel experience, with many
interactions having symbolic importance for the individual
and for the group. Through role play and other techniques,
the group is able to provide its members with symbolic fulfillment of long-frustrated needs, and thus to facilitate present and future growth. The work with internalized parental
voices described in Chapter Eleven exemplifies the ability of
a therapy group to facilitate symbolic experiencing.

Implicit in this discussion, and in this book, is the
concept that needs are not neurotic and that dependency
needs, in particular, are not insatiable. Group cohesiveness
and the establishment of a therapeutic atmosphere occur more
rapidly when therapists meet rather than frustrate the group's

initial cue dependency on the leaders. In the following chapters, the underlying theory is that therapists can and should meet the group's needs for leadership. The procedures described in Chapter Five for starting a group are based on this assumption and on the assumption, resulting from decades of clinical experience, that initial group dependence on the therapist decreases rapidly and without rancor when those leadership needs are met. These recommendations and assumptions are in line with Dies's (1980) research-based recommendations for an initially active therapist who gradually decreases directiveness as the group matures.

A constant problem for the group therapist is whether or to what extent to focus on individual intrapsychic, individual behavioral, client-therapist, group-therapist, or group-as-a-whole phenomena. I take the position that group is an interpersonal context for the resolution of interpersonal difficulties. It is, therefore, generally preferable to focus on observable behavior and its sequelae within the group rather than on clients' verbal content. However, it is important to acknowledge rather than to ignore what the client is actually saying. It is also important for clients to discover that both their personal issues and their intrapsychic mechanisms have common as well as idiosyncratic aspects. That discovery cannot be made without some delving into personal and intrapsychic realms. The interpersonal focus advocated here should not restrict therapists from exploring other realms as they seem pertinent.

The question of what is effective in group psychotherapy cannot be separated from the theoretical framework of the individuals evaluating the question. For the psychoanalytically and psychodynamically oriented, the development of insight is an important component. Empirical research in this context seeks to evaluate the extent to which insight has been attained. For those with a more interpersonal orientation, interpersonal learning is likely to occupy a more central place, and empirical research focuses on interpersonal issues. For the behaviorally oriented, research documents the change in frequency of emitted target behaviors.

In the following chapter, factors that have been shown to be related to improvement and/or outcome in group psychotherapy—therapeutic factors—are discussed. The study of therapeutic factors is an approach most congruent with the interpersonal group theories. However, one need not subscribe to the interpersonalist position in order to apply the therapeutic factors.

There are many ways of looking at both the theoretical and empirical facets of therapy groups. The best way is the one that makes the most sense to you and that has the strongest empirical support. People differ with regard to what makes sense to them, to what importance they place on empirical data, and to what constitutes convincing empirical support. With these differences in mind, your respectful consideration of a variety of theoretical frameworks is most likely to facilitate development of your own subjective theory of group therapy—the one you take with you into the group room when you leave supervision and textbooks outside the door.

4

Techniques to
Enhance Therapeutic Factors
in Group Work

What is supposed to happen during a group therapy session? The answer to this question depends on a variety of factors: the purpose of the group, the nature of the agreements between therapists and clients regarding the therapy, and the theory espoused by the therapists, to name a few. Most group therapists, particularly when they are starting out, assume group members are supposed to talk with one another. Specifically, clients are supposed to talk about feelings, and, ideally, to express or show those feelings. Thus, group therapists may seek to facilitate client self-disclosure and catharsis, after which the client may feel better and report relief from feelings of distress. How much encouragement and guidance the client gets toward behavior change depends on which theory the therapists use, and probably on the therapists' personalities and therapy experience as well.

But self-disclosure and catharsis are only two of the factors that have been identified as therapeutic in group therapy. Review of the literature suggests that there are five lists of therapeutic factors that have been compiled over the years. The first of these is by Corsini and Rosenberg (1955); the second, by Hill (1957); the third, by Berzon, Pious, and Farson (1963); the fourth, and probably best-known, by Yalom in 1985; and most recently, by Bloch and Crouch (1985). There

...able overlap among the lists, which have nine to
...actors. In what follows, I rely most heavily on the
... of Bloch and Crouch, whose review of the group ther-
...py literature on therapeutic factors is the most scholarly and
whose suggested factors are the most solidly empirically based.
The factors they name are:

- Insight
- Learning from interpersonal interaction
- Acceptance (cohesiveness)
- Self-Disclosure
- Catharsis
- Guidance
- Universality
- Altruism
- Vicarious learning
- Instillation of hope

It may be a formidable task, particularly for relatively inexpe-
rienced therapists, to try to keep these factors in mind along
with all of the other things that they are supposed to keep
track of—what is taking place in the group, what the coleader
is doing, the individual agendas of patients, the agenda of the
group as a whole, and so on. To make matters more complex,
some of the therapeutic factors are primarily therapist issues
(guidance, instillation of hope); some are primarily group
issues (universality, cohesiveness); some are primarily client
issues (self-disclosure, altruism, catharsis); and some are interactional issues (learning from interpersonal interaction, vicarious learning). The conceptual complexity here is formidable
indeed.

In this chapter, I will discuss each of the therapeutic
factors in terms of therapist technique: what to do in order to
maximize the effectiveness of the therapeutic factors. I will
start with guidance and instillation of hope because those are
factors that you control and because they are present in the
screening interview as well as in the first sessions of group
the client attends.

Guidance

Bloch and Crouch (1985, p. 170) define guidance as "the imparting of information and the giving of direct advice." (Yalom calls this factor *imparting information*.) Information is usually provided by the therapists, and advice giving is offered primarily by group members. Yalom and Bloch and Crouch are no more than moderately positive about information giving by therapists, and they are more negative about advice giving by clients. Yet both refer to Flowers's study of advice giving in group therapy with sex offenders (1979) in which this type of guidance was shown to be effective. Curiously, neither Yalom nor Bloch and Crouch refer to the explicit instruction and advice characteristic of behaviorally oriented groups (see, for example, Rose, 1977) that have been shown to be effective in the modification of maladaptive behaviors.

Information Giving. In a general, interactional therapy group, there are several situations in which information giving is particularly helpful. The first of these is in the screening interview, when you give clients information about how the group works, about what they can expect from the group, and about what the group will expect from them during the group sessions. During the session itself, information giving is helpful and appropriate at the following stages.

1. Early in the life of the group, or during the first few sessions a new client attends. The information you provide (in essence, the teaching you do) enables clients to learn how to be good group members. The information pertains to the way the group works: starting on time, not interrupting people, issues of confidentiality, and the like.

2. After the first few sessions, as you begin to teach clients how to use the theoretical language you use to understand, predict, and explain or interpret events. How much explicit teaching you do depends on the theoretical approach you use and on the purpose of the group. In a short-term, special topic group, for assertiveness training or bulimia, for example, such teaching might be an agenda item. In a general therapy group, the teaching is often implicit in ther-

apist comments. If you keep asking group members how they feel about what they report, they will sooner or later get the idea that they are supposed to talk about feelings. If you keep focusing the topic away from there-and-then issues to here-and-now issues, or to historical antecedents, the group members will begin to talk more in those terms. You will facilitate learning if you tell the group what you are doing as you are doing it. For example, after asking how a client feels about something he or she has just said, you might comment that it is important to let the group know about feelings and reactions as well as events.

3. When the group addresses a particular content topic about which you have knowledge or expertise, as, for example, personality characteristics of adult children of alcoholics, or characteristics of victims of sexual abuse, or how to be assertive without being aggressive.

4. When the group gets stuck and you know what it needs to do to get unstuck. In the early sessions, the group will not know what to do and will fall silent unless you provide leadership. Later on, the group may fall silent, or become repetitive, because the group members are reluctant to talk about some potentially difficult topic or to confront a member who is generating hostile feelings in the rest of the group. The first few times this happens, you can point out that the group is avoiding a topic, without necessarily specifying what the topic is. (In dealing with very seriously impaired clients, though, it would be facilitative to take that extra step of specifying the topic as well.)

Guidance, in the form of imparting information, frequently has a bad name among therapists. Reluctance to guide, in this sense, may be related, as Bloch and Crouch (1985) observe, to a fear that supplying information to a client may foster undesirable dependency and inhibit growth toward self-sufficiency.

Whatever validity this assumption has in individual therapy, it may not hold in group therapy. Consider the difference between a novel and a play. In a novel, it is possible for the author to describe, and the reader to see, events that are entirely intrapsychic. In a play, everything must be visible; even when intrapsychic events are discussed, the necessity for translating them into the spoken idiom limits the depth and detail in which they can be explored. In a novel, the locus of the action is within and between the characters; in a play, it is between the characters and the audience.

Group therapy is much more like a play than like a novel. In individual therapy, guidance can set up an undesirable dynamic between client and therapist in which the client becomes accustomed to, and then dependent on, the therapist for the resolution of intrapsychic tension. In a group, the establishment of such a dynamic is difficult precisely because of the presence of other group members. In the interpersonal context of the group, guidance—specifically, the imparting of information—becomes a process of making your expertise available to the group.

In addition to providing information the group is likely to find useful and helpful, guidance helps reduce anxiety by reducing ambiguity and by providing leadership. Reducing anxiety facilitates the effectiveness of the therapeutic factors.

Advice Giving. This other component of guidance is more frequently encountered from other group members than from the therapists. An exception is the psychologically naive group therapist, who may have much clinical experience but little formal education in therapeutic techniques. There are at least three kinds of advice giving:

1. Instructions about specific behavior, generally of the form, "What you should do is . . ." or "If I were you, I would . . . ."
2. Proffering of alternative solutions, as in "Have you tried . . . ?"
3. Facilitation of problem identification and problem solving, as in "That looks like it would be a lot for one person to take on. You might need some help."

Of these, the first is probably the most common and the third the most helpful. Generally, the answer to the second type, "Have you tried . . . ," is "Yes"; the recipient of advice is likely to have already thought of all of the alternatives that other group members might think of.

In group therapy, guidance can be facilitative, or it can be irrelevant. I have found, in the group therapy literature, virtually no empirical evidence that guidance in groups fosters unwarranted dependency. On the other hand, the potency of guidance as a therapeutic factor may not be as great as some other factors.

Instillation of Hope

Bloch and Crouch define instillation of hope as the expectation, based on the client's own observations of other group members, that group therapy will work, and on his or her conclusions, drawn from those observations, that their improvement is attributable to experiences in group therapy.

It takes some time before improvement becomes apparent. How much time depends on the severity of the initial disturbance and on its duration and chronicity—in short, on its etiology and prognosis. Rapidity of improvement also is affected by client attributes such as age, education, and intellectual level. Other influences include the techniques and theory employed by the therapists, the ambience of the group, which is a function of the way the group members interact, the length of time they have been together, and similar factors. The length of time needed for improvement to be seen varies greatly. In groups of college students in student mental health clinics, for example, visible improvement can be expected within a month. But in some clinics offering long-term treatment, improvement may not be convincingly apparent for a year or more.

A year is a long time to ask someone to attend a group before becoming convinced that it will help. Therefore, long before improvement is undeniably apparent, or (in an ongoing group) before a new member has been in the group long enough to assess the progress of other group members, it is essential for the therapists to provide and nurture hope.

When clients come into therapy, they have stories to tell: the stories of the life events that led them to become clients in your clinic. Almost always, these are stories of tragedy and defeat, of sorrow and loss. There is also another component to these stories: the clients' continuing sense of hopelessness, helplessness, and futility in the face of intolerable events. The instillation of hope must come initially from your refusal to accept these feelings as definitive.

For example: Sonya had come to the group with a presenting complaint of difficulties in interpersonal relationships. After she had been in the group for two months, she talked during one session about her troubles. Her life had been a series of brief, intense relationships characterized by a month or two of great happiness and satisfaction followed by three or four months of painful breaking up. She had concluded that she was incapable of maintaining an intimate relationship, that she was basically unlovable, and that men generally were unpleasant and self-centered creatures who would only use her as long as it suited them and then cast her aside.

The therapist acknowledged the validity of her feelings, for herself, but said that he did not share her conclusions. Intimate relationships, he said, are difficult to establish and to maintain. Most people manage only one major intimate relationship at a time, and it takes a while to learn to maintain such a relationship over a span of years. Sonya, the therapist suggested, was in that learning process. He acknowledged Sonya's belief that she was unlovable, but suggested that she had that feeling, at least in part, because she had difficulty accepting and acknowledging love but no difficulty concluding that people did not like her or were hostile to her. And he acknowledged that some men (as well, he noted, as some women) are unpleasant, selfish, and manipulative. Perhaps, he said, the group could help Sonya to look at how she chose the men she became involved with, and could help her devise ways to evaluate their desirable and undesirable qualities before reaching a state of intense involvement.

In this example, the therapist accepted Sonya's feelings, but not her beliefs or conclusions, and suggested some possible alternative outcomes. This kind of therapist comment is appropriate early in the life of a group, or at the time a new group member first engages in some major self-disclosures. One reason for the relatively high level of therapist activity at this early point in the group's life is the high probability that the other group members will respond with Type 1 advice giving: "you should . . . ," "what you need is . . . ," and the like. Such advice is seldom experienced as helpful by the recipient.

Thus, the instillation of hope is primarily a therapist function early in the career of a group or of a group member. The two important points for the therapist are acceptance of the client's feelings and refusal to accept the client's negative conclusions about eventual outcome. As the group matures and the members see each others' improvement, instillation of hope becomes more of a group function.

Sometimes clients come to group upset, they discuss what is troubling them, and, within a single group session, they experience the relief that accompanies the acceptance of reassurance or the decision to engage in some course of action. New group members who see the process may conclude that similar help and relief is available to them. The difference between such quick conclusions and the therapeutic factor of instillation of hope is that the latter is based on the observation of changes in behavioral patterns over time while the former is based on such changes within a single group session and thus may be more transitory.

Universality

This therapeutic factor is listed as a group issue rather than a therapist issue because it depends on the presence, in the group, of people who are willing to say they have had experiences or feelings similar to those being expressed by the speaker. Universality, thus defined, is one of the moves that even beginning therapists seem intuitively to facilitate. "Has anyone had similar problems?" or "I wonder if anyone else here has ever felt that way" are typical therapist comments during the early group sessions in response to client self-disclosure.

If you have done the screening interviews or have read the charts of the group members, you will know the background and issues they have in common. However, contents of the charts are private, and referring to them would be a breach of confidentiality. So you cannot use information in a chart until the client talks about it, and even then you can talk only about what the client has told the group.

Suppose a group member, John, talks about his relationship with a troubled sister and about his feelings of resentment about all the attention she received from other family members as they were growing up. You might know that another group member, Marianne, has a schizophrenic brother and has to deal with some of the same issues of resentment and guilt. But even in a small town clinic, where group members probably know each other, it would be inadvisable to ask Marianne how she felt about her brother until she had mentioned him herself.

So, even when you know that there are some major issues in common, you have to wait until the clients themselves have opened the door to exploring the common ground. The most you can do is invite participation. "Other people in the group have similar issues" is about as specific as you can ethically get.

There are two components to universality as a therapeutic factor. One is, as Yalom (1985, p. 8) puts it, "the disconfirmation of a client's feelings of uniqueness [which] is a powerful source of relief." The other is the important role universality plays in social discourse as a prelude to self-disclosure and in the potential development of feelings of closeness or intimacy. People thrown together by circumstance, as in airplanes, in hotel lobbies, or in the waiting rooms of mental health clinics, go through a ritual of acquaintance and search for common ground: Where are you from? You are? Do you know so-and-so? Really? I went to school with his dad! Do you know so-and-so?

Sometimes, when this common ground is established in casual encounters, little else follows, for common ground is not common cause. Nonetheless, strangers who have established some common ground in this rather ritualized way will tend to be friendlier toward one another, more supportive and readier to engage again, than those who have not. Universality in groups serves a similar function, facilitating self-disclosure and the development of group cohesiveness.

Acceptance (Cohesiveness)

This is a complex factor, which Bloch and Crouch (1985) regard as multidimensional. As does Yalom (1985), they accept Cartwright's (1968, p. 91) definition of cohesiveness as "the resultant of all forces acting on members to remain in the group." Acceptance is the individual's sense of warmth, friendliness, and belongingness, and sense of being valued by the other group members. Cohesiveness pertains to the group, acceptance to the individual. Bloch and Crouch suggest that cohesiveness is a condition for change, one that facilitates the operation of the therapeutic factors.

A less complex way to look at cohesiveness is to consider its role in the development and maintenance of an atmosphere of warmth and supportiveness. In such an environment, the individual can be confident that others will listen carefully and respectfully, and that they will respond gently when he or she engages in intimate self-disclosure. The development of cohesiveness is largely a therapist responsibility, but it also requires the presence of group members who are capable of accepting and offering verbal support to other group members.

There is, surprisingly, not much literature on the therapist's role in influencing cohesiveness. Bloch and Crouch (1985) mention two papers (Liberman, 1970a, and Krumboltz and Potter, 1973). In his discussion of cohesiveness, Yalom (1985) does not mention therapist role at all. Yet it seems clear that therapists influence the development and maintenance of cohesiveness in therapy groups.

Therapists facilitate group cohesiveness by reducing anxiety, by providing structure, and by manifesting attitudes of warmth, acceptance, and positive regard. In the initial group sessions, member anxiety is generally reduced when therapists exercise leadership, provide instruction, and offer a credible amount of praise when group members clearly meet explicitly stated performance criteria.

Providing structure, in the early stages of a group, involves telling the group what is going to happen next, doing it, and then telling them what happened. This sequence is followed by a description of what will happen after that. The *opening survey*, described in the next chapter, is an example of the initial provision of structure. After the early stages, once the group is in a working phase, it maintains its own structure with little intervention from the therapists. Occasionally, however, structural issues arise that require therapist intervention. Perhaps the most common example is the group member who introduces a major topic five minures before the group session is to end. In such instances, it is important to end the group session on time. Assume that the client was counting on you to do that, and purposely waited to introduce the topic until time was nearly up. It is important to start the following session by inviting that client to continue with what he or she started the week before.

Another example is a situation in which one or more group members engage in some particularly intense or poignant work. It is important in such a case to start the following session by asking how they are feeling, and whether there are any leftovers from last time that should be talked about today. Usually there will not be, but it is reassuring for group members to know that if they leave something major incomplete, they will have an opportunity to finish in the next group session.

Perhaps the most important way therapists provide structure is to keep the group on task: to encourage support, to facilitate self-disclosure, and to orient group members toward change in painful or maladaptive behavioral patterns. There are also some housekeeping functions that can reduce anxiety if the therapists take the initiative rather than waiting for group members to assume the responsibility: getting the session started (and ended) on time, instilling hope, keeping the interactions from becoming too hostile or too vapid, and the like.

Manifesting an attitude of warmth, supportiveness, and acceptance is not a technical skill to be wielded and put aside when no longer needed. Rather, warmth, empathy, and positive regard are personality characteristics, and people differ in the magnitude of these characteristics, both in general, and in particular situations (Truax and Carkhuff, 1967). Some people are characteristically warmer than others, who may show warmth only with difficulty; but even people who are characteristically warm are not consistently so in all situations.

Common sense, clinical experience, and the empirical data reported in Bloch and Crouch suggest a curvilinear relationship between therapist warmth and group cohesiveness. That is, cohesiveness will be slower to develop in groups led by therapists who are cold and distant and in groups led by therapists who are effusively warm and charismatic (Lieberman, Yalom, and Miles, 1973). Too much and not enough are no good. If you are usually perceived as cool or cold in most situations, social and otherwise, you can expect that cohesiveness will be at least somewhat slower to develop in your groups than in groups led by therapists who are interpersonally warmer. If you are naturally a warm, outgoing person, let those qualities show in the group room.

There are other limits to therapist influence on group cohesiveness, including the group members themselves. Some people are referred for group therapy because they are regarded by others as unpleasant and hostile. Frequently, their hostility masks underlying fears—fears often based on a perception of the world as having a limited quantity of emotional resources. These people have the view that approval is in short supply and that if others get some, there is that much less of it for them. For some hostile individuals, there is a different kind of underlying fear—a fear that positive feelings or emotional support or just plain friendliness will lead to closeness or intimacy, which in turn will result in power moves within intimacy, and obliteration of, or at least challenge to, one's own ego boundaries. Such individuals may respond to emotional support with rage because of the unconsciously perceived threat to their own identity—their sense of self. This pattern of fear is sometimes found in individuals who have been diagnosed as having borderline personality disorders.

A related pattern, but one that does not usually lead to quite so much overt hostility, is found in people who believe implicitly in the limited availability of emotional supplies, and who are so involved in holding onto any such supplies that come their way that they can offer no support and little attention to the other group members. This behavioral pattern is characteristic of narcissistic personalities.

In groups, these people retard the development of cohesiveness, in part because of their defensive posture characterized by attack or nonsupport. A group consisting of six to eight members can handle two people with these characteristics. If you end up with three or four such individuals, cohesiveness will develop quite slowly, if at all, despite your best efforts—even with optimal initial levels of warmth, empathy, and positive regard.

There are other types of groups in which cohesiveness is likely to remain low or absent despite therapist characteristics and skills. One example is the group of regressed, withdrawn, chronic schizophrenic patients found, not infrequently, in day hospital or post-hospital clinic programs. When the level of pathology is high, and when most or all of the group members have difficulty forming any kind of tie or relationship with other people, cohesiveness is likely to be low regardless of therapist characteristics. A similar situation may obtain in groups consisting of status referrals (see Chapter One), in short-term groups, or in groups with high member turnover, such as those on short-term inpatient units.

The challenge for the therapist in such group situations is to make the group experience therapeutic in the absence of cohesiveness. In groups that are not cohesive, interactions are likely to be one-to-one, client-therapist. When the absence of cohesiveness is due to the presence of several hostile group members, it is important for the therapists to provide safety for the nonhostile members. Some measure of safety is attained when you are equally protective of the group member who is being criticized and the one who is doing the criticizing. It is not easy to do. Yet, by the time you get to be a therapist, you have had substantial experience in mediating conflict, in stepping between two potential antagonists, and in taking care of or being protective of the feelings of other people. These social skills are appropriate for you to use in a therapy group. When there is hostility in the group, follow your protective instincts.

It could be argued that a therapy group is a place for people to learn how to express hostility appropriately, and that expressing anger toward another group member represents progress or improvement. Sometimes that is true, and most group members are amazingly tolerant of verbal attack from other members for whom such an expression constitutes a step forward. However, we are talking here about people characterized as hostile, who typically have no difficulty expressing their hostility. Indeed, what they may have difficulty with is meeting their interpersonal needs without being angry and defensive. Thwarting such a person's expression of anger, without rejecting that person or counterattacking, contributes to the feeling of safety and thus of cohesiveness within the group. In a later chapter, we will discuss some techniques for dealing with hostile clients. The points here are that (1) you know how to be protective of people, and (2) your use of that knowledge in the group, even when it impairs the expression of anger, may contribute to group cohesiveness. Furthermore, I should note that there is some evidence that venting anger is among experiences regarded by group members as least helpful (Lieberman, 1983).

Insight

This factor has considerable theoretical importance because of the belief among psychoanalytically oriented group therapists and theorists that the development of insight is one of the major goals of group therapy (Wolf and Schwartz, 1962; Foulkes and Anthony, 1965; Kaplan and Sadock, 1972). The term *insight* is used to refer to a number of different concepts. Bloch and Crouch (1985) apply the term *psychogenetic* to the traditional psychoanalytic concept of insight, which involves an understanding of the causal role played by past events in the development and maintenance of present problems.

Defined this way, insight is an intensely personal intra-psychic event, which is fine for individual psychotherapy and analytic group therapy, but poses some problems for the inter-personally oriented group therapist. Yalom (1985) challenges the psychoanalytic formulation as lacking empirical support, and, though he does not offer a formal definition, he seeks to put insight into a more interpersonal framework, specifically, the context of interpersonal learning.

Bloch and Crouch do not really define insight either. Following Yalom, they emphasize learning as a central component of insight. They describe insight as operating when clients (1) learn something important about themselves, (2) learn how they come across to the group, (3) learn more clearly about the nature of their problems, and (4) learn why they behave the way they do and how they got to be the way they are. The first two of Bloch and Crouch's components of insight appear to stem from group interaction and feedback; the latter two seem related to therapist intervention.

Bloch and Crouch then discuss insight from the psycho-analytic and existential points of view, and they proceed to a careful examination of interpersonal versus psychogenetic insight. They conclude that an eclectic approach to insight is best. Theirs is a scholarly theoretical discussion. The empiri-cal research they summarize suggests that insight, as they have defined it, is complex and multidimensional, and that it is not always beneficial.

Probably the most useful point Bloch and Crouch (1985) make for the clinician is that psychological-mindedness is a necessary precondition for insight to have therapeutic value, and is "of no relevance in noninsight-orientated groups" (p. 48). Hence, if you have a group of people who are not particularly psychologically-minded, such as are frequently found in community mental health settings, the development of insight in group members is not something you need to strive for. This conclusion recently has received some empirical support (Piper and McCallum, 1988).

My own definition of insight is not based on learning, but on the client's comprehension of relationships among subjective, behavioral, and interpersonal factors. I define insight as clients' awareness or understanding of the relationship between their internal emotional experiences and their behaviors; or between their behaviors and the behavioral responses of other people; or among their internal emotional experiences, behaviors, and the behavioral responses of others. Using this definition, it is relatively easy to see what to do to facilitate the development of insight. It becomes a matter of commenting on the relationship between feelings and actions, and between actions and consequences.

Valerie was referred for group because of problems in interpersonal relationships. During the sessions, she appeared sullen, withdrawn, and silent most of the time. She occasionally had angry outbursts at the men in the group, whom she accused of being unsupportive.

The vehemence of her outbursts was such that the men were reluctant to confront her. Finally, the therapist intervened. He asked both men (there were also three other women in the group) if they felt supportive of Valerie. They both replied that they would like to be supportive of her, but found it difficult because of her pattern of silence punctuated by angry outbursts. Both said that her outbursts made them want to keep their distance from her. Initially, this interchange provoked yet another tirade by Valerie.

This scene was repeated several times over the next several sessions, with some reduction in the intensity and length of Valerie's tirades. Each time, the therapist pointed out that her outbursts led to an interpersonal outcome different from the one she said she wanted. That is, he emphasized the relationship between action and consequence. Two weeks later, Valerie spoke at some length about her stormy relationship with her boyfriend, and acknowledged that her anger was driving him away. The therapist wondered if she then became more angry as he became more distant and rejecting, a pattern that he had observed with the men in the group. Valerie again acknowledged the accuracy of his suggestion. She then said, "My father was like that, too."

There are a number of ways this situation could have been handled by the therapist, and a number of different ways it could be interpreted. There is seldom one clear-cut right way to do things or to understand a therapy situation; there is always more than one correct interpretation.

In any given situation in group therapy, and in individual therapy, correct interpretations result from a mix of general and specific factors related to therapist theory, training, and experience. The general therapist-related factors include (1) mastery of at least one theory of personality and the basic principles of psychopathology, (2) familiarity with basic principles of individual therapy, and (3) knowledge of group therapy theory, including therapeutic factors. The situation-specific components of a good interpretation by a therapist include (1) knowledge of the client's history, problems, and goals in the group, (2) knowledge about the other group members, and (3) some sense of the flow of group experience. These are all components of a frame of reference, a way of thinking about group therapy, influenced by theory, training, and experience. It takes time, study, and supervised experience to develop such a frame of reference. But once developed, the framework helps the therapist rapidly decide what to say and when to say it. It also provides a reference point for assessing goodness of fit between theory and the specific situation.

From my own frame of reference, the above example is a good illustration of the slow development of insight in a difficult group member.

Another component of insight is historical: the client perceives the relationship between past events (assumed to be causal) and present emotions and behaviors. There is, however, little evidence that the historical component is related to the improvement of clients in group therapy. Psychoanalytically oriented group therapists are frequently criticized by interpersonally oriented therapists for emphasizing historical insight. Yalom's criticism (1985) is a case in point. However, it is probable that most psychoanalytically oriented group therapists are more sophisticated and less dogmatic about curative factors than their critics imply. Rutan and Stone's recent (1984) book on psychodynamic group psychotherapy is an example of the psychoanalytically oriented view.

Self-Disclosure

Bloch and Crouch define self-disclosure as "a patient's direct communication of personal material about himself to other group members" (1985, p. 127). This definition has two components. One is historical, pertaining to events or feelings that occurred at some point in the past, that is, there-and-then. The other component is contemporary, and refers to the individual's reactions to and expectations of the ongoing inter-personal events in the group, here-and-now.

It is important to note a third component having to do with depth or importance to the individual of the personal information. What I had for breakfast this morning, or how many children I have, is personal information, but it is of relatively low importance and relatively easy to disclose. It is a disclosure with low information value: it does not say very much about me. Self-disclosure ranges from this type of infor-mation to the communication of information experienced by the individual as highly personal and intimate.

I have elsewhere defined intimate self-disclosure as "an individual's (usually verbal) report to the group about how he feels and/or thinks *at this moment* about some topic that is of great importance to him—that is, in which he is invest-ing considerable feeling. It involves taking an interpersonal stance from which there is no retreat: this is how I feel, now, really and undeniably, about this topic. Later, the individual may report that he has come to feel differently, which may involve a change in his earlier stance but not a denial that he once held it" (Friedman, 1979, p. 28).

Intimate self-disclosure is not likely to occur in the first sessions of a group. There is usually a gradual increase in level of self-disclosure as the group develops. Cohesiveness and self-disclosure are related: cohesiveness fosters self-disclosure, which in turn enhances cohesiveness. If there is little cohesiveness in a group, either because the hostility level is high or because of the sparseness of interaction, intimate self-disclosure is unlikely.

As a therapist, there are two ways you can facilitate and enhance self-disclosure. One is by modelling, that is, by engaging in self-disclosure yourself. The other is by inviting or requesting self-disclosure by group members. Both methods are more important in the early sessions of a group than they are later on; they help establish group norms and procedures. Similarly, when you first come into an ongoing group, it is more important to do some self-disclosing than when you have been in for a while and the group members know something of what to expect from you.

Modelling. In considering what to reveal about yourself, and when, it may be helpful to remember that the group is far more interested in information about you that pertains to how you will relate to the group and its members than they are about any other kind of information about you. Accordingly, telling the group some of your thoughts and feelings about ongoing here-and-now interactions is facilitative of client self-disclosure and group cohesiveness. When you first come into a group, or in the opening minutes of a new group, it is appropriate to tell the group members you are feeling anxious, if that is true. But it is important to avoid saying anything that reflects your uncertainty about what to do next or about how to lead the group. It is generally appropriate to let the group know when you approve of some interaction or some member disclosure, but criticism or negative feedback should be avoided as much as possible. "Thanks for telling us that," or "I'm glad to know that about you," or "I like what just went on between you and Jack" are examples of therapist self-disclosure pertaining to ongoing here-and-now interactions.

Sometimes group members will ask questions about you that pertain to outside-of-group matters, and sometimes they will ask questions you consider personal. You are most likely to encounter such challenging or probing questions when you are least prepared to handle them comfortably, that is, early in your career as therapist with that particular group. Such questioning may also occur in the first or second session of a new group.

There is a tradition in individual psychotherapy that the therapist should not answer questions of this sort, and frequently therapists bring that tradition with them into group therapy. If you follow that tradition, or if you have observed an individual or group therapy session led by someone who does, you have seen the results—patients or clients frustrated and angry because of the therapist's refusal to respond to the question, and the whole therapy session sidetracked onto "Why won't you answer my question?" versus "Why is it so important to you that I answer it?" ad infinitum and ad nauseam. The best that can be said about this tradition is that its therapeutic purpose is unclear.

If a group member asks you a question, answer it. That is a simple, straightforward principle to follow, and it keeps you and the client (and the group) from getting caught up in what is essentially an iatrogenic argument. (This principle also holds for individual psychotherapy.) If you regard the question as impertinent or too personal, or if you would be uncomfortable answering it, say so. But rarely do group members ask inappropriate questions.

Generally, the kinds of personal questions group members ask you during the early group sessions (rarely, in the screening interview) are of two types. One pertains to your professional qualifications: are you a doctor? a student? a social worker? how long have you been doing this? Seldom are there more than two or three such questions about professional qualifications and identity. The second type of question is more personal, but still largely demographic: Are you married? Do you have children? Where are you from? How long have you lived here? Do you like it here? Where were you before this? The answers to these questions are, in a sense, a matter of public record. Perhaps that is why clients react so negatively when therapists refuse to answer them.

The function of this questioning is to permit the group to obtain information about how you will relate to them and how you will react to them. Early in the life of a group, or early in your career with a group, how you answer these questions is considerably more important than what your answer is. If you answer easily and openly, you are modelling self-disclosure; if you do not, you are slowing the development of a group atmosphere in which intimate self-disclosure can occur. Even saying that you are not comfortable answering the question is still sufficient self-disclosure: it lets the group know unequivocally where you stand.

Requesting Self-Disclosure from Group Members. The first self-disclosure you ask group members for should be innocuous and easy. In the opening survey of a new group (see Chapter Six), you might ask the clients to say their names and something about themselves that they would be comfortable telling about. You might then ask them to say a word or two about how they are feeling at that moment; if such a request is likely to elicit words or comments like "fine" and "I feel OK, I guess," you may find it helpful to ask a different kind of question. In the initial session, you should avoid asking clients to tell why they are in the group. Such a question might come in the second session; it represents a different level of self-disclosure. Start small and proceed in small steps toward deeper self-disclosure.

Clients sometimes resist accepting referral for group therapy because they fear being pressured into revealing more about themselves than they would like to. There is a certain amount of popular misconception that being in a group means having to share personal information with strangers. In the early group sessions, people are strangers, and the sharing of personal information is inappropriate. This should be made clear in the screening interview, and perhaps again at the start of the group session. It is important to make explicitly clear to group members that self-disclosure is not required, though it may be encouraged. When you first ask people to do some self-disclosure, even the rather minimal amounts described above, it may be helpful to remind them and the group that the exercise is voluntary.

Self-disclosure by itself is not necessarily therapeutic. The effect that intimate self-disclosure has on the individual and, to some extent, on the group depends on what happens next, after the self-disclosure is made. If self-disclosure is followed by criticism, then further self-disclosure by anyone in the group is less likely to recur. Intimate self-disclosure followed by no reaction at all from the group is also likely to be experienced by the discloser as negative. Therefore, when a group member has done some significant self-disclosure, it is a good idea to respond with positive reinforcement, followed, appropriately, by some exploration of possible alternatives.

Catharsis

This refers to the "ventilation of feelings (either positive or negative and about either life events or other group members), which brings some measure of *relief*. The factor operates when a patient releases feelings, leading to relief, within the group, either of past or here-and-now material. These feelings include anger, affection, sorrow, and grief which have been previously difficult or impossible to discharge" (Bloch and Crouch, 1985, p. 162).

Catharsis presupposes self-disclosure, and in most group therapy techniques, is related to it.[1] It has at least two components: (1) the experiencing of emotion followed by (2) feelings of relief. The experiencing of emotion is not itself cathartic. The frequency and intensity of catharsis, and whether it occurs at all, depend on the group members themselves and their willingness to risk cathartic experiences during group therapy sessions. What you, as therapist, can do is establish and maintain the conditions under which catharsis is most likely to occur, and then to help it along. Those conditions are the same as for intimate self-disclosure: the presence of an atmosphere of warmth and supportiveness in which the group members trust that their experiences will be responded to gently and respectfully by the group.

The most commonly expressed emotion during catharsis is grief, and its expression is usually weeping. The cathartic expression of anger is a distant second. There are various ways of encouraging clients to weep, if that is what they need to do. One is to give explicit permission—"It's OK to cry," for instance. Another is to offer a comforting arm, or to approve the offer of one if made by one of the other group members. It may help to point out that, although it may feel like the tears will never stop, in fact they do. People generally know how to be comforting when someone is on the verge of tears; so do you. In this instance, as in so many others, follow your human instincts.

It is not unusual for people to get very red in the face during a cathartic experience. Sometimes when anger is being ventilated, their color may turn almost blue. If there is emotional release, the person's color returns to its normal pink; if the release is inhibited, he or she is more likely to turn pale. If that happens, it is worth commenting on: "you look pale," or "it looks like you held back there and didn't finish letting go," or some such comment. And that is all you need to make of it.

Catharsis involves a letting go, which may be experienced as a loss of control. People generally avoid even the possibility of such loss of control unless (1) they believe it is safe to do so, (2) they have permission to do so, and (3) they have some faith that the outcome will be satisfactory—that they will feel better. Catharsis is not likely to occur in a group when those conditions are absent, despite the best efforts of skilled therapists. However, it is important to note that catharsis is only one of the therapeutic factors and that individuals can experience improvement without it. Actually, Bloch and Crouch (1985) report little evidence that catharsis per se is therapeutic. They cite a study by Liberman (1970b) that showed therapist prompting increases the frequency of expression of hostility. However, this kind of catharsis was not related to various outcome measures. The study of encounter groups by Yalom and his associates (Lieberman, Yalom, and Miles, 1973) also did not find a relationship between catharsis and outcome. However, their findings must be viewed with some caution since they are not based on the ratings of patients or clients in therapy groups.

In sum, catharsis may be regarded as desirable but not necessary for improvement in group therapy. If you have been putting a great deal of effort into encouraging group members to express and experience feelings, which is frequently quite difficult for clinic patients to do, the absence of positive results may not be due to any failing of yours as a therapist, nor of the clients. The probable reason is simply that catharsis in group therapy is not as potent a therapeutic factor as you might have assumed.

Altruism

Bloch and Crouch define altruism as operating "when the patient: . . . can forget about himself in favour of another member; and recognizes that he wants to do something for a fellow member" (1985, p. 192). The desire to be of help to others is quite common; indeed, the absence of such a desire may be regarded as an indicator of psychopathology. Most group members are willing, to a surprising extent, to help other group members, and to sit through an entire group session that focuses on only one person. (If the group focused on the same person every time, that would be another matter.) Being of help to another person is apparently related to enhanced feelings of self-worth and self-esteem and to a reduced sense of incompetence and dependency (Maxmen, 1973).

In therapy groups, altruism is most frequently seen in clients' willingness to yield group time to another group member. When this yielding occurs, the feeling in group, the ambience, is different from those situations in which one group member is drawing the tension (and attention) onto himself or herself in order to help the group evade some confrontive work it needs to do. What differentiates the two kinds of focusing on one person for an extended length of time is the difficulty of the work and the intensity of the self-disclosure. You might, for example, help a reticent group member express some of his or her feelings toward others in the group, a difficult exercise which might occupy most of the session. As you do so, you are likely to find other group members also trying to be facilitative of the reticent client's self-disclosure, and, at the end of the session, trying to reassure that client about the amount of time he or she took. Clients who get large blocks of group time, as well as the therapists, are often concerned about time distribution. If you are, or if you think the client is, ask the group. Asking the group how they feel about one client's taking so much time provides reassurance to the client, and to you, and gives the other group members the opportunity to express altruistic support.

A second place you will encounter altruism is in the willingness of other group members to give interpersonal feedback. An example is a group member who, in her efforts to be helpful to others, was quite critical, and then was surprised when people rejected her or kept their distance. After an interaction in which this woman, whose name was Beth, was highly critical of another group member's story about his relationship with his roommate, the therapist asked Beth what her intent was. "I'm trying to give Chris some ideas on how he can handle that problem better," she said.

"You're trying to be helpful to Chris?" the therapist asked?

"Yes, to be helpful," said Beth.

Turning to Chris, the therapist said, "Did you know that?"

"No," Chris said, "I thought she was just being critical and tearing me down like she always does."

After some discussion of the fact that Beth's efforts at being helpful were frequently misperceived in this way, the therapist, with Beth's consent, asked the other group members to give feedback on how they perceived her. Most of them said that they thought she was being critical and were surprised to learn that her criticism was intended as helpfulness.

uism here is not Beth's critical help, but rather
ss of the other group members to give her this
rmation about herself. Such feedback might yield
imal benefits attributable to self-disclosure on the
ie other group members, but it was not enough of an
r them to have much invested in it. It was clearly a
i issue for Beth. Such feedback from group members—
a.. ction that offered those members little direct gain—is
altruistic behavior.

You will also encounter altruism in the willingness of
group members to engage in role play, if you use such techniques in group. These techniques are discussed in more
detail in the chapters on working with internalized parental
voices and on dreams in group therapy.

Learning from Interpersonal Interaction

This is perhaps the most important of the therapeutic
factors. Bloch and Crouch define it as "the *attempt* to relate
constructively and *adaptively* within the group, either by
initiating some behaviour or responding to other group
members" (1985, p. 70).

One might quibble with this definition of learning as
an attempt to relate. Bloch and Crouch use this wording in
an attempt to retain the emphasis on interpersonal rather
than intrapsychic issues. More commonly, however, learning
is regarded as a change in behavior not attributable to developmental or transient factors. Learning from interpersonal
interaction, then, would be reflected in a change in behavior
resulting from the individual's behavior in the group, from
the responses of other group members or of the therapists to
that behavior, and from the conclusions the individual draws
about the relationship between his or her behavior and the
responses of other group members. Put more simply: learning
from interpersonal interaction is a change in behavior resulting from the influence of the group on its members.

Interaction is a necessary (but not sufficient) condition
for the benefits obtainable through interpersonal learning.

After the interaction, the individual evaluates both the outcome and the relationship between interaction and outcome. Such evaluation involves an awareness of the interactive network of relationships in the group and of the individual's own place in that network. As a result of the evaluation, the individual makes either (1) an attitudinal change intended to lead to a more reproducible outcome, or (2) a behavioral change intended to produce a different, more satisfactory outcome. Interpersonal learning may be said to have occurred only when the individual reports the attitudinal change or manifests the behavioral change.

This issue can be complex. Yalom (1985) takes considerable care to lay a conceptual groundwork for his discussion of interpersonal learning, which he acknowledges is multidimensional. During a group session, however, it is difficult for a therapist to retain the full richness of all that cognitive complexity. A simpler working formulation recognizes interpersonal learning as having taken place when a group member figures out what he or she has to do in order to relate with greater satisfaction, first to the therapy group and then in social contexts.

You can facilitate interpersonal learning by getting clients to look at the outcomes or consequences of their interactions with other group members. In early group sessions, a client may solicit advice from the other group members, only to find that he or she already has considered, and has rejected, all of the proffered suggestions. The end result frequently is that the recipient of advice feels bad because nobody else could come up with an acceptable solution either, and the advice givers feel bad because their advice was rejected or ignored. Yet, the client got what he or she asked for—advice.

Indeed, if you ask the client, "Did you get what you asked for?" he or she frequently will answer in the affirmative. However, if you ask about the level of satisfaction (for example, "Are you satisfied with what you got?") or about how other group members are feeling at that moment, you are likely to get some expression of dissatisfaction with the transaction.

Frequently, people want encouragement rather than proferred solutions. But if they ask for advice, the group usually will proffer solutions; so, the outcome is discouragement rather than the desired encouragement. In this case, you can facilitate interpersonal learning by pointing out that the strategy they used—advice seeking—did not produce the desired interpersonal outcome. The extent to which you should present alternative strategies depends on the resources available in the group. Long-term inpatient groups and some outpatient groups are characterized by limited interpersonal experience and resources, and you may have to describe alternatives in some detail. In other groups, people are more able to devise alternative strategies on their own or with the group's help. Generally, the greater the impairment in overall functioning, the stronger the need for you to suggest alternative strategies.

Vicarious Learning

Bloch and Crouch define vicarious learning as "the patient experiencing something of value for himself through the observation of other group members, including the therapist" (1985, p. 195).

Vicarious learning is said to take place when the patient or client identifies with another group member's experience, or when he or she sees another person (usually, the therapist) model behavior that the patient or client would like to emulate. "I know how you feel" may be a typical comment for someone who engages in vicarious learning. It is difficult to know when vicarious learning based on modelling has taken place, unless you later see client behavior that imitates behavior that you or a group member has exhibited.

Vicarious learning is passive learning. It does not involve the client interacting directly, but indirectly by observing the interactions of others. Learning from interpersonal interaction is active learning. Active learning is better remembered and is, therefore, more likely to result in lasting behavioral change. However, interpersonal interaction, even in the context of a therapy group, may be so fearsome for some individuals that they feel unable to risk it. For such individuals, vicarious learning may be all they can do.

Vicarious learning is difficult to facilitate. For one thing, it depends on the presence of interaction between you and the group members, or among the members. The interaction must be of interest to the vicarious learner, it must not provoke too much anxiety, and it must involve situations with which he or she can identify or from which he or she can learn through observation and imitation. For another thing, vicarious learning is intrapsychic. It is impossible to discern whether it is really occurring, or whether the attentive audience is just watching the show.

So, perhaps the best way to regard the therapeutic factor of vicarious learning is as a bonus: it is not something you have to work to facilitate; it provides an attentive audience; and it requires neither time nor energy from other group members or from you. How credible is the claim by vicarious learners that they benefit in this way? It is difficult to know.

Concluding Comments

As we have seen, there is considerable conceptual and technical complexity involved in attempting to deal with the therapeutic factors. The concept of therapeutic factors can serve as a frame of reference as you go through a group session. It is pointless to say, "OK, today we will work on instillation of hope and learning from interpersonal interaction." The unfolding group experience, as the session progresses, determines which therapeutic factors might be brought into play. The concept of therapeutic factors helps you to recognize what is happening in the group, and it provides some guidelines for therapist interventions. Familiarity with the therapeutic factors, and with the techniques you can employ to facilitate them, helps keep the group therapeutic. However, as with individual psychotherapy, technical facility is secondary to personal qualities, and the most potent therapeutic

factor may well be the warmth, empathy, and genuineness of
the group therapists (Truax, 1966).

Notes

1. Some of the so-called nonverbal therapies are exceptions. Therapists using these techniques may encourage the
nonverbal expression of emotion (frequently, copious weeping
or angry bellowing) while at the same time explicitly dis-
couraging verbal reporting of thoughts or of words connoting
feeling. Examples include neo-Reichian techniques like bio-
energetics (Lowen, 1958) and primal screaming (Janov, 1970).
Fortunately, these techniques, which do not distinguish
between emesis and catharsis, are now largely out of vogue.

5

Opening Moves in
New and Ongoing Groups

The first session of a new group is most likely to start in anxious silence. Your first task is to reduce anxiety, and you are the first person whose anxiety should be reduced. You come into the group room with a workable set of skills for reducing anxiety in ambiguous interpersonal situations. Use these skills. For example, some people tend to talk more readily when their anxiety levels are moderate or moderately high. Such individuals might open the group session by reminding the group of the guidelines discussed in the screening session pertaining to confidentiality, for instance. Other people, at those same levels of anxiety, tend to be quiet. If you are one of the quiet ones, it is important to identify a cotherapist who is comfortable with talking (or who talks to reduce anxiety). If you both come into the group at its first session, sit down, and say nothing, anxiety will increase rather than decrease; there will be a lengthy silence, and the first interactions are likely to be hostile and defensive.

Starting a group by waiting until a group member breaks the silence is a time-honored way of getting started. There is no evidence that such an approach is facilitative of cohesiveness or of client self-disclosure; the dropout rate (unilateral termination) is high.

Once you have reduced your own anxiety to tolerable levels, you can begin to reduce the group's. People are anxious initially because they are in a new situation in which the rules of social discourse may or may not apply. They are not sure what you expect of them, what is appropriate, how to relate to the other group members (or to you), or what to do. That is, they are in a highly ambiguous interpersonal situation, with few cues to guide them. Under these circumstances, providing them with cues reduces anxiety.

I usually start groups by talking briefly about the group guidelines; that is how I reduce my own anxiety. Next, I tell the group members I will ask them to tell us something about how they are feeling right then, and, if they are not too anxious, to tell the group one important thing about themselves that they would like the group to know and that they are comfortable in telling. That is, first I tell them what I am going to ask; then I ask it. It goes something like this:

> I'd like for you to take a moment now to ask yourself how you are feeling right now. Then I will ask you to tell us, in a word or two, how you're feeling. I will also ask you to tell the group one thing about yourself that you would like the group to know about you and that you would be comfortable telling us. Go ahead, take a moment, take a look inside you, and then tell us how you're feeling, how it feels to you to be here, in this room, at this moment.

Usually people will close their eyes or look down or off into the distance for a moment or two. Then someone will look up. This is one of the more tense moments of the early group: everyone knows you are going to call on someone to be first.

People feel varying degrees of reluctance to go first, and they will generally use body language to tell you something about their readiness to engage. Some people will stay bent over, staring at the ground. Others may sit with arms and legs crossed, silently warding you off. Sometimes an individual will look quite distressed, head buried in arms.

Look around. Call on the person who looks most ready to respond. Usually that will be someone who is making eye contact with you, or who looks expectant and not lost in thought. Occasionally no one will look really ready, but almost always there is one person who looks less unready or least unapproachable. Say that person's name. There may be a moment's hesitation or even a "Who, me?", but usually he or she then goes on and says something like, "I feel anxious." If that first client does not volunteer the first small self-disclosure, you might have to ask for it: "What one thing are you willing to tell us about yourself?" It matters not at all, for present purposes, what that one thing is—only that some minimal self-disclosure has occurred. Thank the client, and go on to the next.

Your first choice point in interacting with the group is deciding which client to call on to begin the self-disclosure. Your second choice point is deciding whom to go to next. Some therapists wait for a second client to volunteer, in which cases there is likely to be a long silence and a return to, or a continuation of, high levels of anxiety. Other therapists may call next, with little delay, on the client who looks second most ready to respond, and then on to the next, and so on until everyone has been called on. A better method is to use the geographic position of the first client called on as the starting point, and to go around the group in order from there. That way you do not have to keep track of who has spoken and who has not, and neither does the group.

This procedure, which is called the *opening survey*, provides a considerable amount of structure in a short time. Yet, it is not so rigid that there is no leeway for individual expression, and occasionally a client may opt out of the exercise altogether. You begin by telling the group what you are going to do, and what you expect of them. Then you do it. You also begin to establish a group norm of self-disclosure. Your starting with the person who is readiest to respond tells all the other members that you will be at least somewhat sensitive to their nonverbal messages about readiness to engage in interactions. Your actions say that you will not go to the person most reluctant to interact, but rather to the least reluctant. Clients seem to realize that they are not likely to be called on if they are not ready, and that realization reduces the initial anxiety sharply and quickly.

Going around the room in order, after the first person, lets all members of the group know when their turns will come. The person who speaks second has perhaps the second most difficult task, with the last speaker having perhaps the easiest time of it. But knowing when their turns will come, and hearing what other people have to say, help reduce anxiety and provide cues as to what to say about their own feelings. And listening to others provides an indication of the appropriate initial level of self-disclosure. The opening survey, then, reduces anxiety by giving the group members a great deal of information about what to do and what to expect in the opening minutes of the group.

Unless you have thought about it beforehand, a third choice point comes when it is your turn to say something. Should you self-disclose in much the same way the clients do, or should you remain silent and opaque by indicating that the client seated on the other side of you should proceed? The answer depends almost entirely on your own sense of comfort or discomfort with joining in. If you do join in, it is important to share your excitement but not your anxiety with the group. At that point, the group has enough anxiety of its own. The literature on the effects of therapist self-disclosure has been nicely summarized by Dies (Dies and MacKenzie, 1983; Dies, 1973).

The initial structure I am describing is a classroom question-and-answer interaction. It is all one-to-one, client-therapist, with no effort to get clients to relate to each other or to initiate anything. That interaction will come later, when group anxiety is lower, when the ice has been broken, and when the other people are better acquainted.

Your next choice point comes when the opening survey has been completed. If you think of the initial go-around as a request for bids for attention (yours or the group's or both), then you turn to the person who has made the highest, most urgent bid and invite him or her into further discussion.

When deciding which person to turn to, follow the same principle you used in choosing the client to start the opening survey. Some of the comments in that survey will let you know you should keep your distance, at least for a while; and it is important to do so, to be sensitive to and to respect the person's wishes. Usually, in the initial survey, there will be one or two people whose opening statements will make it clear that they need to be or want to be attended to. Consider these client responses to the opening survey:

> I'm feeling a little anxious right now. But I always feel anxious in new situations. I will watch and listen, and pretty soon the anxiety will go away by itself.

> There's a lot on my mind. I'm always anxious. I haven't been sleeping well. I'm really hurting. I don't know what to do.

Clearly, the second of these offers more opportunity for intervention.

Sometimes, as you do the initial survey, there will be several bids for the group's attention. You can rank-order them in terms of salience, and go first to the person whose bid is loudest, and then to the second, and so on. If people's bids are of approximately equal urgency, or if you cannot distinguish readily among them, it will not matter much which one you go to first. It would not be a disaster even if you went to the third readiest person.

If you are not sure how to rank the bids in terms of urgency, here are some guidelines:

1. Go first to the person who expresses present anguish. When that happens, it is easy to determine whom to attend to. Usually, but not always, that will be the person who expresses the highest level of anxiety and does not indicate an unwillingness or unreadiness to respond. Sometimes the person who expresses the highest level of distress also lets you know, verbally or nonverbally, that he or she is not ready to engage; so you go to the person with the next highest level.

2. In the absence of present anguish, attend first to the person who expresses the most difficulty in being here now, in the sense of being able to pay attention to what is going on and to commit his or her own energies to the present interactions. This kind of comment is unusual in the initial session of a group, because the overall level of anxiety is so high and is more likely to occur in the second or third session when anxiety is lower. For example,

> I'm feeling that it was really hard for me to get
> here today because there's so much stuff to do at
> work. I can't get my mind off it.

A therapy session is a special kind of interaction, one which involves communication between people. Anything that impairs the communication process or clogs the communication channels reduces the probability that effective therapy can take place. Therefore, attending to factors that impair communication should take precedence over any other issue. Anxiety impairs communication because it reduces the client's ability to engage with other people and to hear and integrate what is being said. That is why you deal with anxiety at the outset. A client whose mind is elsewhere cannot engage fully with the group if he or she is anxious. Therefore it is important to help that client refocus his or her mind on the present situation. This principle of attending first to factors impairing communication is one that holds throughout the life of a group. It is also applicable in individual therapy, and may constitute the principal therapeutic work in family therapy.

3. In the opening survey, the amount of energy will vary from one person to the next. People differ in the amount of energy they put into what they say about their feelings and into what they tell the group about themselves.

In this context, the term *energy* is a metaphor for a number of behavioral cues. A person who is regarded by others as energetic will usually move at a faster pace, talk with more apparent enthusiasm, and maintain more eye contact than one who is regarded by others as less energetic. In practice, the judgment of whether a person is energetic is subjective and intuitive. In deciding where the energy is in the group, follow your intuition. Invite the client who seems most energetic, or whose response seems most energetic, into further discussion.

4. Most of the time, if you follow the first three guidelines, something emerges. But suppose that you have gone through the first three, and all you hear are noncommittal low energy responses with little energy variation in the group. At that point, do another go-around, asking for another minimal self-disclosure. If the group is frozen with anxiety, you could decide to stay fairly close to the wording of the previous go-around and ask each person to say one additional thing that he or she would be willing for the group to know. If the problem is not as much anxiety as it is difficulty in verbalizing (that is, if you have a nonverbal group), you could ask for a little higher level of self-disclosure—using your own judgment about what a small self-disclosure would be for this group. The specific content of client responses will vary from place to place and group to group; but the principle of requesting small but gradually increasing amounts of self-disclosure does not change.

Small self-disclosures are items of information about oneself which are relatively public: where or in what part of town one lives; what kind of work one does, how long one has lived here or there, and the like. A step up from that in terms of personal information might be marital status, number of siblings, and the like—essentially demographic information like that found on applications of one sort or another. The next step up involves opinions or preferences: answers to questions such as, do you like fishing? or what is your favorite television show or sport or other pastime?

One possibility would be to ask people, what is most important for us to know about you? Some people might say that there is nothing important for the group to know about them, but experience suggests that they are a small minority. Others are likely to say something significant with regard to how they present themselves initially to the group. One man responded by saying, "I'm a farmer and my father and grand-father before me were farmers." Another said, "People tell me that sometimes I sound angry when I'm not." The latter would be relatively easy to follow up ("Is that something you'd like to work on in group?"), and both are examples of comments people make in a second or third or fourth go-around, but seldom in the first.

5. Perhaps the worst-case situation is one in which all the group members say, in the initial go-around, that they are feeling fine and that there is nothing special that they want to tell the group about themselves. This occasionally occurs in inpatient groups and in groups in which participation is involuntary, as in court-ordered treatment for alcoholics or sex offenders. When it happens, your best response is to provide an agenda the group can follow. In some situations, however, it may be necessary to wait out the silence until the group develops its own interactions and its own agenda. We will discuss each of these possibilities briefly.

When All Is Said to Be Well

In an outpatient group where people respond to the opening survey of the first group session by saying that they are fine, you already know you are dealing with people who are, at best, marginally appropriate for group. It just does not happen otherwise—not in the first session. You may have a group of people who are chronically mentally ill, or are very reluctant to engage verbally, or are significantly below average in intelligence (IQ less than 85). Or everyone in the group may have two or all three of these characteristics. Such groups work best if they are structured and informational. The thera-peutic factors most likely to be effective here are instillation of hope, guidance, and universality. The application of those three factors, as discussed in the preceding chapter, constitutes the initial agenda for the group, at least during the first several months of its existence.

In an inpatient group where people respond to the opening survey by saying they are fine, the agenda to follow depends on whether they are in a long-term residential facility, such as a state hospital, or in a short-term unit, such as a psychiatric ward in a general hospital. In the long-term settings, the range of groups—high functioning, low functioning, therapeutic community, behavior therapy, and so on—is so great as to preclude brief generalization here.

In short-term psychiatric wards, group agendas can be formulated around three content areas: adjustment to the ward and to inpatient status, change needed before the patient leaves the hospital, and resources available post-discharge to help the patient and to reduce the probability of readmission. If you are working on the inpatient unit where you do group, you already know what the ward issues are and some of what needs to change in order for post-hospital adaptation to be successful. Take the ward issues first. But, if your group gets into discussions about needs for change, be very careful to avoid introducing patient information that comes from charts or from individual sessions. You might, for example, know that a patient is an incest victim but, unless he or she says so in the group, you can't suggest that he or she should change living arrangements after leaving the hospital. Yalom (1983), Erickson (1984), and Maxmen (1978) have written extensively about inpatient group psychotherapy.

Involuntary therapy is a special problem and is discussed in the chapter on special problems. Usually, in court-ordered treatment, there is an agenda you must impose on the group members. Seldom, in the initial sessions of such groups, do the members indicate any willingness to be in the group or receptivity toward therapy. But, an initial survey is worth doing for your own information about the levels of resistance and hostility with which you will be dealing. Even if all group members say they are fine and do not want to talk, you still have to go ahead with whatever you are supposed to do.

When You Have to Wait It Out

If left alone, groups almost always start in silence. The opening survey breaks the initial silence and begins to reduce the anxiety level, facilitating self-disclosure. But sometimes you have to wait it out. In the initial session, the only time you should wait out the group's opening silence is when you have some very clear reason for so doing. Such a tactic is not inappropriate if you find yourself coleading a training group consisting of therapists or of students of the group process. And if you are being introduced to group by a more experienced coleader or supervisor who believes in starting groups this way, it would be unwise to break the initial silence.

Starting a group session, other than the first several, by waiting for a group member to break the silence is sometimes necessary. Occasionally during a session, a group that has been moving along quite nicely will come to an issue that no one wants to talk about even though most or all group members recognize that nothing else will happen until that issue is discussed. The most common content of such issues is anger or sexual feelings, though on occasion there may be other themes. When a group hits such a point, the usual result is silence; and if that silence occurs during a group session, it is necessary to wait it out. Sometimes it will occur toward the end of a session, and the session will end in silence. If the next group opens with a continuation of the silence that began in the preceding session, it is still necessary to wait it out. Sooner or later the most anxious group member, or the one least able to tolerate silence, will break it, and the group can go on.

Silences of this sort are sometimes broken by group members who have no intention of acknowledging or dealing with the underlying issue the group is trying, by its silence, to avoid. The person who breaks the silence may try to go on to another topic or may make some banal comment that other people may respond to. If you are sure of what is going on, you can comment that that is not the topic the group needs to talk about right then. If you are not sure, wait. Eventually the filler conversation will dwindle and stop.

Having made all of these points regarding silence in groups, I should emphasize that, fortunately, it is seldom necessary to wait out the initial silence of a group session.

Opening Moves in a New Group

Now let us return to the opening moves in the first session of a new general outpatient therapy group. If you follow the format of an opening survey, you will engage in some interaction, one-to-one, with the first person you go to after the survey is completed. The therapeutic factors likely to be most salient in these interactions are instillation of hope and universality. When you reach a stopping point with the first group member, you go on to the second and third and so on, as time permits, in the order you determined from the information in the opening survey. If time runs out before you complete your work with a client, be sure to say you will start with him or her next time.

The transition from these one-to-one interactions to group-centered and group-originated interactions takes time and usually occurs naturally. Each one-to-one, client-therapist interaction provides the other group members with information about that client. The factors of universality and acceptance, along with your own warmth and acceptance of client self-disclosure, enhance cohesiveness. The interaction of these factors and therapist characteristics contributes to the evolving atmosphere of warmth and supportiveness in which self-disclosure is facilitated. In the third or fourth session of a group (longer if the level of pathology is higher, the level of intelligence is lower, or both), when you have engaged with most or all of the group members, they know enough about each other, and about how others will relate in the group, to risk volunteering some comments or initiating some interactions with other group members.

Eventually the opening survey will become superfluous because the agenda will flow from previous group sessions. Group members come to know each other well enough that if one is upset or depressed or angry and does not volunteer that information at the outset, the other group members will ask about it. In some groups, the members will do their own opening surveys and decide on who will have the group spotlight, for how long, and in what order. In other groups, characterized by less verbal activity and less psychological-mindedness, you may have to continue performing these functions.

Session-Starting Moves in an Ongoing Group

A group therapy session usually has two starting points, one informal, the other more formal. If the group assembles in the clinic waiting room, the informal start occurs there; otherwise it occurs in the group room as the members come in. The informal start occurs when the second group member enters the room. The two clients can ignore each other, acknowledge each other but sit silently, or greet each other and begin a conversation. Ignoring each other is rare, unless there is some ill feeling between them. Sometimes the first two people will sit silently, but initiate a conversation when the third or fourth person comes in. When there is conversation, it is almost never about the group or group business, for that would indicate a formal start. Instead, conversation is usually light and social.

If the group has assembled in the waiting room, you and your coleader have considerable influence over whether there will be any informal conversation once they all arrive in the group room. Some therapists prefer to arrive in the group room only after all the members have come in and sat down. This kind of entrance has the advantage of keeping the therapist-client interactions strictly business, with no small talk at all. It also tends to keep the atmosphere chill, stiff, and formal. Unless your theory or your supervisor indicates that it is wrong, cordial acknowledgment of the group members as they come through the door is not inappropriate.

If the group assembles in the group room, you and your coleader should decide whether to wait until everyone has arrived before entering yourselves, to be there already when the first group member comes in, or to arrive sometime between those two points. In some cases, you may not have much choice of arrival time because of a tight schedule that keeps you from arriving before the group's starting time, or perhaps because of a requirement that you arrive early in order to unlock the door so group members do not have to wait in a hallway or outside the clinic.

The time and manner of your arrival, and your actions between then and the formal start, influence the way the group begins. The first few minutes of a group session influence the emotional tone of the session, and probably the topics addressed as well. Deciding with your cotherapist about how you will arrive, and what you will do during the informal group, allows you to set the tone for the session and to remain in control of the situation.

If you have a choice, your handling of the interval between informal and formal start and whether the clients wait in the waiting room becomes a matter of personal preference guided by theory and supervision. It is important to attend to this interval because the informal start of a group session is a real start of an actual session. The apparently light social conversation that people sometimes engage in while they are waiting for the group to start is frequently predictive of the emotional tone of the main theme that day; in reality, it is not light at all. The quandary you are likely to be in, if you sit in the group room waiting for the last group member to show up before you formally start the session, is whether to engage in the conversation. If you are going to be there at all, it is better to join in than not; but remember that you are working even if the clients are not.

The Opening Survey of an Ongoing Group

The first question of the opening survey differs little from that of the initial session of the group. You want to know how people are feeling as they begin the group session. Usually a word or two will suffice. The second question is different. The general form is, What would you like to work on today? There are endless variants, like, What do you want to cover today? What would you like to do in group? What would you like from the group? and so on. Responses to this question constitute the members' bids for the time and attention of the group, as described above. The same principles apply. Go first to the group member who expresses pain or discomfort (that is, present anguish). If there are more than one such expression, take them in order. Then go to those group members, if any, who have expressed difficulty in being there, or who have indicated that something might make communication between them and the group more difficult during this session.

Usually, these moves, and what follows from them, will take most or all of the group session to work through. But sometimes you will work through these issues in short order, or all of the group members may say that they do not have anything in particular to work on. You may have thirty or forty minutes or more of group time available. Then what do you do?

The answer depends on the theory you use. If you do nothing, the likely result is an anxious and unfruitful silence and a rapid increase in group discomfort. The silence is most likely to be broken by the group member who is either most anxious or least able to tolerate silence, and what follows is more likely to represent the group's response to anxious silence than anything else.

Other than silence, there are at least four things you can do:

1. Pick up any loose threads from the last group session.
2. Do another survey, asking the group members what they would like to do until time to stop.
3. Make a process comment.
4. Introduce a topic of your own.

Picking up loose threads from the last session is probably least helpful unless there is some major unfinished business which was not addressed in the opening survey of the day's session. Doing another survey is a convenient way to generate an agenda, and will work even when there is not much time left—fifteen minutes or so. The chief disadvantage of a second survey is that it maintains the one-to-one therapist-client interaction pattern. Making a process comment—

something like, Well, we've worked through that agenda, what now?—may result in the group's doing its own survey, or it may result in an uncomfortable silence. Introducing a topic of your own has the advantage of keeping the group moving and the disadvantage of possibly obscuring a topic the group wants to, or is ready to, bring up on their own. A new topic is a most appropriate move in the early sessions of a group, or when the group's average verbal ability is low— and when you have a definite agenda to follow. If you are not sure what to do, do the survey.

Therapist Activity and Structuring

The method of starting a group session described here involves an active therapist providing structure and direction during the initial sessions of a group. As anxiety diminishes and cohesiveness increases, the group members assume more responsibility for their own structure and direction, and the therapist's role becomes one of facilitator rather than leader.

The position taken here, proposing a high but decreasing level of therapist activity and structuring, has received some research support. Kinder and Kilman (1976) suggest that groups are more productive when they follow the sequence of high and decreasing structure. Bednar, Melnick, and Kaul (1974) found that lack of initial structure is associated with high client distress and premature unilateral termination, as suggested earlier. Dies (1983) has summarized a group of studies relating client characteristics to group structure. He concludes that "clients with dependent, conservative, or authority-oriented personality styles prefer structured group psychotherapy [while] high-status group members and internally oriented, nondependent members favor less structured treatments" (1983, p. 47).

In general, then, both clinical experience and empirical data suggest that an initially active and structuring therapist is most facilitative of early group development. How rapidly the level of therapist activity can drop off depends on the interaction of client, therapist, and group characteristics.

- *Client characteristics* include level of pathology, psycho-logical-mindedness, personality attributes, and intelli-gence. Many of these characteristics are related to socioeconomic and cultural factors.
- *Therapist characteristics* include personality attributes influencing the readiness and comfort with which the therapist wields interpersonal power in providing struc-ture and direction to a group of people. Other therapist characteristics include social skills and theoretical orien-tation in individual therapy, as well as experience level.
- *Group characteristics* include the mix of personalities and problems in a particular group; the setting; long-term versus short-term characteristics; the level and chronicity of distress; and the nature of the contract between the group as a whole, each of its members, and the group therapists. In some settings, the nature of the contract between the group therapists and the clinic may also influence how rapidly the therapists can move from a directive to a facilitative role.

While the position advocated here, of high and decreas-ing therapist activity, has received some empirical support, the difficulties of doing research in group therapy have thus far precluded the collection of convincing data on virtually any point, particularly points that are controversial. Clinical experience, particularly when the clinician's observations are guided and informed by theory, may at times reflect a closer approximation to reality than research data gathered with the best of intentions and with as much methodological rigor as conditions permit. Clinical lore is sometimes based on truths that are difficult to quantify.

Under these conditions, the best way to lead your groups is the way that makes the most sense to you: cogni-tively, if that is how you function, intuitively, if that is the way you work, or with some combination of cognition and intuition. Use what you already know about psychopathol-ogy, about healing, and about being helpful; and use what you have learned about theory and what your own experiences in groups have taught you. If you do not yet have enough group experience to form your own opinions, use those of your supervisor or cotherapist temporarily. The main thing to be wary of is the notion that there is only one best way to start groups.

6

Therapist Responses
to Client Disclosure

When a group member makes a self-disclosing statement during a group session, the therapist is faced with a number of decisions: how to respond, when to respond, or whether to respond at all. In this chapter, we will consider a single self-disclosing statement by a group member, and we will examine some possible responses to that statement. At the same time, we will consider the therapeutic factors involved in each possible therapist response.

During the opening survey of her fourth group session, Marie said she was feeling some distress and wanted to talk about her relationship with her husband. She began as soon as the opening survey was completed:

> Carl is so unresponsive and critical of me. I told him last night how much I hate it here—I have no friends and I don't like my job. He told me very calmly that he has a good job and he likes it here and besides, he doesn't want to move away from his brothers and sisters. He was very calm and not emotional at all. I hate it when he gets that way when I am upset.

That was all she said. If you were the therapist in this group, what would you do next? You could (1) remain silent, (2) invite Marie to continue, (3) respond to her comment, (4) invite response from the entire group, (5) invite response from other group members with similar problems, or (6) wait for the group to respond and then comment on the group process. Let us consider each of these possibilities.

Remaining Silent

If you have done an opening survey and you are taking an active role in structuring the group, now is not the time to change your approach. Remaining silent would be confusing to the group at this point, early in the group's life, because your silence would be a sudden switch to a different leadership model. If you have not done an opening survey, and if you are following a more impassive therapist model, perhaps remaining silent would be appropriate.

Inviting Marie to Continue

Marie's statement is an incomplete story. There are some gaps in it, the point is not clear, and neither is it clear why she has chosen this time to tell her story to the group. When a story is incomplete, inviting the client to continue is a cautious and reasonable move. You might say, simply, "go on," or make some such comment that suits your interpersonal style. If the client then indicates that she has said all she wants to, you can decide to leave it at that. But preferably, you would attempt to elicit further information to fill in the gaps and to reduce the ambiguity of the story as much as possible.

If you attempt to have Marie fill in the gaps, get your own questions answered first. One question might be about the context in which the interaction of interest occurred. What was going on when Marie told Carl how much she hated it here? How did it happen to come up? Did Marie want Carl to become upset too? If so, in what way? What about the implied threat that she can go if she wants to, but that he will stay?

These are just a few of the content-oriented, there-and-then questions that might help to fill in the informational gaps in the client's story. There are, of course, dozens of other possible questions. The important result is that the client's initial story leads to questions from you and, perhaps, from the group. At this early point in Marie's group career, it is difficult to determine if getting people to ask questions is a significant interpersonal pattern. It is also difficult to determine if she is even aware of how incomplete her initial story was. Her handling of the request for further information may give you some clues to these issues.

Responding to Her Comment

Responses to comments like this one fall into five categories.

The first response is to the verbal content. Within this category, there are no fewer than eight possible themes to respond to in Marie's story.

- Carl's unresponsiveness and criticism
- Marie's hatred of the locale
- Her lack of friends
- Her dislike of her job
- Carl's implied threat of separation
- His reluctance to move away from his siblings
- His calm demeanor when Marie gets upset
- Marie's dislike of Carl's calm at such times

Some other themes are discernible as well, but the above are sufficient to illustrate the magnitude of quandary that even a short statement can create for the therapist, who must decide which themes to attend to and how to go about understanding them. Marie gave no clue as to which of these elements is most important to her, so a content-oriented therapist is confronted with an eight-choice menu and no recommendations that would help identify the best choice.

If you have done the screening interview or have read the chart, you will have some idea of why Marie is coming to the clinic, why she was referred for group, and what kind of change she is hoping for from therapy. If she came in with marital distress, you might start by commenting on her dislike of her husband's calm when she is upset. Perhaps you could just reflect her last statement or suggest that she might like more of a response than she gets from him at such times. A second therapist option along this line would be to try to clarify the implicit threat. This approach is less satisfactory since it centers more on Carl's possible intention than on Marie's reaction. A third choice might be to focus on her reaction to his unresponsiveness and criticalness in general— the first problem she mentioned in her statement. Usually, if a client is already talking about a specific incident, you should not go back to a more general statement. Discussion of generalities is less likely to be helpful and less likely to lead to meaningful change than is discussion of specific interactions.

If Marie came to the clinic with a primary complaint of social isolation or distress with her job, you would pick up on those aspects of her comment. Or you might comment on these issues if they had been targeted during the screening interview. But you might find yourself in a situation in which the client's statement bears no resemblance to anything that was discussed in the intake, diagnostic, or screening interviews. Marie, for example, might have been referred to the mental health clinic by a primary care physician from whom she was seeking medication for low back pain.

If you cannot tell how a client's comment fits into the pattern or context of his or her life, it may be that the comment is simply out of character, or, more important, it may be that there is little correspondence between the verbal content and the underlying message. In the latter case, which is by far the more common, you may be able to understand the client's initial, significant self-disclosure as his or her staking out a particular interpersonal position relative to the other group members. Such comments are made primarily as interpersonal maneuvers—not to convey significant information about the speaker's life circumstances.

Responding to a maneuvering comment as though its

information were of primary importance will usually result in some strange-feeling interactions in the group; verbal interchanges may become lifeless, boring, and puzzling. You usually do not know a client's interpersonal maneuvering skills or strategies early in the group (whether it is a new group, or new to you or to the client), and you may not yet recognize the maladaptive or unsatisfying ways that he or she relates to other people. In maneuvering comments, the verbal content is like a decoy or feint, and if you try to engage the client on those grounds, the outcome is usually unsatisfying; the client will have reproduced, in the group, the negative outcomes in interpersonal situations that contributed to his or her being in group in the first place.

The main clue you will have as to whether the comment is intended primarily as information or primarily as maneuver is the extent to which it deals with issues you know are of present importance in the client's life. Another sign, not always reliable, is the discrepancy between the verbal content and the client's affect—how the client told the story. If the client seems to have little interest in what he or she is saying, that may, in fact, be the case because the real, meaningful message is not the one being delivered. The client's comment may be so self-contained that it may be difficult to decide on an appropriate verbal response. That is the case with Marie's comment, the self-contained nature of which is a clue that there is at least some interpersonal maneuvering going on here.

The second category of therapist response to Marie is to respond to the interpersonal purpose of the disclosure. If you remain silent, whether you have done an opening survey or not, the most likely responses from the other group members will be to ask questions, to offer sympathy and advice, and to tell of similar situations they have experienced. In Marie's case, none of these is likely to be particularly helpful to her or to the group because the questions, sympathy, and advice address the verbal content, not Marie's interpersonal purpose.

Marie's motivation for making the comment is not

clear. A therapist comment like "Why are you telling us this?" is likely to be perceived as critical; a question like "How would you like the group to respond to what you've just said?" may result either in an explicit request for advice or a denial of any interpersonal purpose. If a client requests advice early in the group, it is probably better to let the group members go ahead and offer it. Advice giving is something that group members like to do, especially in the early stages of a group before members begin to suspect that advice giving may not be the most helpful response.

If the client denies any interpersonal purpose, you might make the point that disclosures in the group have an effect on the other group members, that interpersonal actions have interpersonal results. The point may be pursued more extensively later in the group's career; but in the earlier stages of the group, as here, simply pointing it out is about as far as you can go.

The third response category involves the emotional envelope in which the verbal message is conveyed. You might ask Marie how she feels as a result of her interaction with Carl last night; how she feels about Carl; how she feels about the interaction; how she feels now about what she has just said; how she feels having said it; and the like.

Responses that are more group oriented involve inviting the group members to tell Marie how they feel about what she has told them. Possible focal points for the ensuing discussion would be any of the eight elements mentioned earlier.

Reflection is the fourth possible response. I recently asked clinicians in a training workshop on group therapy how they would respond to Marie's statement. Most participants agreed that they would have reflected her statement in some way. Beyond that they would have been noncommittal and, for the most part, nondirective.

Presumably, you would reflect the main thrust of the statement. But what is its main thrust? Reflection here requires the therapist to be selective, to choose one component from the many to reflect and thus to focus on. This choice by the therapist can be the beginning of a sequence of interchanges that lead to an unsatisfying outcome. In Marie's case, the therapist who ends up making a choice or guess about her real message is relieving Marie of her responsibility for identifying it.

However, perhaps you can think of a way of reflecting Marie's statements that would not involve your choosing the content to be pursued. A comment like "You're upset with Carl," although it seems noncommittal, reflects a choice of this element over the others. It might turn out, for instance, that Marie's lack of friends or dislike of her job is most troubling to her, and your reflecting either of those elements would be equally correct. But, in the final analysis, if you reflect one element, you ignore the others. You may get lucky and choose the theme most important to the client. But it is probably not worth the chance. A better approach is to use a response mode that will lead to the client's own identification of the element most important to him or her.

A fifth possible response is none of the above. There is sufficient ambiguity in Marie's situation that the number of possible helpful responses (including no response at all) is probably infinite. I have listed the most obvious to me. But, there may be others obvious to you—especially if you use a theoretical frame of reference different from mine (see Chapter Three).

Inviting Response from the Entire Group

This therapist intervention is a good choice if your goal is to get group members talking with one another. In this instance, you might ask something like "Would anyone like to respond to Marie?" or, somewhat better, "Who would like to respond to Marie?" This is a content-oriented invitation, likely to elicit content-oriented comments from the other group members. The therapeutic factors involved here would be acceptance (cohesiveness), and, perhaps, learning from interpersonal interaction.

In Marie's case, the content-oriented responses of the group are most likely to be about Carl, although other group members might pick up on one of the other elements of her statement. Carl probably would come in for some criticism because of his failure to try to make Marie happier here or because of his refusal to move somewhere she would presumably be happier. That is, the focus of the discussion could easily be on Carl's behavior, feelings, and motivations. Such a discussion might be of considerable interest to Marie, but it is not likely to be helpful, or even interesting, to most of the other group members. If the group did focus back on Marie, it would probably get into direct advice giving—one of the least helpful kinds of group interaction.

Group members may in general be encouraged to talk about their relationships with people outside the group. Indeed, in making the referral to the group, or in the screening interview, the therapists may explain to clients that group therapy is an interpersonal context for resolving relationship problems. Clients may come to the group expecting to talk about their troubled relationships—as soon as they feel sufficiently comfortable and trusting of other group members.

The invitation from the therapists for self-disclosure about relationships may be quite explicit. The opening survey facilitates such disclosures with its inquiry into what individual clients might like to work on (that is, tell the group about) during that session. Indeed, since so little happens in the group room itself (the group members sit around and sometimes talk), it is virtually inevitable that clients will talk about there-and-then issues. If clients are guided (by the therapists, group leaders, other group members, or their own expectations) to discuss there-and-then relationships, statements such as Marie's will not be unusual and much group time will be taken up with advice giving designed to influence the behavior of nonmembers of the group.

Entire group sessions can be taken up in this way, with most or all of the members being verbally active. If your goal is to get people to talk with one another, then it will appear that you have succeeded. You might even attribute the group's willingness to offer advice to the therapeutic factor of altruism. Advice might be fervently given, though it is seldom received with much enthusiasm. So it might appear that group members are engaged with each other and committed to the interaction, to being of help to one another, and to the group. And maybe they are.

The danger is that you are witnessing an unsatisfactory interactive sequence. Marie's statement, for example, is ambiguous in many ways. She does not say that she wants some response from the group; she just tosses something out. And because she does not take a stand on the issue of what, if anything, she wants from the group, the group members respond as they might in a social situation—by offering advice intended to be helpful. The interpersonal outcome of advice giving, however, is that the giver feels frustrated because his or her advice is not taken or warmly accepted, and the recipient feels frustrated, misunderstood, and dissatisfied. So, the outcome of all this is that the group members may have expended considerable time and energy on the issue and still feel dissatisfied, frustrated, impotent, and perhaps bored. And it may have been a succession of just such interpersonal outcomes that led them to the clinic and to the group in the first place.

It is possible that, left to its own devices, a group would eventually decide that such exchanges were unsatisfactory and would begin to cast about for new ways of communicating and relating. A group of very bright, articulate, psychologically sophisticated people might do it in a relatively short period of time. But in most groups, the repeated experience of loss, failure, and frustration does not lead to mood enhancement, to behavioral change, or to an increasing sense of self-worth and competence. Therefore, inviting the group to respond at the content level is not likely to be helpful or to bring the desired therapeutic factors into play.

Group therapy sessions are characterized by verbal content involving a complex interplay of here-and-now and there-and-then issues. The clients bring the there-and-then issues into the group. To the therapist, it does not matter what those issues are; what is important is the client's handling of those issues in the interpersonal context of the group. Sometimes, there-and-then issues have such clear relevance for a majority of the other group members that it is of value to focus on them; other times, the here-and-now issues are more salient. Frequently, the relationship between here-and-now and there-and-then issues is most important. (The client or group perception of that relationship is called *insight.*) Knowing when to focus on here-and-now and when to focus on there-and-then is something of an art, born of experience, sensitivity, and good instincts. In learning this art, if you must err, err on the side of here-and-now.

Some groups are characterized by a low level of verbal activity. Groups of schizophrenic inpatients, and outpatient groups of people who are withdrawn and depressed, are typical. Group therapists frequently attempt to generate interactions between group members by asking one group member a question and then asking another group member to comment on the response. That is not quite the situation in our example, since Marie has volunteered her comment. But in groups of taciturn, aloof people, it may be tempting to force interaction in this way. Such interactions almost always feel artificial and meaningless, and as soon as you stop directing them, the group members again fall silent.

Inviting an affective response would be something like "How does the group feel about what Marie has just said?" In this context, the word *feel* has some ambiguity. Popular usage is somewhat loose, and in this context the word may be synonymous with *think.* Hence, group members may respond as though you had asked them, "What do you think of what Marie has just said?" If you are intent on an affective response and the group responds cognitively, it may be necessary to rephrase the question.

Asking the group for their affective reactions to the statement or comment of one member seems an almost instinctive reaction of many group therapists. Sometimes it is a good thing to do. For situations in which a group member makes a poignant self-disclosure, or is especially uncertain about the group's reaction, or fears a negative response when one is unlikely, or simply has no idea at all about the emotional

impact of his or her words, inviting the group's affective feedback may be particularly helpful. The therapeutic factor
involved here is learning from interpersonal interaction. Its
effect may be enhanced when it follows self-disclosure and
possibly catharsis, though it need not be preceded by these
factors in order to be beneficial.

Sometimes asking the group for affective reactions is
not such a good thing to do. Some clients are expert at generating negative feedback, and when they do, asking the other
group members for their affective responses may unleash a
series of angry blasts, the effects of which are seldom therapeutic. Asking for affective reactions early in the life of a
group, or when a group member is relatively new, may be
more puzzling than helpful. The group may be reluctant to
engage with the client at this level of self-disclosure, perhaps
because the client is perceived as too fragile or too powerful
to confront. The main point to remember about these issues
is that there are many therapeutic factors, and affective disclosure by the group is not the only approach that can result
in client improvement.

Inviting Responses from Other Group Members
with Similar Problems

This therapist intervention is a bit more specific than
the preceding invitation, which was to the group generally
and no one in particular. You know more about the group
members individually than the group does because you have
read the charts and have done the screening interviews. But,
while clients are free to bring that information about themselves into the group, you are not. You may refer to things
clients have done or said in earlier group sessions, because
those are public knowledge to this group. But bringing information about clients in from outside the group poses serious
ethical and perhaps legal problems pertaining to confidentiality. This principle holds true even if group membership is
restricted to clients whom you are seeing or have seen individually, and even if everyone knows it.

So, here is a situation in which one group member,
Marie, is discussing problems you know other group members

share, or have resolved, or need to talk about. You can remain silent and hope that they will volunteer something, or you can elicit responses from them. You can say something like, "I wonder how other people here, in similar situations, feel about what Marie just told us." Or, simply, "Anyone else here been in that fix?" The people you are referring to know who they are and are free to respond or not.

The therapeutic factor involved here is universality: you want the disclosing client to know that others are, or have been, in the same situation. Such a move is appropriate early in the life of the group, when people discover similarities in each other's there-and-then life circumstances and in their reactions to those circumstances. However, you must take care to keep the group from slipping into unhelpful advice giving.

Not only is universality a therapeutic factor, it is a group builder, enhancing cohesiveness and trust through the establishment of common grounds of experience. Universality is an important factor to emphasize early in the life of a group. It may be desirable or necessary to emphasize this particular therapeutic factor at other times as well—for example, when a new member comes into an open group, or when a group member has described troubles that he or she regards as unique. It is also important to emphasize universality if your group members share the conviction that they are deviant, or that no one could possibly experience or understand their stories, their lives, or their troubles. Such feelings of isolation and sorrowful uniqueness, though painful, may be held tenaciously by clients with diagnoses denoting major psychopathology. It may take a group comprised of such clients many sessions to begin to believe there are commonalities among the group members. In such groups, inviting responses from other group members with similar problems may be one of the best things you can do.

Waiting for Group Response and Commenting on the Group Process

In the real group on which this discussion is based, the therapists remained silent, and the group ended up commiserating with Marie, speculating about Carl, and offering unhelpful advice. One possible therapist response could have been to wait until two or three of the other group members had offered advice to Marie, and then to comment on the group process. For example, "It seems that the group's response to Marie's talking about Carl is to offer advice." The therapist might have added, "And I wonder how Marie feels about all this advice she's getting." But in our example, a group member made a disclosing statement, the group responded to that statement, and the therapists chose to remain silent. The result of the silence was an unsatisfactory outcome consisting of group commiseration, speculation, and advice giving.

The therapists' intervention in Marie's case could have been to describe the group's response and to inquire about its effect on the discloser. The probable effect of this style of intervention is to get the group to look at what is going on between its members in the here-and-now: to invite each member to look at how the initial interaction and the response it engendered affected both the speaker and the group. Thus the whole behavioral sequence and the emotions surrounding it come under review. The therapeutic factors potentially brought into play would be self-disclosure, learning from interpersonal interaction (in our example, for Marie and for the other group members, to the extent they examine their own roles in the behavioral sequence), acceptance, and perhaps also vicarious learning, instillation of hope, and insight. From this point of view, therapist silence, followed by comment on the group process, appears to be the most promising of any of the therapist interventions because it involves each individual, the group as a whole, and, potentially, six of the eleven therapeutic factors.

However, when group members are not psychologically-minded, process comments by the therapist are puzzling at best. In many settings, a therapist comment that the group is offering advice to one of its members is likely to be ignored. It is as though the group were saying, "Yes, that's what we're doing, so what?" The question about the effect on Marie may well be met with some positive response from her, a statement that she is glad to hear the proffered advice even though it involves suggestions she had already thought of and had tried or rejected. Process interventions have as much potential as any other, including therapist silence, for involving the group and bringing the therapeutic factors into play. They also have as much potential as any other for falling flat. When process comments do not work—if the group is puzzled by them—go back to a more concrete level, eliciting individual reactions— affective or cognitive or both—to client disclosure.

Concluding Comment

The purpose of this chapter has been to describe some of the possible responses to a client's disclosure. Each of the possible responses discussed has advantages and disadvantages. A therapist intervention that deals with, or directs the group toward, the interpersonal situation here-and-now is potentially more effective, and has fewer hazards, than an intervention oriented toward the verbal content of the client's disclosure. Therapist interventions oriented toward interpersonal here-and-now situations involve the group's perceptions of and responses to the client's communication and interpersonal purpose, and the resulting changes in the interpersonal context.

However, some theories of group therapy are content- and there-and-then oriented. If you or your supervisor follow that kind of orientation, you may not agree with an interpersonal bias. Since nobody yet has a lock on truth and beauty in group psychotherapy, you have to decide for yourself which approach makes the most sense to you and fits you best.

The quest for certainty is understandably characteristic of people who seek to learn or sharpen skills in a complex undertaking like group therapy—an activity requiring both technical skill and artistry. But, as this chapter illustrates, there are few things that are certainly wrong to do in response to a client's comment. And there are probably no interventions that are certainly perfect or clearly best. In this situation, your most reliable guides are your own knowledge and experience, common sense, intuition, and sense of humanity.

7

Coping with
Difficult Group Members

Difficult clients are those whose behavior has proved to be extraordinarily problematical for the group therapists, for the group, or for the clinic. Such clients seldom regard themselves as difficult.

Erickson (1984) has suggested that difficult clients are those whom the therapist is unwilling or unable to approach in straightforward and commonsensical ways. He attributes this hesitancy to (1) therapist reluctance to give direct feedback, (2) adoption of a passive therapist stance, and (3) interpretation of disturbed behaviors as manifestations of illness rather than interpersonal issues. Taken in sum, these factors suggest that difficult clients are a reflection of therapist experience and competence.

My own view is somewhat different. I suggest that the locus of the difficulty lies in the differing agendas clients, therapists, the group, and the clinic bring to the therapeutic enterprise in general, and to group therapy in particular.

There are many reasons why people come to mental health clinics. They may seek relief from symptoms that are emotional or physical or some combination of the two. They may seek wise counsel or guidance in confronting and surviving intolerable life situations. Or they may come because other people have told them it is desirable, or necessary, for them to do so.

Clinics, like other mental health care delivery systems, offer few therapy services geared toward symptom relief or toward the offering of counsel. Perhaps the most notable exceptions are the treatment of symptoms with medication or with behavioral therapy. Many, perhaps most, mental health professionals prefer to treat underlying causes rather than situation-specific symptoms.

There is, then, at least a potential discrepancy between what the patient or client is seeking and what the therapist and clinic offer. The discrepancy may be greater when clients are psychologically unsophisticated and prone to take action, rather than enter discussion, in order to reduce discomfort. It is not unusual for clients to enter therapy to find out what action to take, only to find that they are encouraged instead to talk about their emotions relative to both immediate and long-past situations.

When client and therapist agendas differ, their concepts of help are likely to differ also. Frequently, clients want pills and answers that will enable them to feel better while maintaining behavioral patterns and relationships therapists regard as maladaptive. Therapists, on the other hand, may seek to provide cognitive understanding (insight), emotional catharsis, and change in troubled behaviors and relationships. When client and therapist agendas differ in this way, clients may experience frustration and anger with their therapists, who in turn may regard clients as difficult.

The solution to this type of difficulty involves reduction of the discrepancy between agendas. For the discrepancy to be reduced, both agendas (the therapist's and the client's) must change. Such change is the result of negotiation. In the context of group therapy, other group members may be party to the negotiation, and to the amended treatment contracts resulting from successful negotiation.

By the time a client gets into a therapy group, there have been at least three negotiations. The first involves the client and the intake worker who must decide the extent to which the clinic's mission and the client's needs are congruent; the client must weigh the potential benefit of clinic attendance with the various costs in time, money, and stress. The second negotiation involves the referral for screening by the group therapists. The referring therapist must convince the client that attending the screening interview(s) offers benefits sufficient to make doing so worthwhile. The topics of the third negotiation, which takes place during the screening interview, include the ways therapists and group therapy will benefit the client and what the client is willing to do in order to obtain that benefit.

It is possible that none of these negotiations addresses the discrepancy between client and therapist agendas. And it is possible that none of them seeks to modify unworkable client agendas. As a result, the client and the therapists may reach the group with implicit agendas that differ but with explicit agendas on which agreement has been reached.

It is inherently difficult to negotiate implicit agendas. Indeed, their very presence may go undetected for long periods of time, particularly if the difficulty is defined by the therapist as inhering within the client. In dealing with a difficult client, then, the first step is to consider the possibility that you and the client are operating from different implicit agendas. The second step is to make the agendas as explicit as possible, and the third is to renegotiate on the basis of the newly explicit agendas.

An example will help here. One of the most common and most vexatious problems with which a group therapist must deal involves clients who engage in self-disclosure ad nauseam, monopolizing the group's time, attention, and energies. It is difficult to know how to shut off the torrent of words without hurting the clients' feelings and, early in the life of a group, without frightening the other group members into silence lest they too be chided for saying too much. Yet it must be done. The true monopolizer is regarded as difficult because the behavior is repetitive.

The high verbal output of monopolizers can be regarded as a symptom. Symptoms are behaviors that have functions and goals, and usually the goals are legitimate or reasonable or healthy. But these symptomatic behaviors of the monopolizers represent maladaptive efforts to reach reasonable goals or to meet normal human needs. Sometimes, the function of the monopolizers' high verbal output is to maintain control of interpersonal situations while the goal is to receive support and admiration from attentive audiences. The clients' implicit agenda, in this instance, might be to determine how to get such support and admiration while maintaining control of interpersonal situations through talking and other attention-getting behaviors. Through some careful and persistent work, it may be possible for the therapists to help monopolizers make the agenda explicit, and then to modify it so they can attain the genuine support and admiration they seek.

Therapists may accept a client into group, or into individual therapy, knowing the client is regarded as difficult. Their acceptance indicates the belief that they can influence the client to change. Frequently, the therapeutic focus is on changing behavior that the client is reluctant to give up because it represents the client's best adaptive efforts to meet his or her needs in any given interpersonal context. The tenacity with which such behaviors are held makes it difficult for the therapists, or for the group, to influence the client toward adaptive change. One source of difficulty, then, is the therapists' belief that the client is not susceptible to influence either by the therapists or by the group. Such an assessment may be related to therapist feelings of frustration, helplessness, and lack of competence. Dealing with these feelings, and with the belief that the client is not susceptible to influence, may help resolve some of the therapist's feelings of difficulty and of impotence.

Difficult clients, then, are those whose behaviors in group present problems you do not know what to do with; they are the clients to whom you are not able to respond in a helpful or effective way. When I ask group therapists in community mental health centers what topics they would like to have covered in training workshops, they invariably include a category of difficult patients or clients that comprises a mixture of diagnostic entities and behavioral problems. Diagnostic categories most frequently mentioned are borderline personality disorder, schizophrenia, and depression. Problem behaviors most frequently mentioned include the silent patient (or the silent group), the unmotivated patient, the withdrawn patient, the monopolizer, and the restless or agitated patient. In a survey of forty-two senior group therapy supervisors, Spitz, Kass, and Charles (1980) found that the most common problem areas for beginning group therapists included monopolizers, help rejecters, and complainers. In this chapter, we will consider some strategies for dealing with the problem of the difficult client, and in the following chapter, we will look in some detail at the borderline client in group psychotherapy.

The Monopolizer

As the name implies, this type of person seeks to keep the group's attention focused on himself or herself as frequently, and for as long, as possible. The problem for the group leader is keeping this from happening without making the other group members reluctant to say anything for fear they too might be chastised.

In a new group, you usually have little warning that one of the members will attempt to monopolize the group's attention; it is difficult to predict from the client's behavior during the screening interview. The monopolizer's high level of verbal activity may be little more than a response to the anxiety inherent in the situation; as the group anxiety decreases, the monopolizer may become less active. Some people talk more when anxious, and the talking helps them feel less anxious. On the other hand, if monopolizing is more characteristic, and is, or is related to, the major problem that brought the client into therapy, the high verbal activity may not appear until the second or third session.

When a group member starts to talk, you do not know whether he or she will go on and on and on from there.

There are people who are long-winded, people who use many words when few would do, and people whose thoughts and feelings have been bottled up for so long that when they finally do begin to talk, the words come pouring out. Monopolizers start out in the same way these people do. At some point, however, it becomes clear that they have gone on for too long, and then for much too long; then it becomes obvious that they have lost the audience. Other group members sit around looking bored or annoyed, but the monopolist continues, apparently oblivious to the group's nonverbal responses.

The other group members are not likely to interrupt the monopolizer. If you have an articulate, verbal, intelligent, and sophisticated group, with one or two members who are comfortable with confrontation, one of them might interrupt. But by this time the monopolizer will have been going on for some time, and the rest of the group is likely to be impatient or angry or both. If you wait until the group interrupts the monopolizer, the other group members may be very angry indeed, and you may have to come to his or her rescue. The other group members may also become angry at you for permitting the monopolizer to continue for so long.

At some point, you have to intervene actively. In order to do so, it is necessary first to be fairly sure that it is a monopolizing process going on, and not merely someone who has much to say and is simply saying it at some length. The judgment of whether or not someone is hogging the spotlight is subjective; here, as with so many other things in group therapy, you will have to trust your judgment. If you are feeling bored, restless, and wishing that the group member would get to the point, you can assume that the other group members are feeling something similar—perhaps even more intensely than you. On the other hand, if you get bored easily, your own feelings may not be a reliable guide.

Active intervention begins with interrupting the monopolizer. How you do this depends on your own personal style. If you are comfortable with interrupting people, you already know how to do it. If you are not, you should let your cotherapist do it—if it is easier for him or her. This is one reason you have a cotherapist. If neither of you is good at interrupting, if it is just not your personal style, you should consult with your clinical supervisor about what to do.

When you interrupt, it is important not to attack or to be critical, though your intervention is likely to be perceived in this light no matter what you do. One approach, which has some tradition behind it, is to ask the monopolizer how he or she is feeling just now, while talking to the group. On occasion, some further persistence will be needed.

Therapist: John, how are you feeling right now?

John: Fine. As I was saying . . .

Therapist: That's not quite what I meant. Take a moment now, like we do sometimes at the beginning of group, and really look inside yourself, and tell us how you're feeling. Wait a moment and think before you answer.

John: I feel a little annoyed because you've interrupted me.

Therapist: What were you feeling while you were talking?

John: A little anxious, I suppose.[1]

John's response would presumably open the door to exploration of more adaptive or more direct ways to reduce anxiety, and perhaps to some realization of what generated the anxiety in the first place.

Another possible intervention is to call the monopolizer's attention to the interpersonal situation in the group. If we assume that behavior is motivated and goal oriented, theory and experience suggest that monopolizing behavior is driven by several motives, including dependency and control needs. Monopolizing requires an audience, so it seems likely that its goals are interpersonal—even if the only audience the monopolizer is concerned with is you and perhaps your cotherapist. However, monopolizers are not usually aware of the interpersonal goals of this behavior, so when you interrupt the monopolizer, one question you ask might involve what he or she is trying to accomplish by telling us these things, whatever these things happen to be. Questions might be of the general form, How would you like the group to respond (or, What do you want from the group) after you've told us all this? What are you trying to give to the other group members? What are you trying to get from them?

Note that these questions center on the monopolizer's own efforts relative to the group. Clients generally have more difficulty looking at what they hope to get from the group than they have looking at what they expect to give to the group. Some therapist patience and persistence may be required to keep the client and the group focused on what the monopolizer is trying to do in the interpersonal situation of group rather than on what the monopolizer is saying, that is, to keep the group focused on the process rather than on the content.

Yet another approach involves calling the monopolizers' attention to the effect they are actually creating in the group. Usually that effect includes boredom and perhaps some anger, and seldom is that the effect the monopolizers are seeking. This approach involves asking monopolizers what effect they think they are having on the group. Monopolizers seldom make use of the visual cues available to them through body language and facial expression of the other group members. Frequently, while they are in their monologues, eye contact with the rest of the group is minimal. So asking monopolizers to look around helps to direct their attention to the effect their behavior is having on the audience. You can then ask them how the other group members look— usually they will look bored rather than angry—or you can ask the group members how they are feeling or what they are thinking just then. The latter is risky if you suspect that the monopolizer has generated anger in the group. However, if the monopolizers respond that the audience looks interested and attentive (which is rare), you may have to ask them to look more carefully.

Most of the time, unless they are quite angry, the other group members will express some mild dissatisfaction with a monopolizer's long-windedness. If you ask monopolizers if that dissatisfaction is what they intended, they will almost always say no. But if you then ask what their intent was, they may well be unable to say.

Communication has an interpersonal goal. There is some effect that you wish to engender in your audience. It is likely that most people attend to these interpersonal effects only in some rather special circumstances, as when one is conscious of wanting to make a good impression. One reason for this relative lack of attention to the interpersonal goals of communication may be that most people are good, most of the time, at producing approximately the effect they want; they have effective social, communicative skills. Another reason for the relative lack of attention to interpersonal effects is that people do not invest much energy in getting others to act or feel in any particular way. Most people seek only a response of some sort—most frequently with a neutral or positive emotional tone.

People come into group therapy in part because these systems are not working. Something in their interpersonal communication patterns consistently produces results that they do not want and they do not expect—results which may have unpleasant consequences for them. Monopolizers are usually seeking attentive, supportive, and admiring audiences that will respond nonverbally with approving looks and smiles. They can maintain the fantasy that their verbal behaviors are producing this desired effect, as long as there is no real or genuine interaction between them and their audiences. However, because of the strong narcissistic component that is characteristic of monopolizers, they may actually have given little or no thought to either the real or the fantasied effect. An important component of the work of therapy is to help them learn to be aware of the interpersonal context in which they function and to be aware of the effects they are producing in their real audiences.

The therapeutic factor operational here is learning from interpersonal interaction. When the monopolizer is holding forth at length, there is little or no interaction going on.

If, upon interrupting the monologue, you ask who the monopolizer is talking to, he or she will frequently say, not to anyone in particular. And this is true: the monopolizer speaks to an impersonal audience, to no one person, to no one. In effect, the monopolizer speaks to an imaginary or fantasy audience, one that is endlessly attentive. Your task is to substitute the real audience for the imaginary one, as when you ask the monopolizer to look around at each group member, and to substitute real for fantasied interactions, as when you help the monopolizer look at the interpersonal consequences he or she is actually producing as opposed to the fantasied effect. Because the monopolizer's behavior is usually well-entrenched, of some years' duration, and because it has multiple determinants, including anxiety, control, and narcissistic issues, it is likely to change only slowly. Many patient repetitions of the pattern may be necessary: interrupting the monopolizers, getting them to attend to what they are really doing, here and now, with these real people as audience, and getting them to recognize the real consequences of their behavior.

In some kinds of groups, none of the above will work, and a different approach is necessary in working effectively with monopolizers. Time-limited groups, groups in which there are many silent or withdrawn members and one or two members who talk a lot, and groups of people who have very little psychological-mindedness are all examples of groups in which monopolizers cause special problems. In such circumstances, you might try contracting with the monopolizer for a guaranteed but finite amount of time. This would involve, ideally, convincing the monopolizer that talking too much is a problem that needs to be worked on, and then proposing a time limit for working on it in each session. Initially, ten minutes is a good maximum; typically, within four or five sessions the client is taking less time than that, and the problem is well on its way to solution. The extent to which this decrease in talking behavior generalizes to situations outside the group, where there are no negotiated time limits, is difficult to ascertain.

Negotiating a time limit for the monopolizer's speeches

does not require agreement that their length is a problem for the client. It is, initially, a problem for the group, and negotiating (or, in difficult cases, imposing) a time limit may be put in those terms:

> Barbara, I'm sorry to interrupt but we need time for other people as well. How about taking another five minutes, and then we'll move on?

Then, the following session, one possibility is to interrupt the monopolizer as soon as she starts:

Therapist: Barbara, how much time do you think you'll need today?

Barbara: About a half hour.

Therapist: I'm afraid we won't have time for other work then. How about ten minutes, and then when we've done our other work we'll get back to you if time permits?

If the monopolizer then objects or expresses some resentment at being limited, it may be feasible to look at some of the interpersonal effects of his or her behavior, as described above. But more often than not, if you have to use the contracting approach, there is surprisingly little objection.

In sum, dealing with monopolizers involves (1) interrupting their monologues early, (2) facilitating interpersonal learning and contracting with them to limit, but guarantee, their time in the spotlight, (3) being willing to repeat (1) and (2) as long as necessary, and (4) helping the monopolizer develop alternative ways of reducing anxiety and meeting narcissistic and control needs.

The Silent Group Member

Silent members are those who do not volunteer comments and who respond only briefly when called upon. They are found in inpatient settings, in residential treatment settings, in day hospital programs, and, perhaps less frequently, in other outpatient groups. Silent patients include

- Chronically hospitalized patients assigned to group therapy because of their presence on a unit where group is offered more than because of any indication that they would benefit from this form of psychotherapy
- Patients in residential programs for which group therapy is one component of a structured program, as in alcoholic rehabilitation centers
- Patients in day hospital programs for which some form of group therapy is one component of the structured program and may be a condition for remaining in the program
- People whose personal problems or psychopathology are associated with minimal verbal interaction with others
- People who are normally quiet, or who tend to be silent in particular contexts, as when more than two or three other people are present, or in the presence of other group members who are highly verbal

The problem is not the group member's silence or consistent failure to volunteer comments. Nor is it even the discrepancy between the therapist's agenda and the group member's. The problem arises when the therapist attempts to modify the client's silence without first addressing the differences in their agendas. Typically, when a silent (that is, nonvolunteering) group member is a problem for you, you try to get that person to talk in group—to engage in self-disclosure. The group member, on the other hand, may be trying to get through the group session without being called upon or focused on, and if he or she is focused on, to escape with as little verbal interchange as possible.

In order to deal appropriately with the problem, you should consider why the silent patient is in group therapy in the first place, and what his or her goals might be—as distinct from your goals, or the clinic's or hospital's. In state hospital settings, and sometimes in short-term inpatient facilities as well, some patients are not motivated to get well. The status of mental patient and the secondary gains of hospitalization apparently seem, to them, preferable to returning to home, family, community, and productive work. Individuals who have reached this conclusion will work as actively as possible to thwart therapeutic efforts. Medication may lead to improvement, and while hospital practices may result in compliance with a medication regime, once patients are released, many stop taking the medicine, become dysfunctional again, and return to the hospital. Prolixin, a long-lasting tranquilizer, saves many from this sequence of events since it requires only an occasional injection; however, its effects can be thwarted simply by not showing up for the clinic appointment to obtain it.[2]

The preceding discussion implies that lack of motivation for improvement, or motivation against improvement, may underlie the reticence of some long-term patients in residential facilities for the chronically ill. However, this should not be taken to imply that all such patients lack motivation or even that improvement, as we usually define it, is negative for them. There are other reasons for chronically mentally ill patients to be reticent in group therapy. They are reasons similar to those of less chronic and less ill patients and of clients in other mental health settings.

In attempting group therapy with the hospitalized, chronically mentally ill, it is sometimes necessary to set aside your long-term goal of overall improvement and to focus on the more immediate task of engaging the patient in verbal interaction in a therapy group. Even this agenda may be significantly discrepant from the patient's own. However, most patients, even in long-term units in state hospitals, will respond in group sessions if asked their names and if they are asked questions that allow one or two word answers. This minimal responsiveness provides a small but definite opportunity for interaction, upon which it is sometimes possible to build. (Group therapy with patients who are totally verbally unresponsive poses special problems beyond the scope of this book.)

The technique of engaging silent group members

involves asking them questions that (1) are easy for them to answer, (2) they are likely to answer, and (3) require minimal self-disclosure. The easiest questions can be answered yes or no, require little or no subjective judgment, and follow social routine. Hence, if you ask a silent group member how he or she is feeling today, the most likely answer is going to be, "Fine." But if you ask a silent group member, during the opening survey, what he or she would like to do during the group session today, the answer is likely to be brief and equivocal at best. So do not ask.

The technique requires some ingenuity on your part to formulate questions to which the patient is likely to respond. Questions such as, Is there anything you'd like to do in group today? should be avoided, because the easiest and most likely answer is No, and then you are stuck. Questions such as, What would you like to do in group today? that are good to ask in most cases, should also be avoided with the silent group member because they seldom elicit a meaningful response, and if the patient replies, "Nothing," then you are stuck again. Probably better is a question of the general form, Did you do this or that recently? as in Did you go home last weekend? Did you go to OT this morning?

Questions that, under ordinary circumstances, would seem innocuous are not necessarily so in this context: Is it cold out today? requires a subjective judgment, the formulation of an opinion, and the public self-disclosure of that opinion, that is, the taking of a position. Such a question is, therefore, considerably more difficult than a Did you? question, and should be avoided in this context. With limitations like this, you may need creativity as well as ingenuity in order to formulate questions that will work.

The next objective for the technique of engaging silent group members is to increase the magnitude of self-disclosure by a step as small as possible. One way of doing that is to make requests of the general form, Tell us one thing about x. For example, Tell us one thing that happened when you went home last weekend.

Initially your goal might be to engage the silent

member in one interaction each group session. Depending on how readily he or she appears to respond, and depending on the quality of the response ("We had a nice dinner" being a somewhat better response than "We went to church" because it has an evaluative component), you might stay at the tell-us-one-thing level for some months. Only when this pattern is well established should you attempt the next step—to invite the patient to comment on some aspect of the ongoing group interaction, and perhaps even to comment on another group member's disclosures.

The technique is similar in outpatient groups with silent members. It involves ensuring that there is at least one client-therapist interaction each group, with a gradual increase in the length of the interaction and in the level of disclosure requested. In effect, you are training the client to respond, to interact. When interaction patterns are established, you might be able to go on to the next step—to contract with the client to volunteer one comment during each session. Therapist monitoring will ensure the terms of the contract are met. How far, and how rapidly, the client progresses from one step to the next will depend on a number of factors: (1) the client's personal resources; (2) the nature, purpose, and ambience of the group; and (3) the discrepancy between the client's group therapy agenda and your agenda for him or her.

Thus far, we have discussed the client whose silence reflects resistance to participation in the group and to therapeutic change. A second type of silent client is one whose agenda for participation and benefit is similar to that of the therapists but whose natural mode of expression, particularly of emotion, is nonverbal. It simply does not occur to such individuals to talk about how they are feeling. Frequently, the absence of verbal communication about affect puts a strain on intimate relationships, and relationship issues of one sort or another lead these quiet people into group therapy.

These people tend to express emotion behaviorally rather than verbally. The housewife who cleans house when she is upset, the husband who retreats to his basement work-bench to build something when he feels stressed, are stereo-typical examples. These people express affection behaviorally also, either through gift giving or by doing something the recipient likes, such as fixing an extra-nice meal or painting the house shutters.

In group therapy, however, the expression of emotion is limited to the verbal sphere. When you ask a person whose characteristic mode of expression is behavioral how or what he or she is feeling, the response may be one of genuine puzzlement because the person may not have a verbal label for the subjective experience. The therapeutic work involves helping the client learn which verbal tags go with which subjective experience, and then encouraging him or her to use these verbal tags in interpersonal interactions in the group, where the effects or consequences of such use can be explored.

In order to do this therapeutic work, it is necessary to get group members to pay attention to and talk about, rather than to ignore or act on, their emotions. If you ask silent members how they are feeling, the most probable response is "Fine," unless they are feeling physically unwell, in which case they may report on their physical conditions.

Emotions have a physical component and a mental or cognitive component. A group member may appear angry, with flashing eyes, flushed face, and pursed lips or clenched teeth, and still say "Fine" when asked how he or she is feeling right now. In this instance, you would call attention to the observable manifestations of anger, comment that most people who look that way are feeling anger, and ask for group comments.

It is slow work, and sometimes tedious. People usually learn verbal tags for subjective experience during the developmental years. Learning those tags during the adult years is like learning a foreign language during the adult years. The later in life you start, the slower the process, and the more likely you are to end up with an accent.

A third type of silent member is one who feels unworthy of the group's time and attention. Such feelings

may be associated with severe psychopathology, as in schizophrenic or borderline disorders, though they are more
commonly associated with depression. Such feelings of
unworthiness may be expressed as something quite different
from what they are, as when a client says he or she is silent
"because the other group members have problems so much
worse than mine." Sometimes the client is right, in which
case the difficulty is not as much the silent client as it is his
or her assignment to that particular group. Usually, however,
the difficulty is, in fact, with the client, in which case you
(and the group) have the delicate problem of reassuring the
client that his or her problems are sufficiently bad to warrant
group time. This kind of reassurance, such as it is, may have
to be repeated each time you or a group member invites the
silent member to speak.

Finally, there are those quiet people who are characteristically not verbally forthcoming. In social settings, they may
be described as quiet and perhaps shy. These are people who
may be attending carefully to the ongoing group interaction,
but it does not occur to them to comment or to participate.
In some ways these are the easiest silent members to work
with. It takes little more than an invitation from you, or from
other group members, for them to become verbally active in
group. But without such an invitation they tend to remain
silent. After some time, weeks or a few months, of inviting
participation every session, it may be possible to contract
successfully with such a group member to initiate one interaction per session. Sometimes progress in getting these people
to talk in group is rapid after that.

A potential group composition problem to be aware of
is the presence of a monopolizer and a quiet person. Somewhat less problematical is the presence in the group of two or
three people who, while not monopolizers, are quite verbally
active and who could easily overshadow the more quiet group
member. The remedy for this situation involves three steps:
(1) making sure there is an opening, in the rain of words, for
the quiet person to speak—to have an equal opportunity for
the group's attention; (2) encouraging the more talkative

members to make such a space if they do not do so spontane-
ously; and then (3) encouraging the quiet person to make
such a space for himself or herself. Of course, you could start
with the last step, which is rather like encouraging a lamb to
charge the lions.

The silent group member will claim that he or she is
attending to the group process in such a way as to suggest
the operation of the therapeutic factor of vicarious learning.
That may be true. However, vicarious learning is one of the
least effective of the therapeutic factors. Self-disclosure and
learning from interpersonal interaction are more potent, but
require verbal interchange. The silent member's claim of benefit without verbal participation may be valid, but a successful effort to increase verbal participation is likely to be
associated with significantly more rapid improvement and
greater benefit. In a study of the relationship of verbal activity
and silence to therapy outcome, Fielding (1983) provided
empirical support for these theoretical propositions.

The Withdrawn Client

The difference between the silent client and the withdrawn client is that the latter is unresponsive behaviorally as
well as verbally. Eye contact with any other group member or
with the group leaders is typically poor or absent. The nonverbal posture of such clients (who are most frequently
encountered in inpatient settings) discourages interaction.
These are people with whom you would not start in an opening survey.

The most extreme case is the client who refuses any
interaction at all. Some group therapists assume that if a
client is in group, one ought to be able to engage in some
interaction with him or her. The question that comes up in
the group training workshops I conduct is, typically, how to
achieve interaction with withdrawn clients. As a purely technical matter, the procedure is similar to that outlined above
for the silent client. You find the smallest, most insignificant,
most minimal intervention to which the client will respond,
and you build from there, gradually, over a period of time.

Sometimes that works. However, if you are working with people who have been hospitalized for a long time, it may take many months, sometimes more than a year, before there is much response at all—other than the person's passive willingness to come into the group room upon request.

Two questions come to mind here. One is, why is the client withdrawn? Perhaps a more cogent question in this context is, why is this client in group? Withdrawn clients are seldom admitted to group therapy as a result of referral from an individual therapist, a screening interview, or a contract between the patient and the group leaders about what will be accomplished in group sessions and the criteria for evaluating those accomplishments. Typically, withdrawn clients are assigned to group by ward personnel, and they come because of passive acquiescence. What they are doing in the group is usually not clear to them. Moreover, the goal of group therapy for the withdrawn client is not always clear to the group leaders, other than they are somehow supposed to reach the withdrawn client.

Putting such clients in a therapy group may represent the hospital's or the clinic's best effort to provide some sort of treatment, other than maintenance medication and custodial care. The few hours a withdrawn client spends in the group each week may be the only systematic psychotherapy available. Ideally, such groups are small, and you should have time to become familiar with each client's background history, even to the point where you will have some understanding of why the client is withdrawn. That understanding will give you some idea of the discrepancy between your agenda (or the hospital's or clinic's) and the client's, and perhaps will give you some idea of the emotional and intellectual resources upon which the client may be able to draw.

If you are leading a group of withdrawn clients, it might help to know that this type of client presents one of the most difficult challenges for group therapy. Other difficult groups are those with institutionalized, mentally retarded individuals with a group average IQ below 65 or so, acute admissions service groups, and groups whose members are present as a result of court action. There is apparently very little in the group therapy literature about the withdrawn client. Erickson (1984), in his fine little book on inpatient group psychotherapy, devotes a page or two to the problem. Yalom, in his book on inpatient group therapy (1983), devotes a chapter to what he calls the *lower level psychotherapy group*, but his focus is on an acute admissions service. Nonetheless, some of the exercises he suggests may be helpful here as well. O'Brien (1975) suggests that the therapist's task with withdrawn clients is to promote social interaction among the group members. However, his group consisted of schizophrenic outpatients. Klett (1966) found no significant improvement in withdrawn patients after twenty-six hours of group psychotherapy.

In dealing with the silent group member, your initial goal is to have one verbal interaction with that person during each group session, and gradually to expand the verbal interchange until he or she is volunteering something each session. In dealing with the withdrawn group member, your initial goal may be nothing more than to have the person acknowledge, nonverbally, that he or she has heard you (or has heard another group member) when something is said to him or her. In general, the greater the impairment of the client, and the longer the duration of the impairment, the slower his or her progress is likely to be.

One of the major issues for group therapists working with chronically mentally ill, withdrawn inpatients is a sense of futility, frustration, and incompetence when repeated attempts to engage these patients in verbal interaction are unsuccessful. Whether group therapy is an appropriate treatment for such patients is not the issue. The probability of improvement and success is quite low unless you define your goals carefully. Under these conditions, any improvement is a significant step forward, signalling that the odds have been beaten and a difficult task accomplished.

The Restless or Agitated Group Member

Restless or agitated patients are usually encountered on acute admissions services in long-term hospitals, and in other inpatient settings. The problem they present for the group therapist involves the magnitude of disruption such patients create for the other group members, for the therapist, and for the group process. It is difficult to decide how disruptive a restless patient has to become before he or she is asked to leave the group.

Most group therapists know how to handle a restless or agitated patient on a one-to-one or a two-to-one basis. The same principles apply in a therapy group, but there are additional constraints. These constraints include the size of the group room, the furnishings, and the level of pathology of the other group members.

If you are going to work with this type of patient, you will want a group room as large as possible, furnished only with objects that are too heavy to throw. It is best to let the restless patient move around, if that is what he or she wants to do; agitated patients also may want to move around. The restlessness is related to anxiety, and you already know some things to do with an anxious patient. You might encourage the patient to sit down while you are talking with him or her, provided that you are not going to talk long. However, insisting that the restless patient remain seated may increase both the restlessness and the anxiety.

Even on an admissions service, other patients are surprisingly tolerant of the behavior of restless or agitated group members. The other patients may be frightened by such behavior, but they tend not to show it or to object much to being in the same group. However, other patients usually are not tolerant of being hit or shouted at angrily. If an agitated patient is combative in either of these ways, it is essential to exclude him or her from the group. Patients who fear for their physical safety during the group sessions are not likely to benefit from those sessions.

For nonviolent restlessness and agitation, the limiting factor is what you and your cotherapist are comfortable with, and what you are willing to tolerate. If you can lead the group effectively while someone is wandering around the room, or going in and out, fine. If not, you may have to ask the restless patient to leave.

The Unmotivated Group Member

A person whose motivation for change and improvement is less than your own motivation for him or her to change and improve, or whose desire for change is significantly less than you think it should be, is regarded as unmotivated. These group members are most often found in groups in which membership is coercive—for example, court-ordered substance abuse treatment programs; inpatient groups, particularly if the patient has suffered involuntary commitment; and outpatient clinics or similar settings where group attendance is prerequisite to other services, such as medication.

In these instances, group members' ostensible lack of motivation may really be little more than their refusal to subscribe to the goals set for them by others. People do not always want to get "well," whatever that means, because sometimes doing so would leave them in a more unfortunate position than if they stayed "sick." Getting well may mean giving up behaviors that have brought relief, solace, companionship, and joy, in exchange for hard work, long hours, loneliness, and uncertainty. Hence, one of the keys to understanding unmotivated group members is to look, perhaps along with them and the group, at the consequences of being motivated to change (in the way that you or the clinic or the courts think they should). Such motivation is not likely to become apparent until the unmotivated group members see, from their own frames of reference, that the changes you are advocating are better than their current behaviors.

In this context, *unmotivated* is a judgment rather than an observation. Such a judgment is similar to calling someone lazy. A lazy person is one who does not act in accord with your wishes or your evaluation of what should be done. In a similar vein, an unmotivated person is one who does not seek the goals you think he or she should seek—a person who does not display the vigor you think ought to be shown.

The first step in dealing with an unmotivated group member, then, may be to examine your own judgments, evaluations, and feelings toward the person. The locus of the

problem may lie with you rather than in a group member
who may be highly motivated to resist pressures toward con-
formity—toward what you, but not he or she, regard as a
more satisfying life.

Conclusions

The above discussion brings us back to the point with
which we started: a difficult group member is not necessarily
one who is having difficulty, but one who poses difficulty for
the therapists, for the group, for the clinic, or for all three. It
would be easy to add more types of difficult clients to those
discussed in this chapter: the intellectualizer, the intermittent
attender, the suicidal group member, and so on. In each
instance, the specifics of handling the difficulty differ, but the
following four general principles are similar.

1. Define the difficulty as primarily a therapist or clinic
problem rather than as a problem client, and seek to remedy
that problem. Sometimes the remedy involves obtaining additional information, from supervisors or other consultants, on
how to respond to client behaviors that the therapist (but not
the client) finds particularly troublesome. In this chapter, I
have attempted to provide such information for the types of
patient or client discussed above.

2. Identify, as much as possible, the therapist's or clinic's agenda, the client's agenda, and the discrepancy between
the two. An important step here is to acknowledge the validity
of the client's agenda, at least for that client. Such acknowledgment does not imply that self-defeating or self-destructive
behaviors or purposes are valid, but rather that, from the
client's point of view, maladaptive behaviors may represent a
valid choice, given the apparently available alternatives and
the client's history.

3. If possible, negotiate or renegotiate the treatment
contract with the group member in order to reduce the discrepancy between agendas. With chronically mentally ill
inpatients, such a negotiation may not be possible, and the
therapist may initially have to yield considerably more than

the patient has to in order to find some common ground. The patient, who in some sense already has lost everything, may have nothing more to yield.

4. Develop a strategy to replace problem behaviors, on the part of both therapist and client. In this context, problem therapist behaviors might include reluctance to seek consultation, assuming that therapist and client agendas are similar and need no reconciliation, and formulating disparaging value judgments about the client's behavioral choices. Problem client behaviors are those that have been described here, and the agendas and choices and history that underlie them.

It is also true that some people are particularly difficult to relate to, and, in addition, pose particular problems for the therapist, the clinic, and the group. When these difficulties are sufficiently severe, such individuals may be labelled as having borderline personality disorders. The magnitude and intensity of the problems posed by these clients for themselves and for others are such that they warrant a separate chapter. But even in cases involving particularly difficult clients, defining the locus of the problem as being primarily with the therapist is likely to be a fruitful way of addressing these most challenging issues.

Notes

1. This is one of those responses that occur more frequently in the literature than in the clinic. Theoretically, anxiety underlies prolixity. However, feelings seldom are as accessible as you would like, or as indicated here for purposes of illustration. John is more likely to have said, somewhat defiantly at this point, "I felt fine." Asking for self-disclosure about feelings works fine with intelligent and psychologically-minded clients. Among the psychologically unsophisticated—and you find them in college clinics as well as in community mental health centers—a psychotherapist's inquiry about feelings is frequently mistaken as a polite inquiry about the state of one's physical health.

2. The implication in the preceding discussion is that

people choose madness, an assumption explicitly espoused by Szasz (1956). The behaviors described here can be understood as well in other terms as, for example, pathology-driven resistance. The presence of resistance is readily observable on any long-term inpatient unit, and the silent patient's resistance to therapy is a problem for group therapists regardless of their theoretical persuasions or theories of deviance.

8

Problems Posed
by Borderline Clients

Clients with borderline personality disorders pose challenging problems for the group therapist, as well as for the group members, the individual therapist, and the clinic. The borderline syndrome has been described by Masterson (1972, 1974, 1981; Masterson and Rinsley, 1975), Kernberg (1975), and Hartocollis (1977), among others. There is a growing literature on the borderline client in group therapy. Most reports are clinical-anecdotal (Flapan, 1983; Horwitz, 1977, 1980; Tahacchetti, 1984; Slavinska-Holy, 1983; Macaskill, 1982; Ondaraza Linares, 1969; Di Minicis and Ranzato, 1969), with few empirical studies (Filippi, 1983; Ruger, 1982).

Reading these reports serves to emphasize the difficulty of working with borderline clients. Characteristics of these clients include pathological narcissism, an unstable self-image, defensiveness, rage, sexual deviance, splitting, weak egos, peculiar defense mechanisms, and a developmental history of narcissistic trauma (Kernberg, 1975; Flapan, 1983; Kolb, 1983; Ondaraza Linares, 1969; Shaskan, 1974). Rutan and Stone (1984, p. 181) summarize borderline characteristics in this way: "Their interpersonal relations may be characterized as unstable, intense, or withdrawn. They may have outbursts of anger directed at others or the self. Their mood is equally unstable, though a chronic depressive element is fre-

145

quently present. They have neither a consistent and clearly
formed identity nor an ability to develop long-range goals or
plans. . . . They are particularly frightened by intimacy, closeness, and feelings of contamination or annihilation by
others. . . . Early in their group membership they often take
on the familiar roles of monopolizer or help-rejecting
complainer."

This is an impressive list of interpersonal and intrapsychic problems. Most of the theoretical literature on the borderline syndrome uses a psychoanalytic or ego psychology
frame of reference to understand the relationship between
these behaviors and the underlying disturbance (for example,
Kernberg, 1975; Kohut, 1971, 1977; Rinsley, 1977). Wolf and
Kutash (1985) differentiate between a disorder they call di-
egophrenic schizophrenia and borderline syndrome. They suggest that borderline clients have a split ego while the di-egoph-
renic schizophrenic clients have a submerged ego and an
introjected parental pseudo-ego. While such distinctions
appear to be important to theorists, their implications for
group therapists remain unclear. Grinker (1977) offers what
he calls a phenomenological classification, while Wolberg
(1985) utilizes a variant of the old frustration-aggression
hypothesis (Dollard and others, 1939) and family dynamics
model to understand borderline clients.

To deal with these characteristics, most authors recommend concurrent individual and group therapy (Horwitz,
1977, 1980; Flapan, 1983; Filippi, 1983; Slavinska-Holy, 1983).
At the 1988 meeting of the American Group Psychotherapy
Association, Pines, in a panel discussion on group therapy
with borderline clients, suggested that a group's meeting
twice weekly obviates the need for concurrent therapy. There
is general consensus, even among the psychoanalytic writers
who generally favor a passive therapist stance, that an active,
confrontive (but supportive) approach is best. Most reports
suggest or imply that at least modest improvement is possible
(Tuttman, 1984; Tahacchetti, 1984; Filippi, 1983; Glatzer,
1978; Rutan and Stone, 1984). However, these reports give the
impression that what is required of the therapist is a Hercu-

lean effort, the wisdom of Solomon, the patience of Job, and the compassion of central figures in the world's major religions. Other writers are less optimistic (Di Minicis and Ranzato, 1969).

One thing that makes borderline clients difficult to work with, and that gets therapists caught up in unhelpful interactions, is the clients' not appearing as sick, deviant, or impaired, as they really are. It is generally difficult to distinguish between the insane and the obnoxious, and this is particularly true with borderline clients, who are frequently exceedingly obnoxious indeed. Borderline clients cling to their maladaptive behaviors with such tenacity probably because they are unable to do otherwise.[1] We may expect them to relinquish their maladapative patterns, or to develop insights, or to become less unhappy far more rapidly than they actually do. Five or more years of combined individual and group therapy may be necessary for some perceptible and undeniable improvement to occur.

It may be helpful to regard what the borderline client does in group therapy in terms of *energy input* and *energy drain*. Underneath the verbal output and the emotional intensity, it is sometimes possible to ascertain the amount of energy the borderline client is really putting into the interaction, and into movement toward therapeutic change. Typically, in any given interaction, the actual amount of energy being expended by the client is far lower than would appear from the content alone.

The task of the therapist is twofold. The first part is to identify the client's energy level in terms of commitment to change or resolution. The second part of the task involves the therapist's matching the client's energy level in terms of that commitment, and not working harder than the client for change.

Typically, borderline clients seek an interpersonal atmosphere characterized by tension, hostility, and negative emotions. Having generated an emotionally intense interaction, these clients typically withdraw from the interaction either emotionally or physically, leaving the other person or the group, feeling angry, frustrated, and impotent. The magnitude of the borderline clients' emotional investments in interaction appears to be far less than the intensity of the emotions they engender. Thus, borderline clients make other group members or the therapists furious with them while appearing to remain emotionally uninvolved.

Whether these clients actually feel as uninvolved as they claim is a question that is important not to answer.[2] A borderline client may engage an individual or the entire group, provoking anger, and then profess indifference when the other group members begin to express that anger. Such a move usually serves to intensify the anger, and the borderline client's denials of feeling (or of involvement) may escalate as well. Trying to convince the client that he or she really does feel something—uncomfortable, for example—is most likely to lead to further denials.

The borderline client appears unable to foresee the reactions of others to his or her behavior (Di Minicis and Ranzato, 1969). Sometimes an apparently unconcerned borderline client, faced with the group anger he or she has engendered, will admit to surprise and bafflement at the intensity of the response. If this kind of interaction happens repeatedly, the group and the therapist may assume the surprise is merely another feigned manipulative maneuver. However, such surprise may be a manifestation of a real defect. Rutan and Stone (1984) suggest that the therapist should empathize with the client's apparent bafflement rather than interpret the interactions or seek the client's acknowledgment of involvement in and responsibility for the interaction.

Borderline clients frequently convey a sense of virtually intolerable suffering from which they seek immediate relief. Buda (1977) describes their efforts to attract solicitous concern as attempts to compensate for early childhood deficits. Such clients usually enlist and then dismiss the help of the group in solving their problems. These clients present problems in such a way as to make them appear unresolvable, and they are highly resistant to helpful efforts to arrive at solutions. Nevertheless, the therapist and, somewhat less often, the group frequently have the impression that resolution is nearly at hand. It seems that with just a little more effort and time, success will be achieved. Needless to say, the proximity of resolution usually proves illusory, and the most frequent outcome of the interactions is anger and frustration.

In general, people enter therapy because they have tried as hard as they can to resolve their difficulties, and increased effort has met with increased failure. Thus, by the time they enter therapy, trying harder does not work. This is especially true of borderline clients. These clients cling very tightly to failed solutions. At the same time, they may encourage you, and perhaps the group as well, to try harder to provide the help they are seeking.

It is possible, though, that a client's goal is not help, however that may be defined, but rather intense, negatively toned interactions. In this case, trying harder does not work to facilitate problem resolution or behavior change; but it may reinforce the client's tendency to seek emotionally intense negative interactions.

The quandary in which you find yourself as therapist, then, is that you have a clearly distressed client desperately seeking solutions, dismissing those solutions proffered, and implying that you should try harder—all the while maintaining that he or she is emotionally uninvolved. When you get to this point with a borderline client, it will seem that whatever you do, including choosing to do nothing, will be wrong.

If you take a borderline client into your group, you can expect to be challenged in three domains: the content of the group session, the structure of the group session, and the context in which the group session takes place. Occasionally a fourth domain becomes involved as well, consisting of client intrusion into your personal life, including the reasons for your vocational choice.

Content

Most borderline clients will occupy more of the group's time, energy, and attention than any other type of client. At the verbal level, they present intractable problems, attracting the solicitous concern of the other group members (Buda, 1977), and then dismissing the concern and rejecting proffered help. At the emotional level, there is considerable variability in behavior. Indeed, subclassifications within the borderline diagnosis have been proposed in order to differentiate among these clients. Grinker (1977) has proposed four subcategories, involving clients who are dealing primarily with primitive rage, and those who are withdrawn, disorganized, or impulsive. Roth (1982) proposes six subcategories. The specific emotions with which you as therapist will be dealing depend in part on which subcategory the client resembles most. However, patients in all of the subcategories take up a disproportionate amount of time—the group's, the therapist's, and the supervisor's.

There is little consensus in the group therapy literature on how to deal with the verbal and emotional content of group interactions with borderline clients. Some therapists recommend analytic group therapy (for example, Pines, 1984); others recommend against it (Persic-Brida, 1984). Most therapists caution against interpretation and favor confrontation (for example, Stone and Gustafson, 1982), though some (for example, Flapan, 1983; Slavinska-Holy, 1983) discuss transference and insight, which are interpretive and content oriented.

This lack of consensus in the literature probably stems from a number of factors. One is the variability found within the borderline diagnostic grouping, which is far from homogeneous even given the subcategories. A second factor is the proclivity of therapists to prescribe what they know how to do. In the case of borderline clients, much of the writing is by psychoanalytically oriented psychotherapists, and they naturally recommend psychoanalytic group therapy or some minor variant. (Goodpastor, 1983, has described group treatment based on social learning theory.) A third factor is the tendency of therapists to report what works for them, that is, individual preferences and experiences. Thus, the lack of consensus also is probably a result of the lack of good empirical studies of borderline clients in group therapy.

The recommendations presented here in this book are

based on clinical and supervisory experience rather than on empirical data. The position taken here is that it is absolutely disastrous to become engaged with borderline clients at the level of verbal content. Both the verbal content and the high level of emotional distress may be regarded, at least tentatively, as smoke screens. The real message, the real interaction, is usually something other than the manifest content. An exception to this general rule involves suicidal content. Suicidal threats or ideation should always be taken seriously.

The real message may be difficult or impossible to discern from the client's observable behavior. The message is likely to be fairly complex, consisting of both a genuine request for help or attention and a host of negative thoughts and feelings pertaining to help taking and help givers. These negative factors are usually too powerful to confront directly, for a variety of reasons. Even if you do discern, or become convinced of, what is really happening between you or the group and the borderline client, the client is likely to vehemently deny the accuracy of your perception or interpretation.

There are several ways to avoid being caught up in verbal content. One, following the suggestion by Rutan and Stone (1984) noted above, is to empathize with the client. Typically, borderline clients present problems or situations that are both intolerable and intractable, as in the following example:

> A client complained bitterly and tearfully that she did not have enough money to buy groceries for herself and her two small children. Initially, the group proffered a number of solutions, all of which she rejected. Finally, one of the therapists commented that it was a difficult situation to be in, and the other said that it must be awful to feel that you cannot provide enough food for your children. The client tearfully agreed, and the therapists moved on to another topic.[3]

Reflecting affect empathetically is a riskier approach. Even when the client is visibly angry and shouting epithets at the therapists or the group, a therapist comment like "you're really angry now" may be met with vehement denial and a claim that the client is not feeling anything. But sometimes it works. Indeed, a general principle when dealing with border-line clients in group is that nothing works consistently, but that a wide range of interventions may work on occasion.

Another way to avoid getting caught up in verbal content is simply not to respond to it at all. It might be prudent, and polite, to acknowledge that the client has spoken, so that he or she will not feel ignored and will know that he or she has spoken loudly enough for others to hear. A noncommittal "I hear you," or "Yes, thank you, now let's go on," or some similar comment, may suffice here.

Yet another way to avoid being caught up in verbal content is simply to agree with whatever position the client takes. People are impossible, life is not fair, the client is being unjustly treated, his or her rage is justified—the range of possibilities is infinite. Such agreement may be regarded as paradoxical, or it may be regarded as therapist passive-aggressive overcompliance, depending on your point of view more than on anything else.

As with any other diagnostic classification, there are some therapists who work well with borderline clients, and some who work particularly poorly with them. The therapists who work well with these clients are able to avoid the verbal tangles into which borderline clients lure people. When these successful therapists are asked how they do it, the most common answer, in my experience, is, "Oh, I just don't let that stuff get to me" or "That's just the way they are. You have to just ignore them and go on." Most therapists, however, do not work well or easily with these clients, and they find it difficult to avoid getting caught up in verbal content.

Structure

A second domain in which you can expect to be challenged involves the contractual arrangements therapists and clients agree upon about fees, absences, and group session starting time, which were discussed in Chapter Two, as well as scheduling issues and the physical setting of the group room.

Fees. Borderline clients sometimes place considerable emphasis on obtaining reduced fees for both individual and group therapy. In those settings where therapists are not involved in fee negotiations, the borderline clients may convince the business office that it is necessary for them to have a lower fee.

The client may then fail to pay the reduced fee. It is not unusual for a borderline client who has successfully negotiated a one dollar per session fee to fail to pay it for months or more, until the matter is called to his or her attention. Then the client often will plead that he or she can not possibly pay such a big bill all at once, and a payment schedule may be negotiated. The probability that agreements of this sort will continue to be violated is high. After some years of successful therapy, clients with this diagnosis may be less likely to need the specialness which such an arrangement connotes, and may agree both to higher fees and to timely payment.

As noted in Chapter Two, it is important to be as specific as possible during the screening interview about the handling of payment arrears. Unless there is an explicit understanding, prior to the client's attending his or her first group session, that fees will be discussed in the group, it is better to discuss them individually. This means, in effect, that one way the borderline client can get an individual interview with you is to avoid paying fees. Borderline clients have many ways of gaining individual interviews if that is what they want; so, in such circumstances, it is far easier and less damaging to the group to conduct privately the discussion of nonpayment.

In these interviews, borderline clients typically give reasons why they have not paid and cannot pay, then threaten to leave the group, and then accept therapist offers of extended payment arrangements. When such arrangements are accepted, these clients may continue not to pay, or, more typically, pay only intermittently. This issue of payment can rapidly become enshrouded in ambiguity.

Clarity is achieved by taking an unambiguous position with regard to fee payment and holding to it. The further you agree to deviate from clinic procedures and standards, the more ambiguity there will be and the greater will be the difficulty of resolving the issue. If your clinic denies services to clients for nonpayment of fees, you can draw a fairly firm line: either pay the agreed-upon fee or do not come to group therapy. Some clients, borderline and others, who have not been paying, may stop coming at that point. If your clinic does not deny services for fee nonpayment, it is a waste of time to make an issue of it in the first place. In my experience, the most common resolution of this particular challenge is to forgive arrears, if that is possible, and to call the client the very first time, after the conference, that payment is overdue. A major reason for forgiving arrears is that the amount owed, and previous clinic fee policy with regard to a particular borderline client, is likely to be indeterminate. Attempting to resolve such issues distracts from the possibility that the client will begin to pay his or her way with some regularity.

Absences. As noted in Chapter Two, problems relating to absences are likely to arise with borderline clients. In my experience, borderline clients, far more than others, miss sessions without notifying anyone. As with fees, the dilemma for the therapists is whether to confront the issue in group or in a private session. The reason for considering a private session is that dealing with absences in group is likely to take up a great deal of the group's time and energy, with not much benefit for the other group members. Handling the issue, whether privately or during the session, should be straightforward and unequivocal; the clinic policy, or the policy you and the borderline client agreed on during the screening interview, should be adhered to. The client may protest, vehemently, that prior notification was not possible and he or she may demand an exception to the policy. It is not usually prudent to yield on this point except for cases in which the client could not conceivably have had the slightest control. If the client chooses to leave group therapy rather than pay for missed sessions as agreed, his or her departure is probably a mixed blessing.

Group Session Starting Time. Borderline clients often seem to find themselves in situations where they cannot possibly get to the group session on time. They may come fifteen or twenty or thirty minutes late. Occasionally a borderline client will want to come in an hour late for a group that lasts ninety minutes. The reasons offered usually seem valid, having to do with bus or meeting schedules.

Whether to yield on this point, to permit late entry, depends on how readily you, your cotherapist, and the group tolerate such behavior. I suspect that therapists who work well with borderline clients are not bothered by tardiness. But if you adhere to a strict starting time, and insist on timely arrival, the borderline client may miss a session without prior notification, and then announce at the following session that he or she arrived late and therefore did not come into the group room. The client was following group policy about late arrival, and therefore may want the fee waived for the missed session.

As with so many other matters in dealing with borderline clients, the issue is whether to hold the line and risk losing the client or to bend. If you hold the line, you may be surprised to discover, after the storm subsides, that the client has unexpected resources and regularly arrives at group on time.

Scheduling Issues. A client may become unable to attend the group on the regular meeting day, and may ask that the group shift its meeting to another day. Or, he or she may ask that the group meet temporarily, or even just once, on a different day or at a different time in order to accommodate the client's special needs. While such a shift is sometimes possible, and may seem reasonable, it is seldom desirable.

Physical Setting of the Group Room. Borderline clients may find the group room unacceptable for a variety of reasons and may seek to have the group meeting elsewhere. While such requests are not usually honored, it is indeed tempting to hold the group outdoors on the first warm day in spring, or in the crisp cool air of autumn, especially when the air inside the clinic is likely to be too warm, a little stuffy, and suffused with just enough cigarette smoke to annoy the non-smokers. Whether to hold the group session outside is up to the therapists. If you can hear the clients, if people are not impossibly self-conscious about appearing together in public, if you can maintain a therapeutic stance, and if you want to, it may be worth trying. There are no data to suggest that moving the group session outdoors would impair the effectiveness of the therapy experience. Here, as in so many ways, it is necessary to rely on your own inner sense of what will work for you, based on your knowledge of theory and your supervised experience in therapy.

Context

The clinic and the larger unit in which the group therapy service is offered constitute the context of a client's group experience. In community mental health clinics, the context subject to challenge by borderline clients usually includes the adult outpatient service, the clinic itself, the clinic's governing board, and on up the hierarchy to the county commissioners. If the clinic is associated or affiliated with an inpatient facility, both the service directors and the administration of the hopsital may become involved as well. An additional component of the context is a third party that has responsibility for payment of most or all of the bills incurred by the client.

The relationship of the borderline client to these larger units is usually characterized by hostility, confusion, misunderstanding, and ambiguity. Frequently, there is considerable difficulty delivering mental health services to clients within the limitations, guidelines, and procedural rules governing the agency, and these difficulties further worsen relations with borderline clients. In any event, borderline clients usually have poor opinions of the medical directors of clinics, of the clinic administrators, and of the psychiatrists who may pre-

scribe their medications. The opinions are usually recipro-
cated.

Early in therapy—during the first few years—you can
expect the borderline client to appear at the clinic or hospital
emergency service, to frequent the clinic's walk-in facility,
and, on occasion, to complain to the unit's board of trustees
about you and about everyone above you in the clinic hierarchy. The main issues for group are the extent of group discussion of the client's behavior and the attempt to understand
and modify that behavior. With the help of skilled group
leaders, such discussions may be fruitful for other group
members, who usually have their own difficulties with what
used to be called *the establishment*. For the group therapist,
there are two points helpful to remember: (1) it is not likely
that the borderline client will leave the group expressing satisfaction with you, with the group experience, or with anything about the clinic, its context, or setting; (2) people in the
clinic, and in the community, are probably already familiar
with a particular client's tendency to complain about various
components of the mental health system's service delivery.
Regardless of how badly the client talks about you, most people will consider the credibility of a person who has reported
similar dissatisfaction with other therapists over the years.

Client Intrusion into Your Personal Life

Borderline clients thrive on therapist self-disclosure.
Indeed, they actively seek such self-disclosure from therapists
in both individual and group therapy. A common complaint
of these clients about former therapists is that the therapists
were unwilling to talk about themselves. During group sessions, when you are engaged in the exploration of the personal or family lives of other members, you can expect
borderline clients to ask you for a similar level of self-disclosure. Whether you should oblige depends on a number of
factors, primarily your theoretical approach and your personal comfort. The most commonly asked questions are fairly
innocuous: how old are you? are you married? do you have

children? how old are they? how long have you been living here? and the like.

If you do not answer questions like these, your refusal to answer might become a group issue, involving not only the borderline client but other group members as well. Sometimes a group will press the issue; usually, there will be some clients who defend your refusal to disclose such information on the grounds, appropriately enough, that it is not relevant to the purpose of the meeting. If you do answer such questions, the matter usually is dropped. I have seen many instances of therapist refusal to answer these questions that led to increases in hostility and distancing, decreases in group cohesiveness, and decreases in client self-disclosure. But I cannot recall, in a quarter of a century of group work, an instance of answering such questions that led to any kind of negative result or outcome. Although borderline clients seem to need this level of therapist self-disclosure, almost as a condition of staying in therapy, I cannot recall an instance of a borderline client using this kind of information to intrude on a therapist's personal life.

The intrusions come in other ways. Borderline clients seldom hesitate to call therapists at home, sometimes in the early hours of the morning. They also may contact the clinic's emergency service or they may appear at the hospital's emergency room, in which cases the on-call worker will contact you. If these clients are in concurrent individual and group therapy, usually only the individual therapist is involved; but sometimes, group therapists are included as well.

The question, then, is whether to discuss these extra-group contacts during group sessions. To make that decision, you have to start by asking yourself how angry you are about the intrusion. If you are angry, it is better to resolve the issue with the client privately rather than in the group. Therapist anger is generally destructive of group cohesiveness, and therapist anger with a client skilled at generating anger can quickly degenerate into a scapegoating interaction, with further damage to the desired atmosphere of warmth and supportiveness that you generally try to maintain.

If you are not angry about the intrusion, it may be possible to bring the issue to the next group session, and to discuss it in much the same way that any other client behavior might be discussed. Sometimes, what a borderline client is seeking, with the after-hours phone calls or the emergency room visits, is more interaction with another human being, and in these cases, the need often can be met by negotiating a schedule for after-hours calls. Giving the client permission to do what he or she is trying to do anyway, but putting some limits on it, may be one of the more consistently successful interventions you can make with borderline clients.

Thus, you might offer the client a time slot that is not too inconvenient for you, during which he or she will have guaranteed telephone access. It need not be evening time. One therapist who had been bombarded with after-hours calls from a borderline client offered to talk with her each day between noon and 12:10 P.M. He told her in a private interview that when she called at other times, he became too angry to be of help to her. She tried one more after-hours call after that. Within a month, the noontime calls had decreased in frequency as well, and within about six months such calls had ceased entirely.

Similar behavior is likely to occur if other group members make themselves available, either by phone or in person, for the borderline client during crises. The offers may be taken up once or, rarely, twice, but virtually never more than that.

A Final Note

This discussion of borderline clients in group therapy has been quite negative. You might wonder why such clients are referred to group in the first place, other than for negative reasons such as rejection by an individual therapist.

It is a grim picture. These clients are the most difficult and most unpleasant of all; indeed, the magnitude of such qualities helps make the diagnosis. There is a dearth of empirical research on the appropriateness or effectiveness of group therapy for clients manifesting this kind of disturbance. While the clinical literature is mixed, it does not, as a whole, indicate that borderline clients benefit significantly from group therapy. At the same time, the literature makes it clear that borderline clients are disruptive of group in various ways. On the basis of available empirical data and clinical reports, it is difficult to avoid the conclusion that referral for, and acceptance into, psychotherapy groups is inappropriate for clients with borderline personality disorders. It is also clear that such referrals and assignments will continue to be made in the absence of supporting data.

Usually the problem facing the group therapist is not whether to admit borderline clients to the group, but rather what to do once they are there. The most promising solutions proffered in the literature are either to limit the number of such clients to one or two per group or to form a group consisting solely of people with this diagnosis, led by cotherapists who either do not mind or who enjoy working with them. Unless you are one of these, it is probably best to deny admission of borderline clients into your group. Refusal to accept referral may be based on the absence of evidence that these clients benefit from group therapy. If you cannot refuse, there is a high probability that you, and your group, are in for a challenging time.

Notes

1. If you prefer a learning deficit rather than a disease model of mental illness, it might be said that clients with borderline syndrome have not learned healthier or less obnoxious alternative ways of behaving, and that they may have a learning disability that prevents them from learning such alternatives.

2. One characteristic of work with borderline clients is that you can easily become ensnared in attempting to resolve issues marginally relevant to your goals, while major issues are unattended. Whether borderline clients feel as uninvolved as they claim is such a diversion. Much time and energy can

be devoted to this question in clinical supervision and in the informal discussions therapists have about their clients. It is impossible to determine the veracity of the claim. Whether it is true or not makes no difference in terms of how the group therapist should handle the borderline client's claim of emotional uninvolvement. Thus, it is important not to attempt answering the question in order to maintain therapeutic focus on the interpersonal consequences of the client's behavior rather than on something that may or may not be going on in his or her head.

3. Such successes are more readily found in textbooks than in group therapy rooms. Less pleasant outcomes are equally plausible and more likely.

9

Special Issues
in Group Therapy

In this chapter we will deal with several special problems that arise with some regularity in therapy groups. These include cotherapist issues, involuntary therapy, sexual issues, therapist anger with clients, and problems with the clinic. These problems are usually more difficult to resolve than problems with clients (for example, monopolizers) or problems with groups (for example, silent groups). The greater difficulty may stem from the more directly personal involvement of the therapists in these special situations. Therapist competence and ego strength may be called into question when these special problems arise, and the resultant therapist defensiveness further contributes to the difficulty of their resolution. Nonetheless, if they do arise, these special problems must be confronted; the alternative is a group process that becomes thinner and more filled with silences until finally the group ceases to function.

Cotherapist Issues

Cotherapy relationships are characterized by the sharing of many hours of emotionally intense intellectual work in a setting characterized by the interplay of complex, ambiguous, interpersonal strategies. Disagreements between cotherapists are therefore likely to arise. The disagreements may pertain to the perception of events: what happened, what is happening, and what will happen next. They may involve interpretation: the meaning of events. Disagreements may involve, more or less subtly, leadership or power issues—simply, who is in charge. Given the potential intensity of the shared cotherapy experience, it is not surprising that disagreements often develop between two human beings whose reactions may differ under the same set of circumstances.

In a functional cotherapy relationship, disagreements are identified, discussed, and resolved with some degree of ease and rapidity. Anger tends to be transient. In a dysfunctional cotherapist relationship, disagreements may or may not be identified and acknowledged, but they are seldom discussed or resolved. However, not all disagreements require discussion or resolution; the importance of resolution depends on the magnitude of emotional energy bound up in the disagreement.

Group is not the place to attempt resolution of cotherapist disagreement; group members do not come to sessions to see cotherapists argue. In general, resolution of cotherapist differences should occur after the group meets. If competent supervision is available, major differences can be resolved with the assistance of a supervisor.

Some issues are not easily resolved. The most common of these difficult issues arise when cotherapists do not use the same theoretical framework and do not easily share or delegate power. This situation occurs most often when cotherapists are from different disciplines with different levels of experience, training, status, and power. In most mental health settings, there are formal differences in therapist status. Power (defined as the ability to influence the outcome of events) is a more complex issue in that actual power may differ from that described by the clinic's formal administrative structure. When cotherapists differ in power and in ways of conceptualizing group events, it is sometimes difficult even to find a common language or common base of understanding for discussion of differences.

The problem may be further compounded if both therapists use the same words to denote different concepts. The term *ego*, for example, is used in different ways by psychoanalytically trained therapists and by those with an Adlerian or Sullivanian orientation. When this kind of overlap occurs, people may think they are communicating and understanding each other quite well. However, at points where their respective theories lead to divergent interventions, cotherapists may experience surprise and a sense of betrayal as their partner leads the group off into a seemingly irrelevant discussion. The lack of a common conceptual base, compounded by these differences in use of technical terms, makes identification and resolution of the issue difficult.

Perhaps the most common difficult-to-resolve issues are those that stem from differing therapist temperaments. The differences may be expressed in a variety of ways: one therapist will be more impassive, the other more nurturing; what one will understand as an unacceptably high level of emotional intensity the other may see as desirable and cathartic; what one may see as calm and rational the other may see as cool, distant, and intellectualized; and so on. It is difficult to negotiate such differences in temperament.

All of these differences between cotherapists are usually associated with strong feelings of anger, disappointment, frustration, and distrust on the part of both therapists. Their relationship tends to take on the characteristics of a distressed marriage. Each partner attributes much power to the other and feels unable to influence him or her. Each rationalizes his or her conclusion that discussion and negotiation are futile and would lead to harmful confrontation. Consequently, the behavior that generated the anger in the first place continues, and the anger and disaffection with the relationship continue to grow. Verbal and behavioral interchanges become strained, ritualistic, and trivial. The facade of pleasant and respectful cooperation becomes more and more difficult to maintain, until there is an angry interchange or a sullen withdrawal or both. The problem becomes particularly acute if both clinicians believe that they can neither withdraw from the situation nor improve it.

There is no single solution to this problem. If it were easy for cotherapists in this situation to talk about their relationship, they probably already would have done so. If the supervisor is aware of the problem, he or she can urge the cotherapists to assess those factors that seem to indicate talking about the problem would make it worse, and then urge them to try to modify those factors. Or the cotherapists can talk with their friends or colleagues about the situation. Such discussions may help the cotherapists minimize or manage the real or imagined risks involved in discussing potentially painful issues with a valued colleague. The alternatives to discussion are an angry withdrawal from the group or a continuation of the status quo. Given the relationship between cotherapist agreement and client outcome reported by Kosch and Reiner (1984), the latter is not acceptable. I do not know of any empirical research on the relationship between therapists withdrawing from the group and client outcome. However, it is difficult to imagine that the probability of good outcome would be enhanced.

Reluctance or refusal to talk about a cotherapist problem is usually based on the belief that talking will make things worse.[1] This belief precludes successful resolution of the problem. If discussion of painful issues with a colleague is not likely to be fruitful, as is sometimes the case, there is always someone else with whom you can talk—ideally, but not always, your supervisor. Discussion can lead to conclusions and potential resolutions that you probably would not have thought of on your own. If you cannot talk with your cotherapist or your supervisor, then find someone you can talk with. Giving yourself permission to talk about the unspeakable is the first sure step toward resolution of an intolerable and ostensibly unresolvable problem.

Clinic administrators or medical directors occasionally insist that groups be led solo. Their concern is, usually, the conservation of scarce clinic resources such as therapist time. Although the literature on cotherapy is large, there are many clinical reports and, unfortunately, few empirical studies. I do not know of any convincing evidence that a cotherapy model is superior to that of an individually led therapy group in terms of outcome, that is, patient or client improvement. Consequently, the clinician, confronted by the administrator's request or demand for the solo therapy model, may be hard-pressed to present a convincing argument in favor of cother-apy. A clinical report by Russell and Russell (1980) succinctly lists the pros and cons of cotherapy. Other recent contributors include McMahon and Links (1984) and Bowers and Gauron (1981). But these are not reports of empirical research; and even if such could be found, they would not necessarily con-vince a skeptic of the inherent superiority of the cotherapy model. Indeed, in the absence of data, one may wonder why the cotherapy model persists and prevails.

One answer to that question may be that therapist need for the cotherapy model far outweighs whatever inefficiencies result from two therapists seeing the same group of clients at the same time. Interpersonal interaction in group therapy can be quite complex at times, and the burden of keeping track of all that happens is halved, at least, if there are two therapists. Other advantages include mutual support and the opportunity to work with a colleague conjointly. These are issues that have more to do with therapist morale than with the effectiveness of the cotherapy model in producing behav-ioral change in group members. Sometimes administrators are responsive to the notion that higher morale is associated with greater productivity, lower absenteeism, and lower staff turnover; sometimes not. If there is already conflict between clinic staff and administration over issues of productivity, the cotherapy model may be drawn in; it then becomes a special problem because of the lack of empirical support for that model.

Involuntary Therapy

Involuntary therapy is the name given to certain activi-ties involving the meeting of mental health professionals with individuals whose presence is required by others, usually the courts. The situation of involuntary therapy is probably most often encountered in various programs for individuals convicted, or threatened with conviction, of drunk driving. Involuntary therapy is also performed on people who are committed to inpatient units on which group attendance is required. Sex offenders, gamblers, thieves, and other miscreants may be offered psychotherapy in lieu of trial and conviction, or as a condition of parole in lieu of imprisonment. While therapy is thus in some sense a choice, in reality the alternative is so strongly negative that acceptance of this choice constitutes involuntary therapy.

The practice of requiring individuals to attend psychotherapy sessions raises professional and ethical issues for the mental health worker. For some, the practice raises civil rights and human rights issues as well. These issues, while cogent, are beyond the scope of the present discussion. Our concern here is necessarily limited to the problems presented to the mental health worker who must lead groups having involuntary members. The question of whether involuntary therapy ought to be done seldom arises in the clinic. It is done. Some mental health professionals like doing it; others do not, but feel compelled in order to keep their jobs. Most clinicians involved in this kind of situation do the best they can, whatever their personal reservations and ethical concerns might be.

In an earlier chapter, I suggested that the locus of the problem in dealing with difficult clients lies in the differing agendas that clients, therapists, and the mental health service delivery system bring to group therapy. Situations involving involuntary clients also present problems of differing agendas. The involuntary client's agenda, at least initially, is usually to comply with the court mandate but to resist efforts to get him or her to want to change in ways deemed desirable by others. If change in behavior is unavoidable, the client's agenda frequently includes a commitment to such change that is as minimal as possible, but not so minimal as to provoke sanctions for noncompliance.

The group leader's agenda usually also includes compliance with the court mandate, but, beyond that, there is little correspondence with the agenda of the involuntary client. Group leaders usually want to have a therapy group. Involuntary clients, virtually by definition, do not want therapy. Group leaders want clients to talk in group, to engage in self-disclosure, to orient toward change, to commit to change, to exhibit change, and to report the change to the group, preferably with gratitude. People whose involuntary participation in therapy is a result of drunk driving are not likely to be interested in any of those.

These opposing agendas can easily result in a kind of stalemate involving both therapists and involuntary clients going through a kind of charade that, to an outside observer (for example, a court), might resemble group therapy. Such a stalemate is likely to occur if group leaders use their training in therapy to lead a group of involuntary clients without recognizing and adjusting to the difficult realities of involuntary groups. For instance, in a therapy group, the leaders are usually careful to avoid any kind of administrative responsibility for group members. But when the therapy is involuntary, the leaders have considerable power over the group members. That power is delegated by the court for a purpose: to assist the therapist (functioning here as the agent of the court) to obtain compliance from the involuntary client and to ensure that such compliance will persist indefinitely. The power consists of the therapist's ability—duty, perhaps—to report to the court any noncompliance of the involuntary clients.

The group leader, then, has at his or her disposal a powerful tool that maximizes the probability of client compliance with the therapist's requests. "Talk or I will send you to jail" is indeed a powerful motivator likely to result in group discussion, whether it is an implicit or an explicit message. But because it is forced, such discussion lacks genuineness.

Therapists who lead involuntary groups are sometimes troubled by overt compliance and covert defiance, for they feel they cannot fault their involuntary clients who are exhibiting the requested behaviors. In a therapy group, this would indeed be a problem, but in an involuntary therapy group it is not. When you agree to lead an involuntary group (perhaps, when you accept a position at an alcoholic rehabilitation clinic that lives on court referrals), you agree to accept the power to force various types of compliance from your group members. You may pretend that you do not have that kind of power, and you may promise yourself and your group that you will never use it. Nevertheless, that power is there, and you exercise it every time you walk into a group room with involuntary clients.

So use it. You can command behavioral compliance, but not genuineness. But behavioral compliance is all you need. Attitude change is likely to follow; and behavioral change linked to attitude change has a higher probability of persisting. John Erlichman is reported to have observed, "when you have them by the balls, their hearts and minds will follow." Situations involving involuntary therapy tend to be considerably easier to understand and to deal with effectively when therapists stop pretending that they do not have these involuntary clients by the balls. At the very least, stopping the pretense may help therapists to treat clients in this situation with great gentleness;[2] at best, it may spur efforts to seek alternatives to involuntary therapy.

Sexual Issues

Sexual issues include erotic attraction between cotherapists, on the part of a therapist toward a group member, on the part of a group member toward one or both of the cotherapists, and between group members. The development of such feelings is not particularly surprising, but it is clear that acting on sexual feelings toward clients or patients is not appropriate or acceptable under any circumstances.

Between Cotherapists. The legal, ethical, and moral guidelines are less clear about acting on sexual feelings toward one's cotherapist, particularly if he or she is a peer. Professional guidelines remain clear: development of a sexual relationship with one's cotherapist is likely to impair the effectiveness of both therapists, impede group cohesiveness, and inhibit whatever group norms of self-disclosure have evolved. It should be noted that these guidelines are supported by clinical and theoretical papers (Bowers and Gauron, 1981; Yalom, 1985; Weiner, 1984; Rosenbaum, 1978, writing from a psychoanalytic perspective, cautions against selecting friends as cotherapists). But there is apparently no empirical research directly addressing the question. Nevertheless, two mental health workers who are having an affair probably should not lead groups together because of the likelihood that the ups and downs of their relationship will be played out in the group.

Whether or not married couples should colead groups, they do it. There are no empirical data addressing this point either. Low and Low (1975) describe their experience (and the effects on their marriage) of leading a couples' group. They report strains in the marital relationship that they attribute, at least in part, to their differing styles of group leadership. My own experience in supervising a married cotherapist pair is consistent with the Lows' report. Transient strains in the marital relationship seemed to be related to an increase in group tension and conflict, and at times the converse seemed to occur as well. The interaction of group and cotherapist conflict seemed more closely related to the intimacy and intensity of the relationship than to marital status; similar interactions may well have arisen if the couple were intimate but not married.

Prudence and common sense suggest that if sexual issues arise between you and your cotherapist, they should be discussed, but not acted on, because of the probability that sexual issues will influence the way you and your cotherapist relate in the group. However, you may find it difficult to initiate such a discussion. The place to start is to examine what makes it difficult to talk. At this point, talking with a close friend or trusted colleague may be helpful. Sexual attraction between peers, in this situation, is seldom unilateral, and you may find that your cotherapist has been, at the least, aware of the sexual tension between you.

Between Therapist and Client. In most group therapy

situations, your own subjective reaction to the group members is an important and reliable guide toward understanding what is happening in the interpersonal interchanges. If you feel angry toward a group member, that person is probably doing something in group to cause your anger. Normally, you would report on, rather than act on, that anger, as in "When you say that, I feel angry." That is not an angry interchange, but the report of a subjective state, in the context of interpersonal feedback; the therapeutic factor here is interpersonal learning. But when your own subjective reactions to a group member include sexual feelings, it may be difficult to sort out feelings generated by your own sexual needs—as a natural response to an attractive member of the opposite sex— from those that are primarily a situationally determined response to client seductiveness. If you are not sure of what is happening, talk to your cotherapist or supervisor or both.

One special problem arises when you do not acknowledge these feelings, either to others or to yourself—that is, when you do not give yourself permission to feel something that is natural to feel. Another special problem is whether to acknowledge these feelings to the client. "When you do this I feel angry" is very different from "When you do this I feel sexually attracted to you." When group leaders favor one member over the others, cohesiveness is impaired. The group members have equal access, in a sense, to your anger, and also to your approval. But they do not have equal access to the attention and favor associated with sexual interest, which is, by its nature, exclusive rather than inclusive. Acknowledging, in the group, sexual feelings toward a group member is therefore not recommended, in the same way and for the same reasons that any expression of special favoritism should be avoided.

Sexual feelings of clients toward group leaders can be understood in terms of transference. Therapists are presumably neutral figures who are imbued with various attributes, including sexual attractiveness, by group members. In most instances, sexual attraction on the part of clients is based on limited knowledge of the therapist, and client generalizations of how the therapist would act in other situations are based in part on that limited knowledge and in part on the client's own needs or fantasies.

These issues are perhaps more clearly seen and more easily explored in individual therapy. In group therapy, client sexual attraction toward therapists is most likely to be expressed in requests for individual meetings, attempts to gain or keep the therapist's attention, and sometimes in seductive behavior. A major advantage of cotherapy is that if you are the target of such behavior, your cotherapist can facilitate the necessary group work. This facilitation involves pointing out that the behavior is seductive (though not necessarily in those terms), facilitating the exploration of the client's feelings and your response to them, and perhaps working through some of the transference issues. If there is an underlying sexual tension in the group, as sometimes happens, this kind of interaction can be helpful to each person in understanding, accepting, and perhaps coming to terms with his or her own sexual issues—particularly the difference between sexual feelings, which are not under conscious control, and plans for sexual activities, which are.

Occasionally, therapists and clients come to like each other and to realize that they would be social friends if they had met somewhere other than the clinic. Sexual feelings may arise as part of that liking and that realization. However, approaching or responding to that client, even years after the conclusion of therapy, places you and your professional career at considerable risk. Many therapists do not believe that a genuine social relationship with a former client can ever develop; transference and countertransference issues will always distort it. If the possibility of such a relationship arises and tempts you, remember that (1) you are not alone, and (2) this is one of the times in your life when it is truly important to seek wise counsel.

Between Group Members. Sexual feelings between group members almost always arise in groups of late adolescents and young adults, for example, in college student mental health settings. Such feelings also occur in groups in which the average age is much higher. In most groups, it is possible to talk about these feelings in the same way that you would talk about any other feelings, usually with the clear understanding that talking about them is not a prelude to acting on them. Usually the discussion of sexual feelings is possible only when the atmosphere of warmth and supportiveness has developed, and group cohesiveness and trust are high.

A special problem arises when you have reason to believe, or when you know, that clients in your group have started a sexual relationship. Most group therapists frown on such relationships, and some prohibit them. The development of a sexual relationship, usually referred to as *sexual acting out* by those who disapprove of it, is regarded as damaging to group cohesiveness and as impairing the ability of the guilty couple to benefit from group therapy. While there are no empirical data on this issue, there is a considerable amount of clinical opinion.

Mullan and Rosenbaum (1978, p. 204) suggest that "sexual intercourse between two members of a group is an emergency." Rutan and Stone (1984, p. 146) refer to the "powerful feelings of envy, frustration, and distrust" that sexual relations evoke in other group members, and they suggest that one or both of the involved individuals might be asked to leave if they are "unable to discuss and explore their relationship openly in the group." Rutan and Stone do not mention, however, the intrusive and potentially punitive nature of their requirement for public (group) discussion. Flapan and Fenchel (1983) similarly require that extragroup contacts be reported, and express concern about sexual acting out. Weisselberger (1975) suggests that negative transference toward the therapist is an important element of sexual acting out, prescribes group involvement in exploring the dynamics underlying the sexual relationship, and discusses some countertransference feelings that may develop in the therapist when sexual acting out is occurring in the group. Rosenthal (1980) echoes Freud's ([1922] 1949) warning about the disintegrative effect of sexual activity between group members. Grotjahn (1983, p. 24) is apparently unconcerned about deleterious effects of sexual acting out in inpatient groups, but he seems to be referring to flirtatious or reductive behavior rather than sexual intercourse. Yalom (1985) mentions sexual acting out only in the context of a leaderless group session, commenting that therapist fears of sexual acting out in such a context are generally unfounded.

In determining how to handle the situation when you find that clients in your group have started a sexual relationship, the first step is to decide what, if anything, would be gained by disclosure, in group, of the relationship by one of the pair or with mutual consent. Take into account both the potential benefit for the couple, or for either of them, and for the group as a whole. In some situations, disclosure is likely to be highly beneficial to all concerned, but in some situations, it is not. Forced disclosure and the possibility of banishment from the group are not likely to be beneficial either to the couple or to group cohesiveness. The authors mentioned above who favor such a procedure in order to reduce acting out may never hear about sexual relationships that might develop after the first confession.

If disclosure is likely to be beneficial, your approach to encouraging that disclosure depends in part on how you know, or how well you know, what is going on. If one of the pair has made the disclosure to you in an individual session, you should take that opportunity to discuss with him or her the benefits and hazards of group disclosure. If you surmise, but are not sure, that a sexual relationship has developed, you may have to wait until an opportunity presents itself to encourage, more or less indirectly, greater openness with the group by one or both clients. Considerable care must be taken to avoid raising the issue as though it were an accusation. In some cases, the opportunity may never present itself, and, if the couple is reasonably discreet, the anticipated impairment of group cohesiveness may not materialize.

Occasionally you may find yourself in a situation involving one group member, almost always male, seducing other group members (almost always female) one by one. I have not encountered the situation outside of student mental health settings, though that may be fortuitous. This situation may be one for which disclosure in the group is not beneficial. Men who do this sort of thing—here I think the term *acting out* is justified—usually have a characterological disorder and are not likely to benefit from group therapy. If you are reasonably sure that this seductive behavior is going on and if you can confront the individual without violating someone's confidence, you should arrange an individual interview, do the necessary confronting, and refer the client to individual therapy. This kind of behavior is seldom encountered, but when it happens, it takes the group and the clients a long time to recover.

Therapist Anger with Clients

It is highly likely that at some point you will become angry with a group member. The level of anger I am referring to is well past the point where you can effectively say "When you do that, I feel angry" or some similar move reporting rather than acting on anger. The problem is handling that very high level of anger.

One possibility is to acknowledge it, to say to the client, "I'm really angry with you." Theories of therapy that favor openness and therapist disclosure might favor such an approach: be honest with the client and the group about what is going on and about your reactions. However, it is important to think through, very carefully, the possible consequences of such a statement directed at an individual who presumably came to the clinic, and to you, for help. I suppose there are situations in which such a therapist statement would be helpful to a client. In group therapy, however, telling a client you are angry with him or her will affect not only that person but also the group; the other members will feel vulnerable and fearful that your anger sometime may be directed at them. The result is likely to be an increase in relatively superficial discussions and a decrease in group cohesiveness.

On the other hand, denying that you are angry when you really are probably would have serious consequences for cohesiveness and trust. Such a denial is a lie—a reflection of personal dishonesty that impairs trust and faith in therapist competence. The special problem here is a double bind: it is not good technique to tell a group member you are angry and neither is it good technique to tell him or her that you are not.

The principle to follow here is *primum non nocere,* the Hippocratic injunction to "first, do no harm." In the group setting, you have to consider possible harm to the group as well as to the individual. One possibility is not to deal with the issue at all, not to volunteer that you are angry with a person, and to evade questions from the group about whether you are angry. This evasive position is most attractive to therapists who are not comfortable with personal self-disclosure, particularly about anger, or who are in settings where such self-disclosure is frowned upon by supervisors. If you are good at being noncommittal about your own feelings, an evasive stance may work for you. If you tend to be more of an open book, an evasive stance, at best, will have the same effect as denial—trust and cohesiveness will be impaired and your integrity may be reevaluated by the group members. Failure to acknowledge something that is known to be true may suggest to the group that you share rather than transcend their fear of reality. In group therapy, as in life, evasiveness does more harm than good.

Your therapeutic approach when you become angry with a group member depends on a number of factors including your own personal issues, your relationship to your cotherapist and to the group, group composition, and the group's stage of development. Personal issues include your willingness and resources to deal with what psychoanalytically oriented therapists call countertransference. Intense anger is intensely personal, and if you experience anger in a group situation, it is because you have taken personally something that a group member has said or done.

In the preceding discussion of sexual issues it was suggested that client attraction to therapists is based on a limited range of observed therapist behaviors, on interactions in a special situation (the therapy session), and on the client's own needs and fantasies. A similar situation obtains in the case of anger and anger-generating behaviors. There is likely to be, in fact, a largely impersonal element in client reactions to the therapist, such that the client's reaction to another therapist, or to virtually any therapist in the same situation, would be similar. These reactions may, in other words, be transference issues. Therefore, taking a client's actions or words so personally as to respond with intense anger may be a misreading of the situation (just as taking a client's professed sexual interest personally would be) or it may be the result of unresolved countertransference issues. Under these circumstances, and in the presence of intense therapist anger, disclosure to the client is unlikely to be therapeutic.

One of the best ways to deal with countertransference issues is to discuss them in supervision. To do so, you have to trust both your supervisor and your cotherapist. Unfortunately, in many clinics supervision of group therapy is either absent or poor, and cotherapy relationships are not always such that one is comfortable discussing personal issues pertaining to the group. Even when supervision is both available and good, clinicians do not always avail themselves of it, perhaps in part because of the pressures of time and the need to see as many clients as possible.

Another way of dealing with countertransference issues is to discuss them with your cotherapist. Many times a group member whom you dislike or who quickly angers you will not bother your cotherapist at all. Your discussion with your cotherapist need not include exploration of countertransference issues to be fruitful. But it is important that you both are able to accept, in a nonjudgmental way, each other's quirks as well as your individual likes and dislikes of group members—and your differential responses to them. In discussing your anger toward a group member, you do not have to go into specifics about your own background that may contribute to your reaction. But it is important to talk with your cotherapist about the group situation, and about what to do next. Talking out your anger may be as much help to you as your group members' talking is to them. One possible outcome of your talk may be some agreement with your cotherapist that he or she, instead of you, will engage or respond to the group member who angers you easily. This sharing of chores, in effect diluting the countertransference, is one of the most important advantages of the cotherapy model; it maximizes the potential for therapist effectiveness (since you each deal mostly with those group members with whom you work best) while minimizing the potential for damaging, angry interchanges between you and the group members.

If your relationship with your cotherapist is strained, it may be difficult to talk with him or her about your anger with group members. Indeed, the lack of support and help that a good cotherapy relationship can offer may increase your own strain and sense of burden while coleading the group. This increased stress, in turn, may reduce your own tolerance and patience and may make it more likely that you will respond angrily to group members. In such circumstances, it is usually difficult to discuss issues of anger and strain during supervision because of the presence of your cotherapist.

Confronting cotherapist issues is the most rapid and effective way of resolving those issues. You may feel that such confrontation is more likely to lead to a negative outcome than to a positive outcome. You may come to feel that you have nowhere to turn: not your cotherapist, not your supervisor, and not your professional colleagues and friends. Such a sense of hopelessness is invariably conveyed to the group, with a resulting general lack of progress. Under these circumstances it is easy for a downward spiral to begin. But the therapeutic factor of instillation of hope can be effective for therapists as well as for group members: there will always be someone in your environment, in your life, with whom you can talk about these issues. Who that person is may not be readily apparent; but even the most interpersonally isolated therapist lives in a social or professional network where an accepting and trustworthy ear is somewhere available.

In some groups, it is particularly important to acknowledge anger, whether minor irritation or towering rage. Many schizophrenic patients are particularly sensitive to the presence of therapist anger. Because of their sometimes tenuous hold on reality, and their usually low confidence in their own perceptions, it is especially important to validate these patients' awareness of your anger. When leading either inpatient or outpatient groups composed primarily of people diagnosed as schizophrenic, acknowledging anger takes precedence over other considerations, such as the damage that such an acknowledgment might do to the atmosphere of warmth and acceptance and to group cohesiveness. If you try to deny your anger, or even if you fail to comment on it, you are likely to see an increase in pathological behavior on the part of the schizophrenic patients in your group.

In early stages of group development, the group depends on the therapist to provide cues indicating how to act and what to expect. The group members also rely on the therapist to reduce situational anxiety about the group sessions. If the therapists do not deal with these issues, but wait for the group to do so, the result is likely to be silence. This opening silence is sometimes frustrating for the therapists, particularly if it continues for several sessions and group members start dropping out. It is possible for a therapist to become angry with a group early in its life because of its passivity and dependence. Such anger is virtually always a result of therapist countertransference; it is not unusual for therapists to fear and to feel threatened by dependency needs. If you find yourself angry with the group early in the group's life, the place to look is within yourself, and then perhaps at your relationship with the clinic and with your cotherapist.

In general, the longer a group has met, and the more cohesive it is, the less damage a therapist acknowledgment of intense anger will do. Indeed, late in the life of a group, when transference and power issues have largely been resolved, the group may be able to handle such therapist disclosures with relative equanimity, and to see that neither personalities nor relationships need be destroyed by the presence and appropriate handling of strong anger. However, in many community mental health clinics, it is difficult to resolve power issues within the group, in part because of social-class differences, education-level differences, and other differences between therapists and group members. In such circumstances, disclosure of therapist anger, even in a group that has been meeting for some years, may not be in the best interests of the group. When in doubt, be cautious: therapist caution is more closely related to successful outcome than is therapist risk taking (Berzins, Friedman, and Ross, 1972).

Problems with the Clinic

Think of the mental health care delivery system as a kind of pipeline through which clients or patients move. They enter the system by way of referral and intake; they move through the various therapeutic modalities, usually with referral at each point; and they exit when the last of the therapeutic modalities is terminated.

The group therapy program functions within that system. It requires therapists, a supervisor, a room, a time to meet, patients or clients, a referral and screening procedure, and documentation and fees. The clinic usually provides therapists and room and is usually supposed to provide a competent supervisor. Patients or clients are provided by a referral network of other clinic therapists or of therapists not on the clinic staff. The group therapists provide the screening and the necessary documentation, and deliver the service.

Problems can arise at any point in this process. Therapists may be so burdened with other clinic responsibilities that they do not feel they have time to run a group. In some clinics, group therapy as a treatment modality is not valued, or perhaps not understood, by administrators. They argue that a group session should count as one contact hour with clients, rather than six or eight, and they insist that the group therapist maintain a clinical load accordingly. Appointment secretaries, who are sometimes influenced by clinic directors, may then load the therapist's schedule with appointments that are difficult to reschedule or cancel, such as meetings with families, committees, or members of outside agencies.

The potential for conflict is especially great on inpatient units. When group therapy is not highly valued, group leaders will find themselves scheduled for important meetings that conflict with group time; patients may be in occupational therapy or in recreational therapy or may have been taken out for a walk by another staff member; physicians may decide that the group hour is the only time they can possibly see their patients, and they may walk into the group room (or send a staff person) to get them; psychologists may insist that the hour the group meets is the only possible time to do testing; and on occasion the only room really suitable for group may be occupied by other members of the hospital staff who are not involved in direct patient care.

Usually, when some of the above problems are present, supervision is also problematical. It may be available only from an individual who has administrative responsibility for the group therapists, in which case clinical supervision inevitably has an evaluative component. It is difficult, and perhaps imprudent, to discuss mundane clinical problems with the person who decides whether you continue to work at that clinic.

The competence of supervisors varies almost as much as the competence of therapists. Competent supervision may not be available, or available only infrequently, or it may be available only grudgingly from a clinician who has group supervisory skills but is subject to the same performance pressures that the group therapists are. The availability of supervision is especially difficult in some settings, where both clinicians and supervisors are penalized for supervisory meetings unless they are held at mealtimes or after hours.

All of these are symptoms indicating the group program is not highly valued in the setting where they are in evidence. The therapist staff may not place high value on the program as a result of personal bias against group therapy (or, simply, in favor of individual therapy, chemotherapy, or some other therapeutic modality) or because of a lack of familiarity with group or a lack of training in group therapy. The professional staff, which does not always value therapeutic services delivered by ancillary health care professionals, may also place a low value on the group approach. In the clinic support staff, antigroup bias is usually attributable to lack of appreciation for the potential benefits of group therapy, and to their awareness of the demands of a group program (for time, space, appointment arrangements, the pulling of multiple charts, generation of multiple progress notes, and the like). And, perhaps most important, the low value placed on the group program may stem from an administrator's bias, which then pervades the whole system.

The people most affected by the clinic's low valuation of group therapy are the patients or clients who are deprived of the benefits of this therapeutic modality, the therapists with group skills and enthusiasm, and therapists whose job descriptions require them to do groups in a clinical setting that makes it difficult and then ignores or denigrates their successes. The problem is compounded by the infrequency with which potential clients come to the clinic requesting group therapy. More often, a certain amount of persuasion is necessary to get them to accept referral. Thus, group therapy has little or no constituency among the people it benefits most.

If your job description requires you to do groups in a clinical setting where group therapy is not valued, your biggest long-term obstacle to delivering an effective service is likely to be apathy. Clinics which insist on the appearance, but fail to support the substance, of service delivery usually have other problems as well, staff morale being chief among them.

Many, but not all, of these clinic problems can be influenced by a therapist who has group skills, enthusiasm for group, a sufficiently high energy level, and persistence. But no matter how much skill, enthusiasm, energy, and persistence are invested in the group program, some staff therapists will remain unalterably biased against groups, and will not refer their clients under any circumstances. Other staff therapists may change their minds about group therapy if they can see its benefits for their clients. Usually the issue is one of intrapsychic versus interpersonal therapeutic modalities; as therapists begin to see the interpersonal components of their clients' problems, these therapists are likely to be more willing to refer and more supportive of the group program in general. It takes time, enthusiasm, and persistence to make a skeptical therapist staff aware of the benefits of group therapy, but the rewards are usually well worth the effort.

Turf issues frequently underlie the antagonism of ancillary staff toward the group therapy program. In inpatient and day hospital settings, occupational and recreational therapy frequently compete with group therapy for patient time and, occasionally, for physical space. These professionals have their own needs for recognition and status and may be especially sensitive to issues of professionalism. The relationship of the group therapy program to these programs, and of the group therapists to these therapists, can be collaborative rather than competitive; but usually it will be up to the group therapists to make the collaborative moves. Sometimes occupational and recreational therapists have group skills, or sufficient educational background to develop them in a cotherapy model. If the clinic's quality control criteria can be met, inviting these people (after suitable training and with appropriate supervision) onto the cotherapist staff can solve many issues of turf and scheduling.

The attitude of the clinic administrator toward the group program is especially important since his or her attitude is likely to be pervasive throughout the mental health care delivery system. Sometimes administrators, like therapists, are biased against group therapy, and for similar reasons. However, their opposition to group may decrease if they can be shown that group therapy is an efficient use of clinic resources and, in settings where third party payments are important, potentially lucrative as well. In inpatient facilities, group therapy services are sometimes included in the room charge. This is true even in some proprietary hospitals operated for profit by health care corporations. Where there is no separate line item for group therapy income, it is more difficult to enlist administration support for a group therapy program. However, it is a rare administrator who will fail to respond to the persistent enthusiasm of a staff member seeking to improve service delivery and patient satisfaction with the clinic or hospital.

Concluding Comment

Special problems are those that seem both unavoidable and unresolvable. In this chapter we have reviewed some of the more common ones. Every clinical setting is likely to have its own set of special problems. While such problems may in fact be unavoidable, they are seldom truly unresolvable. There is always someone with whom you can talk about an unspeakable situation or unspeakable feelings, even if that person turns out to be your own personal therapist. It is highly likely that there is someone on the clinic staff who feels the same way you do, or who has had similar experiences and can understand and genuinely empathize with your situation. You can sometimes resolve difficult or intractable problems by redefining them in such a way as to minimize their negative effects while bringing your personal resources to bear optimally on the situation. Talking helps you to perceive workable alternatives.

Notes

1. It is ironic that such a fear is found so frequently and so strongly in people whose professional lives are predicated upon the assumption that talking helps. We are apparently not immune to the misconceptions that bring so much misery to the lives of our clients and patients.
2. When the power differential between two people is great, it is easy for the more powerful person, if he or she is unaware of the discrepancy, to inadvertently hurt the less powerful one. Most people who are powerful take care to avoid inflicting this kind of pain. If therapists realize—in some cases, admit to themselves—the enormous power differential between them and their involuntary clients, they are less likely to inadvertently hurt those clients.

10

Achieving
Successful Termination

It is difficult to know when a client is finished with group—
when it is really time to terminate. There are few firm guidelines, so unless the clinic imposes some upper limit on the
number of group visits, factors influencing termination decisions are usually subjective. Yalom (1985) suggests that group
members are ready for termination when the group becomes
less important to them than it was initially and when their
behavior in leaderless sessions is similar to their behavior
when the therapist is present. Rutan and Stone (1984) link
termination criteria to clients' presenting problems but they
also note the subjectivity involved in termination decisions,
as do Mullan and Rosenbaum (1978) and Yalom.

Let us consider why clients terminate from group. The
best reason is marked improvement in or resolution of the
problems that brought them into group in the first place.
Other reasons include changes in clients' life situations: new
job, moving, getting married or pregnant, and the like. (These
changes in situation sometimes cause premature termination.)
And sometimes clients terminate because they are dissatisfied.

Other reasons for termination have more to do with
the clinic than with the client. The referral flow may be insufficient, so the group slowly dwindles in size to an unworkably
small number. One cotherapist may have to leave, so both

185

therapists decide to terminate the entire group rather than to bring in a new therapist. If both cotherapists are trainees (psychiatric residents), they may both have to leave without finding suitable replacements. The clinic administration may decide it can no longer offer group therapy under the conditions in which groups have been meeting. An example of this would be a decision that the group room has to be used for something else, or that it is not possible to continue to keep the building open after a certain hour. And, finally, sometimes the therapists just get tired of doing group, either in general or with this particular bunch of clients, and so they grind to a stop.

Clients or therapists or clinics may terminate therapy groups for a variety of other reasons, but these are the ones I have encountered most frequently over the years. Of course, in short-term, time-limited groups, these issues do not arise; but for long-term groups, the reasons I have mentioned above warrant further discussion.

Improvement in Resolution of Initial Problem

How you define client problems in the first place depends largely on the theory of psychopathology you use. The theory I have been following in this book is based on the assumption that people come for therapy because they are experiencing subjective distress, primarily in interpersonal relationships. Under this theory, termination should occur when there is an improvement in interpersonal relationships and a corresponding reduction in subjective distress. Ideally, in this model, termination occurs when three conditions are met: (1) the client reports low subjective distress; (2) the client describes satisfactory interpersonal relationships outside the group; and (3) the client's ways of relating within the group are consistent with his or her claim of improvement in relationships and in subjective distress.

The same phenomena can be described in other terms, depending on the theory; but the essential question always is how to decide whether the client has improved sufficiently to warrant termination. It is not a simple determination.

Frequently, clients complete the work that was agreed on in the screening interview and then want to go on to other things. If you are behaviorally oriented, along the cognitive-behavioral rather than the dynamic-insight dimension, it will be easier for you and the client to determine when goals have been reached because cognitive-behavioral people negotiate for specifiable goals. But more often, you have to deal with a vague initial definition of the problems that brought the client to group therapy, and therefore it is difficult to ascertain whether, or to what extent, the problems have been alleviated.

It is not unusual for the client to have a goal involving symptom reduction while the therapist's goals for the client are to deal with the underlying behavioral or personality patterns that give rise to specific maladaptive behaviors. That is, the therapist may feel it is not enough to simply fix the problem; it is also necessary to fix the cause of the problem. So, you are confronted with two different agendas related to two different goals. The client, and perhaps the group, may be more concerned with symptom relief while the therapists are more concerned with the modification of underlying maladaptive patterns. When that is the case, the client may be ready to terminate long before the therapist is. (This is true in individual as well as group therapy.) If the therapist is insistent, the client may terminate unilaterally. In these instances, as we might expect, the client's own ratings of improvement, at termination, are likely to be higher than the therapist's.

To a large extent, the secret of successful termination (when you, the client, and the group agree the client's goals for therapy have been met) lies in the negotiation of clear contracts between client and therapists. These contracts specify the goals of group treatment, how those goals are to be reached, and how the assessment will be made of the extent to which the goals have actually been attained. The first of these contracts is typically negotiated during the screening interview, and it is amended, or new contracts are negotiated, as treatment progresses and as underlying or longer-term problems become more apparent. It is easy to note, in writing, the treatment contract negotiated during the screening interview. (Yalom, 1985, sometimes tapes these interviews and replays the tape when the client is ready to terminate.) It is more difficult to keep records of treatment contracts negotiated during group sessions, when your attention is divided among the group members. Nonetheless, the more specific, in behavioral terms, you and the client can be about treatment goals, the easier it will be to determine the time to terminate and the easier the termination process will be.

A surprising theme in the literature on client improvement is that the client, having had many years of individual therapy or group therapy or both, is not competent to evaluate his or her own progress. In many studies, improvement is evaluated solely by the therapists while in others the ideal evaluation is said to include the client's significant others— spouse, boss, relatives, and so on. Yet, for many clients, it was subjective distress that brought them into therapy, and it is that same subjective self-evaluation that may lead them to conclude that they have improved and that it is time to stop.

The consumer of services is the best person to evaluate the effectiveness of those services. Some clients will come to the clinic for crisis after crisis and will terminate as soon as the crisis is resolved. For them, this is apparently a viable pattern. Others may realize, perhaps with a little help from their friends and others, that crises will continue to recur until the underlying issues are dealt with. When they come in for the n*th* time and say they are finally ready to deal with the underlying issues, the contract with the therapist will be different, and there will also be a difference in the therapy.

When clients tell you they are ready to terminate before you think they are, you might try a time or two to dissuade them and the group might try as well. But if clients are determined to terminate, then terminate they will, with or without your or the group's blessing. If you see that a client is set on terminating at a time you regard as premature, your strategy should shift from trying to persuade him or her to remain in the group to a strategy designed to facilitate reentry if and when the need arises. Beyond a certain point, more strenuous therapist efforts to retain a client in group may make it less likely that he or she will return to therapy (at least in your clinic) when it becomes necessary in the future.

A different problem is the group therapy client who reports or describes improvement in problems and improvement in relationships but does not take the step of suggesting termination. Similarly, some clients in individual therapy have to be nudged from the nest, as it were. In more extreme cases, clients carefully keep their improvement a secret from the therapists because they are convinced that improvement will lead to ejection from the group, an event for which they are not ready. Again, as in individual therapy, sometimes the therapist is the last to know that the clients are improving.

In a good termination resulting from client improvement, there is consensus in the group and between client and therapists that improvement has occurred and that the client is ready to leave the group. If you are good, lucky, and willing to have at least a little trust in the client's own judgment, this kind of termination will occur about half the time.

Changes in Life Situations

There are many reasons for change in a client's life situation—new job, new spouse, pregnancy, and so on. Sometimes, the changes themselves are indications that progress sufficient to warrant termination has been made. Sometimes, the changes are evidence of a client's resistance to continuing therapy and his or her reluctance to confront that issue more directly. But frequently it is difficult to determine exactly what the changes indicate.

Some theories of psychotherapy, especially those of the psychoanalytic schools, are highly deterministic. These theories tell you to assume anything that impairs the client's ability to continue with group treatment is nothing more than resistance. Sometimes that is true. But sometimes it is the case that bosses decide, for reasons of their own, that they cannot continue to let a particular employee (your group member) take off from work a half hour early every Wednesday, and sometimes spouses are transferred to other locales. It is unrealistic to hold clients responsible for these changes. Given a choice between group therapy and job, the client will usually choose to remain employed, and that is a healthy choice. Similarly, clients are more likely to move when spouses do rather than split for the sake of being able to remain in the group.

If there is clear agreement between therapists and client that termination because of changes in life situation is premature, your goal in the termination process is to make a successful referral for further therapy. A successful referral is one that the client acts on by accepting transfer into a group that meets at a time the client can go to the clinic, for instance, or by seeking therapy in the new locale.

Some people who come to community and other mental health clinics are not experiencing subjective distress; they might have been referred by courts, or by physicians who will not prescribe medication unless the clients are in psychotherapy, or by spouses who threaten to leave, and so on. Some of these coerced people eventually see that psychotherapy has something to offer them, and they stay on of their own volition. The vast majority of these coerced people, however, leave as soon as the coercion stops. For such people, termination is simply an issue of meeting some external requirement, and when that is met, they stop coming. The change in life situation is simply the ending of the coercive threat that kept them in therapy.

Client Dissatisfaction

A client's exit from group because of dissatisfaction is a special kind of termination. Clients may leave because they are dissatisfied with their progress in group therapy, with their relationships with other members of the group, with one or both therapists, or with both group members and therapists. Because of the multiplicity of relationships, the issues are different from and far more complex than they are in individual therapy.

This kind of termination usually occurs in one of three ways: clients simply stop coming to group sessions; they tell the therapists, outside of the group, that they are not coming back; or they tell the group (usually, just as the session is ending) that they will not be back.

Clients Withdraw from Group Without Notification. When clients simply stop coming to group sessions, the question is how much energy to put into contacting them for follow-up, for closure, or possibly for return. Terminations because of dissatisfaction seldom come as surprises. Indeed, both the therapists and the group may experience some relief, and concomitant guilt, when a dissatisfied client stops showing up. Generally, the cotherapist who is least angry with the client should try to contact him or her. Although you might be tempted to ask the clinic secretary to make the call, it is a task that you cannot properly delegate. The purpose of the call is to ascertain whether the client has indeed terminated unilaterally and whether he or she has no intention of returning to the group. You should invite the client back, either to the group for one final time or to your offices, perhaps to vent anger or to come to closure, and you should ensure that the client understands he or she will, or will not, be allowed to return to this particular group. (Mullan and Rosenbaum, 1978, insist that a group member's decision to leave should be regarded as irrevocable.) Inviting the client back for one last group session is preferable unless he or she has generated so much anger that the other group members will be likely take the opportunity to launch vicious personal attacks. There is no point in subjecting anyone to that. In any event, the ethical thing to do is try to contact the client by telephone. And you should persist despite the difficulties associated with the task.

The other unpleasant task you have in this situation is that of notifying the referring therapist of the client's unilateral termination. This is usually the right thing to do even if the client has terminated individual therapy as well. Notification is both a courtesy and a service to the referring therapist since there is some probability the client will contact him or her, and it will be helpful to that therapist to know what has happened.

Some of the same factors that make calling the client difficult also make it difficult to talk with the referring therapist. In the first place, there is a certain element of failure when a client withdraws from the group, and it is seldom pleasant to face one's colleagues with that news. The referring therapist expected the client to get some help from you in the group, or he or she would not have made the referral. So there is an element of having to say, in effect, "I know you were counting on me to be of help to this client, but I wasn't, for whatever reason." Despite the reluctance that such feelings can generate, it is important that you contact the referring therapist—regardless of difficulties with telephone availability.

It is as important to let referring therapists know about unsuccessful outcomes as it is to keep them informed of your success stories. Not only will the referring therapist be better prepared to handle the disgruntled group member who returns for individual therapy, but the therapist will then have a better idea of how to refer clients to your group. After all, the failure of a referral is a two-way street: the referring therapist may feel that the client's failure to benefit from group therapy is in part a reflection of his or her own poor judgment in making the referral in the first place. Information about clients who fared poorly in group is at least as valuable as information about those who fared well. Both kinds of information help therapists learn how to make appropriate referrals to your group. Thus, informing the referring therapist that a particular referral client terminated unilaterally will not necessarily reduce the referral flow from that source, and might even increase and improve it.

Clients Inform Therapists of Withdrawal. When clients tell you, outside of the group, that they will not return, it is usually possible to invite them for individual interviews (which both cotherapists should attend) or to invite them to return one more time to the group. Usually, getting the clients to return to group is preferable. When clients drop out without closure and without farewells, it is likely that at least some of the group members will feel they drove the dropouts away. The result is that group members may become reluctant to engage in confrontations that would be both appropriate and therapeutic, for fear of driving others away; and there will be a residue of guilt. The situation is reminiscent of a divorce that causes the children to assume for years that they were responsible for their parents' separating.

If the client agrees to return for a final group session, you must deal explicitly with these issues of responsibility and guilt. Like the children of divorce, group members seldom voice their fears that they have driven someone away, and they seldom talk about the guilt they feel. So, it is up to you to introduce the topic and to help people talk about it.

Dissatisfied clients who are willing to come back for a final session are unlikely to get into fault-finding confrontations with the other group members. Even when there have been angry confrontations between group members in the past, it is far more likely that those involved will, perhaps surprisingly, make conciliatory rather than angry moves.

People who inform you outside the group that they are quitting usually already have made their decisions, and most are not likely to be willing to come back just to have more angry interchanges with another group member. But if it appears that confrontation is on the agenda of a client who has agreed to attend group one last time, you should reconsider the invitation.

Conciliatory concluding moves provide the group with at least some information about the client's termination and make it less likely that group members will fantasize about their responsibility for the client's leaving, or about the client's being in terrible shape. (People who are really in terrible shape usually do not return for a final session.) It is important for the group members to see that there is life after group, and for the withdrawing client to hear from the therapists about alternative therapeutic opportunities—other groups, return to individual therapy, and the like. In addition, the withdrawing client may discover considerably more positive feeling in the group toward him or her than had been evident up to that point.

If the terminating client refuses to come back for even one final group session, you should offer an individual meeting. Both cotherapists should be present at this meeting. Its purposes are the following:

1. To ascertain the reasons, both overt and covert, for the client's withdrawal. While these may be obvious, it is frequently helpful and instructive to discuss and confirm them directly with the client in a relatively formal meeting—and not in the hallway just outside the group room.
2. To give the client an opportunity to express any thoughts or feelings that he or she was unable to express in the group. These may be hostile feelings about other group members, the therapists, or both. On rare occasion, the feelings may be positive rather than negative; if the client is fleeing from positive rather than negative feelings, it may be more difficult, and more important, to persuade him or her to voice them.
3. To get the client's permission to discuss with the group at least the ostensible reasons for withdrawal. This permission will enable you to deal with the underlying group feelings of responsibility and guilt about the client's withdrawal.
4. To make an effective referral for further therapy, unless doing so would be grossly inappropriate. It may also be a good idea to get the client's explicit permission for you to discuss the matter with his or her individual therapist—though there is always the risk that the client will refuse, in which case you would be in a quandary with regard to how to provide the individual therapist with feedback.

Note that the primary purposes of the exit interview do not include making a last-ditch effort to get the client to change his or her mind about withdrawing. It would not be fair to do that, unless, at the time you made the appointment for the interview, you and the client agreed explicitly that you would use the time for that purpose. It is legitimate to discuss the possibility of a change of mind, but you should not push it. Sometimes when clients look at the real reasons for withdrawing, they will choose to remain.

Since the exit interview is, to a large extent, for your benefit and for the benefit of the group, it may be appropriate to waive the usual clinic fee for individual interviews. Such a waiver might also increase the possibility that the client will show up.

The client may, of course, refuse either an additional group session or an exit interview, and go storming off into the void. But clients will usually agree at least to an individual interview unless they are very angry or very frightened.

Clients Inform Group of Withdrawal. When a client tells the group that he or she will not be back, how you handle the announcement depends on the amount of time remaining in the group session and on the interpersonal context of the group at that point. It is reasonable, and perhaps necessary, to assume that the client wants the issue to be discussed, or he or she would not have made the announcement. Under these circumstances, the announcement may be treated as would any other opening move—in terms of the interpersonal effects the client is trying to achieve.

Termination announcements made just as a group session is ending are difficult to deal with and are probably very carefully timed. The client may want, on one hand, to create a stir or, on the other hand, not to deal with the issue at all. Generally, you should not extend the session time in order to respond to the announcement; it is important to end the session on time. However, you might have a brief discussion with the withdrawing group member after the other clients have left. The goals of this discussion should be first, to get the client to return one more time; second, to have an exit interview; and third, to obtain permission to discuss termination issues with the group.

Occasionally, you get none of the above. In those cases, you should open the subsequent group session with an announcement that the withdrawing client has indeed left, and you should help the group members verbalize their feelings about the withdrawal. Above all, keep the discussion focused on the feelings of the group members still present, without violating the withdrawing client's confidentiality.

Occasionally, group members and some therapists will say they should not talk about the withdrawn client because that person is not present. This notion apparently stems from the idea that discussing one's feelings about another person is the same as talking behind his or her back. However, in this case, the group is not talking about that person, but rather about their feelings toward him or her. So, the focus of the discussion is on here-and-now feelings—a focus which is permissible and probably necessary.

There is no particular reason to squelch group discussion about a client just because the person is not present. If this kind of issue arises during a regular member's absence from a single group session, you might encourage people to postpone discussion until he or she returns. Allowing the members to talk about their feelings about absent members in group may give you the opportunity to direct and modify the discussion so that such gossip—if it is that—is less noxious. Talking permits exploration of the feelings that generate the discussion by focusing on the here-and-now issues.

Some therapists ask, during the screening interview, that the client agree to give notice of termination two or more sessions in advance. But the usefulness of this type of agreement is questionable. When there is consensus that termination is approaching and appropriate, such a contract is not necessary because the client will initiate discussion of termination well in advance. And if the client is leaving because of dissatisfaction or because of unexpected changes in life circumstances, fulfilling the advance notice requirement may create further stress and dissatisfaction. If you cannot persuade the client to return for a time or two, trying to obligate him or her to do so is unlikely to fill any therapeutic purpose.

Insufficient Referral Flow

If client referrals are too infrequent, the group may slowly dwindle in size to an unworkably small number. The acceptable minimum number of clients for a group depends on your personal preferences, on the composition of the group, and on the availability of two therapists to meet for an hour and a half with only one to five group members. If the minimum number of clients is not being maintained, you should attempt to determine why the referral flow is too small. The rate of new client intakes might be low, or the clinic might be overstaffed with therapists needing individual clients, but both of these situations are rare. Probably the most common reason for an insufficient referral flow is inadequate marketing of the group program to referring therapists.

At some point, if the group dwindles down to four clients, with some intermittent attenders, you may find yourself meeting with only two or three group members. Nevertheless, it is important to go ahead and meet. These people have taken the time and effort to get to the clinic, and you have agreed to provide them with a group experience; so you have an obligation to come as close to that as you can under the circumstances. If just one client shows up, have an individual interview, and if there are differential fees for individual and group sessions, you should ensure that the client is charged only the group fee.

If you lose hope that the referral flow will pick up, you should introduce the idea of group termination. The task is a straightforward one. It involves arranging for other therapy opportunities for the group members. For example, if you have other groups, talk with your clients about their merging. If other groups are meeting in the clinic, talk with their group leaders about referring your clients to them. And talk with individual therapists who have been your referral sources. Your task is to pave the way for clients to obtain these other therapy services. It is appropriate to do far more than you would under other circumstances in order to compensate for a failure of the system to deliver services to people in need. The obligation to seek alternatives is yours rather than the client's, which is the usual case. In some settings, it will be necessary to obtain the clients' permission to discuss their cases with other therapists or clinics before starting to make the referral arrangements.

Therapist Exit or Administrative Termination

The same principles apply in other instances of therapist or clinic decisions to discontinue the group, such as the decision to terminate because one or both cotherapists have to leave or the clinic administrator's decision that group has to stop. In these cases, too, clients want a service that you and the clinic have agreed to provide; so it is up to you to find attractive alternatives.

On rare occasions, the group may decide it wants to keep on meeting without you or outside of the clinic. Such moves cannot be prevented, but they should be discouraged. You do perform some unique functions as group leader, after all. If the group decides to meet anyway, you cannot stop them, but almost always, these sessions will rapidly peter out.

Therapist Burnout

The circumstances under which therapists just get tired of doing group therapy, or get tired of a particular group, have to be handled with considerable care in order to minimize the clients' feelings of rejection by people they have counted on to be helpers. Hence, it is important that you be aware of the reasons you are getting tired enough of doing group to want seriously to consider terminating a going enterprise. Common reasons for wanting to terminate may involve clinic factors, cotherapist and supervision issues, or outside pressures such as family or personal relationships. I will refer to this getting tired of doing group therapy as *burnout* in the following discussion.

Clinic factors contributing to burnout include the individual case load, the amount of paperwork, and the burden of other responsibilities. Of central importance here is the way group sessions are counted as measures of your workload. In some clinics, therapist workload is measured in contact hours with clients. In these clinics, an individual therapy hour is the unit, and a group therapy session counts for 1.5 units. It is an utterly unrealistic way of measuring both services provided and therapist workload. In fact, it penalizes you for doing group. The workload, in terms of your time and energy and in terms of the amount of paperwork and extratherapy contact, is much greater than for an individual contact hour. Moreover, you have to meet with your coleader before group sessions and, ideally, afterward as well; so, generally, each group session takes about two hours.

The workload measure, where group therapy is concerned, should be the number of clients seen per day, per week, or per month. Counting group work in this way might seem to give an inflated estimate of your case load; the paperwork involved in documenting a group member's progress might be less than that required for a patient seen in individual therapy. However, your general responsibility for each client in group is not less than for each client in individual therapy. Your accessibility for extragroup contacts with the client, with the referring therapist, with other clinic personnel, and with the client's family is not different. In addition, you have to meet with your coleader, handle screening interviews, and maintain contact with referral sources in order to keep the referral flow adequate. Seeing six clients in a single group session will not take as much time and energy as seeing them one at a time, but it is certainly more difficult and demanding than seeing two individuals for forty-five minutes each.

Therefore, unless there is some reduction in your obligation to see clients one at a time, it is prudent to evaluate carefully whether you want to do group therapy in this particular setting. You probably have other duties in the clinic besides seeing clients in individual and group therapy, and it is important to get some of these nontherapy aspects of your workload reduced as well before you start doing groups. Unless other obligations are reduced, you will pay a heavy penalty for leading your group. And while it may be worth it to you, it is always good to have a realistic grasp of the magnitude of your task. If you do not, burnout is probable, sooner or later.

Cotherapist and supervision conflicts are two of many
issues that can lead to burnout if you do not deal with them.
If issues arise that are not resolvable, terminating the group
may become necessary. Outside pressures may lead to burnout
if, as is frequently the case, you do group therapy during
evening hours. Evening work impairs your social and family
life. The tolerance of children, spouses, and lovers is great
but not unlimited; and when you get home, tired, they may
need you to go at full speed. Clinic compensatory time—a
morning or afternoon off, for example, for every evening
you work—does not altogether replace the evening time that
would have been devoted to family and friends.

Ideally, in these circumstances, you would be able to
find another person with group skills who is willing to take
over. Sometimes, however, that is just not possible, and you
find that you have to terminate an otherwise viable group.
The situation is similar to that in which a group member
leaves the group because of dissatisfaction. That is, you have
to deal with the group's anger at your leaving—even if you
arrange for another group therapist to take over—and with
their fantasies about abandonment, responsibility, and guilt.
You should assume that these fantasies are present in at least
some of the group members although it is improbable that
members will introduce their fantasies for discussion. You
should bring up these issues of abandonment, responsibility,
and guilt, perhaps repeatedly, until it is clear that they have
been resolved as much as possible under the circumstances.

Terminating an Individual Client

Before getting to the specific techniques involved in terminating a client or a group, let us consider how much of an
issue to make of termination. I suspect that mental health professionals in general, and group therapists in particular, make
more of termination than our clients do. Early in the course of
individual therapy, and early in the life of a therapy group, we
teach our clients the language of the theory of psychotherapy
and personality that we are using. And we teach the theory

itself. This teaching of theory probably goes on throughout the course of both individual and group therapy.

Thus, if our theory tells us that termination is a terribly important event, to be made much of, we teach our clients that, and consequently termination becomes a major event. If we were to leave it alone, and if we let the clients themselves make as much or as little of it as they wished, some would probably make a big deal of it and some would not. Sometimes we lead our clients through events to which our theory has given an exaggerated importance. How much importance to place on termination, and how ceremonial to be about it, is something that should be determined on a case-by-case basis. It is not necessary to insist, as do Mullan and Rosenbaum (1978), that termination is invariably some kind of psychic trauma fraught with symbolic significance. So, as termination approaches, you should give the client the opportunity to make a big deal of it, if he or she wants to, without insisting on it.

In open-ended groups, clients usually initiate the discussion of their own terminations. Sometimes they do so in the group, sometimes in an extragroup contact with the therapists. If the contact is outside the group, the therapist should offer an exit interview to ascertain whether the client's decision to leave is the result of some transient issue in group that the client wishes to avoid or the result of an assessment that the course of therapy is nearing successful completion. If the client initiates discussion of termination during a group session, it is not necessary to offer an additional extragroup session with the therapists. The discussion can be completed in the group.

Once the client has announced his or her plan to leave the group, you should simply note for the group that everything that is to be said by and about this client will have to be said in the next three or four meetings or it will not be said at all. It is not necessary to say much more than that, though you might suggest that, at some point before termination, you and the group and the client will want to review the client's progress.

Two sessions before the last, you should make a similar statement at the beginning of the group session. And at the next-to-last session, you should give yet another reminder:

> George has only today and next week with us. So
> everything that is going to happen in this group
> in relation to George has to happen today or next
> time. It's better if it happens today, so that if
> there is anything left unfinished today we'll have
> one more session to tie up loose ends.

As early in the session as practicable, begin your review of the client's progress. Ideally, you will have mentioned to the group the week before that you would be doing this review. If the client indicates that he or she would prefer not to have the review, offer an individual interview. Usually, client reluctance to discuss progress with the group is an indicator that something else is going on—something that may not emerge during the group session but something you should know about if it is so strong that it is driving someone away.

When doing your review of the client's progress, you should discuss only those aspects of the client's problems that he or she already has discussed in the group. As always, it is important to avoid introducing information you have about the client but which he or she has not broached with the group. If you are not sure about a piece of information, err on the side of caution.

Probably the safest and most helpful way to proceed is to discuss the way the client related with the group when he or she first entered and then to contrast that with the present. In some areas there will have been much progress, in some areas not so much. You should acknowledge both, the positive first. Something like the following statement keeps the summary centered in the present and on the group itself.

> When you first came into group you were pretty
> quiet and hard to get to know. You've become
> more open and you look more relaxed about talk-
> ing about yourself and with others in the group.

Inviting the other group members to offer their impressions of the terminating client is also usually helpful. And the final step in the sequence is to ask the client to give an assessment of his or her own progress and perhaps of the progress of others in the group.

Thus, the next-to-last group session is one for review, summing up, and perhaps a bit of reminiscing. The last session is primarily one for saying good-byes. Following this procedure may make the last session seem a bit superfluous, but it performs the function of strengthening the departing member's assessment that he or she is really ready to leave the group.

Doing most of the terminal work in the next-to-last session allows for the possibility that some latent powerful feelings may show up and may have to be dealt with. Some group members are more frank as they approach termination than they have characteristically been with regard to their feelings toward and assessments of the other group members and the therapists. On rare occasions, a long-simmering argument will erupt. But more frequently, people who have been at odds in the group for years will make some effort at reconciliation. Having a final session afterward acts to cement the more conciliatory position, or, at least, to make it more credible.

If the bulk of the work of termination is done in the next-to-last session, you need say little in the client's last session other than to note that it is his or her last. The client may, in the last session, ask you or your cotherapist for a more personal kind of self-disclosure than is appropriate—something on the order of, "Now that I'm leaving, what do you really think of me? And what are you really like?" Clients terminating individual therapy will sometimes do the same thing. As in individual therapy, it is important to stay in the therapist role, and to respond to proffered interest with warmth but not reciprocity. The asymmetry of the client-therapist relationship remains an important factor right up to the end.

Even in a group that has been meeting for some time,

the client may not know the last names, or phone numbers or addresses, of the other group members. As a parting gesture, someone may offer to exchange this kind of information. While such a move may appear to destroy the anonymity that group members enjoy—the anonymity that facilitates self-disclosure—in reality there is almost never much contact between a terminating group member and the rest of the group. Therefore, there is not much cause for therapist alarm or concern, and it is usually not necessary to discourage such activity.

In the process of exchanging addresses and phone numbers, the group members reveal some important aspects of themselves to the other group members, the ones who are remaining. Occasionally, sociopathic group members will take advantage of the situation to contact other clients; and occasionally a new group member will feel uncomfortable about giving out a phone number or address to a bunch of people he or she does not know very well and with whom he or she has little in common except emotional or behavioral problems.

So, if you have someone in the group who is a bit on the sociopathic side, or someone who is relatively new in the group and not yet socialized into the group culture, it is probably better to suggest that the information exchange occur on an individual basis outside the group. That way the group members who want to maintain contact with the departing member can do so, while those who do not can silently slip away. The problem is that this kind of move happens so fast that the exchange can already be started before you have a chance to alter it. It is not a major error, but it is much easier to anticipate it than to stop the information exchange.

Occasionally, clients bring liquor to the group session to celebrate their departure. It is not something you would think to forbid, and, like the information exchange, it can happen very fast. But unless you are in an unusual situation, you should not permit it. If you know this sort of thing is possible, you are more likely to be able to stop it before the champagne cork pops.

Terminating the Group

If you are running a time-limited group, or if, perhaps for one of the reasons discussed above, you decide to discontinue the entire group, the same general principles and time scale apply to group termination as apply to individual termination. If the group has been meeting for six months or more, you should say something, approximately six weeks before the end, about getting all of the group's business finished. A similar notice should be given about a month before the end, and the work of summarizing should start three sessions from the end. In a smaller group, you might not need that much time.

In an ideal situation, you can devote the third-to-last and second-to-last sessions to summarizing, and the last session to reminiscences, good-byes, and discussion of future plans. The general structure of these sessions is for you and your cotherapist to discuss, with each client and with the group, the extent to which the original contract and other contracts that evolved along the way have been fulfilled. The discussion can be structured: this is where you were when we started, these were your goals, this is how you worked on them, this is what it looks like now, this is our recommendation for the next step. Both the client and the group should be invited to participate in the discussion. When you and your cotherapist have completed the rounds in this way, the work of the group is finished, whether or not the time is up. You may choose to stay until the end of the scheduled time, but it is important not to do work after the group has ended.

Unfinished Business

For the individual who is terminating from an ongoing group, and for the group that comes to an end all at once, there will usually be some themes that have not been resolved and for which closure cannot be achieved in the time remaining. It is important to sanction the incompleteness of the theme so that the clients—and you—do not leave feeling that something vital has been left undone.

There are two major kinds of unfinished business at the end of a group. One pertains to group issues, the other to people. Not surprisingly, the underlying group issues that are most likely to remain unresolved when a group ends concern the same great themes with which groups struggle throughout their lives: love and hate, or sex and aggression, in their myriad forms. Some groups are never willing to confront sexual issues between members. And in some groups, a norm evolves compelling people to refrain from expressing negative feelings that nonetheless influence how they relate to other group members.

In these instances, the tasks of the therapists are to identify and acknowledge the unfinished business, to note that it remains incomplete, and perhaps to talk about some of the reasons that things turned out the way they did. You do not have to make a big issue of it, and it is better to wait until after you have had the two feedback sessions described above. So, acknowledgment of unfinished group business should come either in the next-to-last session or in the final session. The reason for waiting is to give group members the opportunity to resolve long-standing issues as they summarize their progress. Here is an example of the kind of thing you might say at the last meeting of a group, about unfinished business:

> There's quite a range of themes that groups can deal with, and no one group explores all the possible themes. Each group selects two or three that are the main life issues the group explores. This group dealt with themes having to do with work and with relationships between you and people you're involved with outside the group. So there was a lot of focus in this group on how to: how to deal with a boss who never says a kind word, how to handle rejection by a friend or lover. There was a lot of information shared here, and it was information that you needed.
>
> In most groups there are things that don't get talked about. There gets to be a sort of silent

agreement that some topics are off limits. In this group, we didn't talk very much at all about sexual feelings within the group—people feeling attracted to one another, or jealous, that sort of thing. It's hard to believe that those feelings didn't come up more often than we talked about them. But that just isn't where this group's focus was. Since this group didn't deal with those issues, they are things you might want to take up with your individual therapists. Or, if at some point in the future you join another group, don't be surprised at how very different it will seem, because groups are as different from each other as people are. Not necessarily better or worse, just different.

A group may fail to deal with a theme of central importance for many reasons including resistance, transference, and countertransference. And the contracts made between clients and therapists in the screening interviews may not be fulfilled. It is not unusual for clients to have sexual issues, for example, they are willing to discuss with their individual therapists but not with the group. Some therapists are more reluctant than others to delve into here-and-now sexual feelings in the group. And there are some communities where there are very strong cultural norms against discussing sexual feelings in public and against angry confrontations. For a group to deal effectively with these issues in such settings, there must be an explicit focus and an explicit agreement among the group members that they wish to overcome the cultural prohibitions. Unless you reach such an agreement with the group, trying to get people to talk about these matters is like trying to get people to row upstream. It can be done, but it takes a lot of energy and not much progress is made. Consequently, these are themes that remain as unfinished business when the group comes to an end.

Another type of unfinished business involves differences between people—minor irritants, not directly related to clients' purposes for being in group and not related to their goals, but irritating differences that pertain more to the particular mix of clients in group than to individual psychopathology or group process. Sometimes, people just do not like each other. The principle to follow in these cases is that not every conflict that can be resolved should be resolved. Some are just not worth bothering with. Nor is it necessary for people to like each other just because they have spent time together in group therapy. Conflicts that arise because of the unique mix of people in the group are probably not worth resolving, because they may represent a unique situation with unique solutions having little generalizability outside of group.

When an individual client terminates but the group continues, you would not expect the terminating client to have major unresolved or unfinished business with the group. When the group terminates, however, there may be members who have not yet begun to experience the benefit of the therapy. For such people, I like to tell the story, attributed to Bart Starr, about how the Green Bay Packers never lost a game. But sometimes the clock ran out before the Packers were ahead. There may be some people in the terminating group who are not finished and who would go on meeting if that were possible. For them, the clock ran out before they were ahead. For such people, a positive outcome would be their accepting referral to another group.

In Conclusion

Termination is a milestone in the career of the client, the group, and the therapist. Theoretically, all sorts of wonderful things are supposed to have happened in order for termination to be achieved. Analytically oriented therapists talk about analysis of the transference and resolution of transference issues (for example, Rutan and Stone, 1984). Others talk about symptom reduction or the completion of the therapy contract negotiated during the screening interview. All of these, in whatever theoretical language, are desirable.

However, most terminations occur before these desirable goals have been achieved. They occur for a myriad of reasons, some of which are relevant to the group and to the therapeutic effort and some of which are not. In a practical sense, then, the criteria for termination should be no more than the following:

- The problems that brought the client to the clinic and to the group are diminished.
- The client has made, or feels confident about making, significant changes in his or her life situation. Such changes may involve work or social relationships or both. Ideally, the client will have made some changes in the style of relating to others in general.
- The client feels confident of his or her ability to manage future stress, and is willing to return for therapy if necessary.

When these criteria have been met, then the work of the group is done. And so is yours.

11

Modifying Internalized Parental Voices: A Role-Playing Technique

In this chapter, we will look at some ways to influence the internal dialogue people carry on with themselves. Most people think to themselves verbally, at least some of the time. You may experience thinking to yourself as an internal dialogue. Actually, of course, it is a monologue. There is only one voice inside your head—your own. It may be regarded, depending on which personality theory you prefer, as ego/superego, as Parent/Adult/Child, or any of a variety of other labels. Here, we will refer to it as your *internal voice*. When the internal voice performs an assessing function, engaging in reality testing, it may be regarded as ego; when it performs an evaluative function, it may be referred to as superego, popularly known as conscience.

People's behaviors are guided, or at least strongly influenced, by their private, personal, internal monologues. It follows, therefore, that if you can influence or modify the internal monologue, you can influence or modify behavior. It is difficult to modify something that is going on inside a person's head. You can ask a client to think about something or to think about something in a different way. But in these instances, even if the client complies, the modification of the internal monologue takes place subject to all the constraints imposed by the client's usual mode of thinking. If you can get the internal monologue out, making the monologue external to the client, he or she experiences it differently and it can be more easily modified.

The way to externalize the internal monologue is through role play. The internal voice can be divided into several components, and other group members can be enrolled to embody the various components. One of the most common components of the internal voice is critical, and usually the criticism is experienced, at an emotional level, as coming from one's parents. Thus, when working with the client's internal voice, you will frequently find yourself dealing with internalized critical parental voices.

As therapist, you will be directing the enrolling process, helping the client to write the script for the other actors to follow, and then making sure that the script is sufficiently explicit and that the other actors follow it precisely, contributing nothing of their own. This faithful reflection by the other actors of what the client tells them to say is the externalization of the internal dialogue and is the most important component of the technique. It is also the characteristic that differentiates this technique from most other role plays, such as psychodrama (see, for example, Moreno, 1946).

When the client has heard the internal monologue coming from outside his or her head, the emotional impact is usually strong. The client may then tell you what to do or may give you clues as to what to do next. Sometimes, however, the client will simply say, "Yes, that's it, that's what I tell myself," or some such thing. At that point, you can suggest different lines for the actors, modifying the outcome so the client ends up successful or reinforced rather than defeated or rebuked. In using this technique, you must ensure the outcome is positive for the client. The experience of positive outcome may be the most significant component of the therapeutic experience.

With this brief overview, we are now ready to describe the technique in some detail.

Indications for the Use of This Role Play Technique

In most group therapy sessions, the focus is on one or two people talking for a time, followed by a more general group discussion in which most of the people present participate. The person talking has a story to tell. He or she may need some help in the telling, usually in the form of encouragement. Early in the life of a group, or early in a group member's participation in an ongoing group, the stories may seem banal or trivial, and may represent the individual's testing the waters of self-disclosure. Later on, the stories may become more dramatic and poignant, or more tangled and involved, as the teller puts more energy into the telling.

Usually, the stories are about events that have occurred, or are anticipated to occur, outside of the group—there-and-then. The therapist must decide how long to allow the focus to remain outside of group, and when and how to bring it back within the group. One way of bringing the focus back to here-and-now is to look within the story for interpersonal situations or for feelings that may have some parallel within the present group. Another way is to explore the effect the story teller has, or is trying to have, on the group through the telling of that particular story. The first is content oriented, the second process oriented. The technique described here utilizes role play that is content oriented but involves other people in the group.

The technique may be introduced at any point at which a group member tells a story that includes a component of criticism, or it may be suggested when a group member describes a desired action that is (or was) blocked by internal constraints. The technique may also be helpful when the desired action is in the near future, is not blocked, but is being approached with considerable trepidation. The technique may also be used when the contemplated action is not interpersonal, as when a group member plans, but hesitates, to build or to write something, to quit smoking, to study more, to balance his or her checkbook, and the like. Usually the involvement of other group members, either actively as participants in the role play or passively as onlookers, is greater when there is an interpersonal component. In general, the technique may be useful whenever a group member appears to be engaging in an internal dialogue.

When a group member's story involves criticism, it may be criticism of one's self or criticism by others; it may be only anticipated or it may be a criticism already made. As the story is told by the client, the principal block to effective action is a subjective feeling (usually, fear of criticism) rather than an external circumstance such as the absence of a person or a relationship. Seldom does the story initially involve internal critical parental voices. Usually, when you first call attention to the internal dialogue, the voice is experienced as one's own, in the present, and directed toward the present story. The story is usually of events in the recent past or in the immediate future; but it is there-and-then relative to the group since it does not involve relationships or interactions actually present in the room during the group session, as illustrated in the following example.

> A group member told of her live-in boyfriend who worked two jobs and was seldom home. According to her, his position was that he worked hard and long to provide her with a good home and with material comforts that he himself had lacked during his poverty-filled childhood. Although angry with him, she felt unable to confront him because she regarded her feelings as unjustified since his absence was for her benefit, and she did in fact benefit materially. In addition, she loved him, and wanted neither to hurt his feelings nor to leave the relationship. She felt stuck.
>
> Other group members began to suggest confrontational techniques that would minimize risk and angry interchange. It soon became apparent that the woman, whom we will call Kim, found it

difficult to plan confrontational strategies
because she had such a strong internal prohibition against bringing up the issue.

"What would happen if you did bring it up?"
one of the group members asked.

"I couldn't bring it up," Kim replied. This
interchange was repeated twice, at which point
the therapist intervened.

"OK," he said, "so you couldn't bring it
up. Why not?"

"I don't know, I just couldn't," said Kim.

"What do you tell yourself when you think
about it?" asked the therapist.

"I tell myself that I shouldn't feel angry
with Ernie, and that I should look at all he's
doing for me and feel grateful," she replied.

Any time a group member tells himself or herself that
he or she should not feel something, the internal prohibition
is usually traceable to an early parental injunction against
the behavioral expression of that feeling.[1] The suspected presence of such an injunction is one of the clearest indications
for the use of this role play technique.

Kim's comment thus brought the therapist to a choice
point at which a number of options were available. One
option was to remain silent. Or the therapist might have
chosen to make a process comment on how the client was
using the group (in this instance, as a kind of consultant), or
how the group was responding to Kim's plight, for example.
The therapist might have invited the client to do a behavior
rehearsal role play, in which Kim would have practiced what
she might say to her boyfriend. Or the therapist could have
suggested the Gestalt two-chair technique, in which Kim
would imagine Ernie sitting in a chair opposite her, talk to
the empty chair, and then switch and role play Ernie as a
means of exploring his imagined or feared response. And
there were other possible choices as well, as is usually the case
in group psychotherapy.

When you are at one of the many choice points that arise during the course of a group session, you always have several options, any one of which would be correct, appropriate, and effective. The more experience and training you have with this treatment modality, the more choices you have at your disposal. When the virtues of these choices are about equal, selection can be based on personal preference, intuition, or other subjective factors.

In the present example, the therapist chose to pursue Kim's internal prohibition against opening the discussion with Ernie about how she wanted to see more of him and how she was angry and in conflict about his absences. In order to understand how the therapist did this, we must digress briefly into a bit of theory.

Some Theoretical Background

A theory is a language for describing events and the relations among them. When the events are inherently ambiguous, they may be adequately described by more than one theoretical language. Most human interactions, especially during a group therapy session, are characterized by high levels of inherent ambiguity and can therefore be satisfactorily described by a variety of theoretical languages.

What is described here is my own adaptation and synthesis of several theoretical languages, principally that of Albert Pesso (1973), and of Freud ([1900] 1955). I have also drawn on the field theory of Kurt Lewin (1935); the reader will find an excellent, and more accessible, summary in Hall and Lindzey, 1957.

Pesso is a truly gifted theorist and teacher who has done considerably more training than he has writing. He is a purist who has resisted the adaptation of components of his approach (Pesso System Psychomotor Therapy) outside the context of Psychomotor Therapy groups led by people he has trained and certified. My adaptation of some parts of his technique, therefore, would almost certainly not have his blessing.

Most theories of group psychotherapy describe the group sessions as multidimensional. The number of dimensions and the ways they are described depend on the theory (see, for example, Bion, 1961; Kadis and others, 1974; Kellerman, 1979; Mullan and Rosenbaum, 1978; Whitaker and Lieberman, 1964). The most useful way I have found for describing this role play technique is to think of a group session as comprising three dimensions or levels:

- The present here-and-now reality, what is actually going on in the room at the moment
- A historical dimension, reaching into the past of the group and of each person in it
- A symbolic dimension, in which the here-and-now real interactions are understood and interpreted as symbolic representations of events located on the historical dimension

Role play has meaning and significance as symbolic interaction; the actual behaviors that take place during the group session are symbols for other behaviors that may or may not have reality in either the past or the future. The technique is contraindicated if anyone in the group might confuse the real and the symbolic.

In this way of looking at interactions, present events have meaning in and of themselves. The past is relevant but does not always have sufficient salience to warrant exploration. However, when a group member reaches puzzling, unrealistic, or irrational conclusions about present or future events, exploration of the past may clarify the reasons underlying those conclusions. Role play is a way of symbolically reaching into the past and modifying unrealistic or irrational conclusions.

When more emotion or psychic energy than appears warranted is involved in a present event, it is probable that some linkage with a past event has occurred. There are other clues that such a linkage may have occurred, as, for instance, when effective action is blocked by apparently irrational fear. The linkage is based on some similarity between present and past events. The similarity may involve emotions, situations, places, relationships, times of day, or other components. The way the mind perceives similarities unconsciously has best been described by Freud ([1900] 1955) in *The Interpretation of Dreams*. The unconscious mind has a peculiar logic all its own, and it is that logic which is at work here, finding similarities of a sort, linking past and present. When such a linkage occurs, both past and present events seem to have more energy. It is similar to the effect of sympathetic vibration on a stringed instrument: if you cause one string to vibrate, an adjacent string set an octave lower will vibrate as well, so that the tone sounded is reinforced and louder than if the concordance were not there and only one string vibrated.

In the preceding discussion, I have avoided using the term *repression* because repressed memories are not readily accessible to consciousness. Here, we are working only with memories that can be easily recalled. And, for our purposes, any past event that has an associative link with the present will do.

It is this past event that provides the initial script for the role play. The therapist will ask the group member to describe the event and to play it out, using other group members as symbolic representatives of the people in the client's own past. When the role play is concluded, the therapist will help the client to reevaluate his or her present situation if such help is needed, to provide a different understanding if the blocked event is in the recent past, or to provide a different anticipated outcome if the block is in the present or near future.

Now, let us return to our example.

Initiating the Role Play

Kim said (back on p. 214) that she tells herself she should not feel angry and that she should feel grateful to Ernie.

Therapist: So who's telling you how you should or shouldn't feel?

Kim: I am.

Therapist: Sounds like a parent's voice.

Kim: Yes, it's my mother's. She was always real critical of me.

Therapist: What would she tell you?

Kim: Basically that she and my dad worked hard to provide me with all this wonderful material stuff, that I didn't particularly want, and that I was an ungrateful bitch.

Therapist: And now Ernie is working hard to provide you with all this material stuff?

Kim: Yeah, and it's nice, but I could do with a lot less of it and a lot more of him.

Therapist: And you can't tell him that?

Kim: No.

Therapist: That's quite a dialogue you're having with yourself, in your head.

Kim: Yeah, it goes on all the time.

Therapist: Would you like to do some work on that here?

Kim: Yeah, but what can you do?

Therapist: I'd like to do some role play.

The therapist then explained what is involved in role play, in terms of giving voice to the internal dialogue and hearing it come in from outside oneself. The therapist then added this note of caution:

> Whenever we do something like this, I'd like for you to remember that you're in the driver's seat. You've got the steering wheel, and your foot on the brakes. I'm sort of like a navigator: I've got the road map, and I can tell you where things are, but you're the one who decides whether to go or not. So you're in control all the way.

However you phrase it, you must emphasize to the client prior to the role play, as you would prior to any group exercise, that he or she is in control and can stop the process at any point. As the group goes on, and as you perform this or other active interventions, it is worthwhile to point out to the client before beginning, even if you have said it many times before, that he or she remains in control.

Now comes one of the most important and distinctive points about this technique. It is clear that Kim was dealing with an internal critical voice that she associated with her mother. But it is also highly probable that she had an internal voice, perhaps fainter or less frequent, that was nurturing and approving—a voice she also associated with her mother. That is, Kim's relationship with her mother was ambivalent, as are most children's, and this normal ambivalence was reflected in Kim's own internal dialogue. If we asked a group member to role-play her mother, Kim's script probably would have reflected this ambivalence which prevented her from dealing effectively with the critical component.

We therefore separate the internal voice into two, or sometimes three, components. One component is labelled the critical voice and represents only those aspects of the internalized parental (in this case, maternal) figure that are negative. The second component is positive and represents only those aspects of the internalized parental figure that are positive and nurturing. This component represents the good parent and is based on things the real parental figure said or might have said or might say in the future. However, it does not represent the real, historical parental figure, but only the positive aspects of the client's own internalized representation of what he or she perceived the real parent to be. This distinction between the client's own introjection and the actual parent is important to maintain throughout the role play.

The third component represents the ideal parent. It is the voice of the parent that every person would like to have had, the absolutely perfect parent for that person, the Cliff Huxtable of the mind.[2] Although there are some important similarities between the good and the ideal parental voices, the chief difference is that the former is somewhat limited by reality, while the latter is not.

Group members are enrolled to role-play these components or aspects of the parental figure. In introducing the technique to the group, the therapist should explain that the group will not be working with actual historical figures. You might say something like this:

> Your real mother is out there [specify where, if possible], and we're going to leave her there. In what we're going to do here, we're not going to ask anyone to role-play your real mother. Rather, we're going to be working with the mother you've internalized, the maternal voice you hear inside your own head. So it's really yours, rather than your mother's.

You then go on to explain the components, and you explain that each person who participates in the role play will symbolize only one part, one aspect, of the client's internalized parental voice. The language you use and the length of your explanations will, of course, be tailored to your audience.

Separating the parental voice into these components enables the client to deal effectively, and sometimes vehemently, with the critical aspects without being overwhelmed by guilt at being angry with a person who has also been positive and nurturing and loving. The separation provides the client with a way to handle the ambivalent feelings without being overwhelmed by ambivalent conflict. The technique of separating central figures into their component parts is one of Pesso's most valuable contributions.

Returning to our example, after reassuring Kim that she would be in control of the role play, the therapist described the technique as being similar to a play. Kim would be the author, the group members who participated would be the actors, and the therapist would be the director. As such, he would work within the script supplied by Kim, but he might at times suggest alternative wordings or alternative ways for the story to unfold. However, as author, Kim would have veto power over these suggestions.

Kim described a situation in which she felt blocked from attempting resolution. The situation involved three people: Kim, Ernie, and Kim's internal negative voice, which is telling her how not to feel and what not to say. The therapist asked Kim to set the stage such that Ernie was home, Kim was angry with him for his absence and was telling herself that she ought not feel that way but ought to feel grateful for Ernie's efforts. This stage was similar to the setting that had evolved from Kim's discussion of the problem with the group. Once Kim agreed, the process of enrollment could begin.

Enrollment

Therapist: We'll need someone to role-play Ernie. Who would you like?

Kim: How about you, George? (indicating a male group member)

George: OK, I'll be Ernie.

Therapist: No, you can't be Ernie. You can role-play him but you can't be him. The way to do this is to say, "I'll role-play Ernie."

George: I'll role-play Ernie.

In describing this technique, I have tried to indicate the information to be conveyed to the group, without being specific about wording. The concepts are more important than the specific words you use. In enrolling, however, the specific words are important; there is an almost ritualistic element to the process. Frequently, in consenting to participate, clients will agree to "be" someone in the role play, as indicated above in the example. It is always necessary to intervene when that happens, and to ensure that the agreement is to role-play, but not to "be," the character. This distinction is a safeguard that keeps it as clear as possible that what ensues is on the symbolic level rather than real. It frees clients from the necessity of dealing with the real person group member who has agreed to portray the character in the client's script.

Note that the therapist asked Kim to select a group member to role-play Ernie. This is preferable to calling for volunteers. There is always the risk that no one will volunteer, especially if the role is a negative one, but as a practical matter the risk is quite small. Group members should feel free to decline nomination for a role, and, if necessary, that freedom should be made explicit by the therapist.

Because the technique involves symbolic interaction, enrollees need not have any actual physical resemblance to the characters they are to portray. Young women may portray grandmothers, and vice versa. Men may be asked to play maternal roles, not unusual if there is a highly nurturant man in the group, and women may be asked to portray paternal figures. This feature of the technique is an asset when sexes are not represented in group in the proportions needed for the play.

It is not unusual for a client to ask the therapist to take one of the roles. If you are doing the group solo, you cannot take a role because you are needed as stage director, and it does not work to be both stage director and actor. If you are doing group with a cotherapist, some fairly complex undercurrents can be set up during and after the role play because of the real therapist-client relationship. In addition, the cotherapist who does take a role functions as a participant rather than as an observer throughout the role play, so you lose valuable assistance. For these reasons, therapists should generally decline nomination. However, there are some situations in which it would be so much more facilitative for one of the therapists to participate that it might be worthwhile.

After George was enrolled to role-play Ernie, the therapist asked Kim where in the room she would like Ernie to be. Each character should be placed before the next is enrolled, and the placement may require that other group members yield their seats. Usually, clients will want positive figures close to them, either sitting next to them or standing nearby. Sometimes, however, particularly if clients are not very forthcoming, they will indicate that the just-enrolled character should remain in his or her present seat. When negative characters are enrolled, and the therapist asks (if necessary) where they should be placed in the room, the client will frequently indicate that they should stay where they are. If this would place them between the client and his or her positive characters, therapist intervention is necessary, along with a word of explanation: the client's support system should be between him or her and the negative characters. In our example, Kim asked that Ernie sit one chair away from her.

The therapist then described the concept of part-characters to the group. This is the idea that the roles portray only some aspects of a character—all negative or all positive—rather than a whole, living, complex personality. The therapist then asked Kim whom she would like to have role-play the negative aspects of her mother. In this enrollment process, the person who agreed should say, "I will role-play the negative aspects of your mother," to make it as clear as possible to all concerned that the character represented only one segment of the client's internalized concept of her mother. Kim asked that this negative character sit behind her, and the therapist suggested that she sit about three feet back. This positioning left room, if needed, for the positive maternal character to get between Kim and the negative character.

The next step was to enroll either a positive or an ideal voice. In our example, the therapist chose to go with the positive voice, reserving the ideal for later on if needed. In this technique, characters can be added at any time as the play unfolds, and need not all be enrolled at the outset. However, the enrollment process, and the agreement to role-play rather than to be, is the same whenever it is done. The therapist explained the concept of the positive aspect character, and Kim chose a woman who agreed to be enrolled. At Kim's direction she took up a position behind Kim and on her other side, but closer than the negative character. The stage was set to begin the role play itself.

The Play

Kim looked at Ernie but said nothing. The two maternal figures sat silent and immobile.

Therapist: Kim, what are you thinking?

Kim: I'm thinking that I'm really pissed and that I love him.

Therapist: Tell him that.

Kim (to Ernie): I'm really . . . *(to therapist)* No, I can't do that.

Therapist: Why not?

Kim: I shouldn't feel angry with him, I should feel grateful, I shouldn't say anything.

Therapist: That's your negative voice?

Kim: Yes.

Therapist: Have her say it.

Negative Mother (to Kim): Don't say that.

Therapist (to Negative Mother): This is really like a play, and Kim is the author of the script. As a character in the play, you read the script, but you don't do any improvising, you don't add anything of your own.

Therapist (to Kim): What should she say?

Kim: She should tell me I mustn't be angry with him.

Therapist: OK, but write her the script. She'll only say the exact words you want, and they should be the same exact words that you hear in your head, that you've been telling yourself.

Kim (turning to Negative Mother): Say, "Don't be angry with him."

Negative Mother: Don't be angry with him.

This interchange illustrates the two most common problems you are likely to encounter once the play is started. The first is that characters start to improvise. You can either emphasize before the role play starts that they should not improvise and spend some time teaching the group how to do the role play, or you can do the teaching as things come up. The therapist in our example chose the latter. If characters in your group start improvising, they should be promptly coached to follow the script.

The client may give the character a longer speech than he or she can easily retain in memory, so you may need to interrupt to ask the client to provide the speech in shorter, more manageable segments. Incidentally, dealing with short segments rather than long speeches yields the desirable result of more opportunity for interaction. You also may need to intervene if a character reads a script that is almost, but not quite, what the author specified. In this technique, almost is not good enough, and the character should be encouraged to echo the client more precisely.

The second common problem is a client's failure to specify a precise script, or, somewhat more rarely, a client's invitation to improvise. Either of these requires therapist intervention in a fashion similar to that illustrated in the above example. If a client is unable to formulate a specific script, you might suggest one if you are sure you know what the client is trying to say. We continue our example:

Kim: That isn't quite right. Say, "You ungrateful bitch, after all he's done for you."

Negative Mother: You ungrateful bitch, after all he's done for you.

Kim: Say it again, louder.

Negative Mother (louder): You ungrateful bitch . . .

Kim (interrupting): Just say bitch, again, bitch, bitch, yell it.

Negative Mother (quite loudly): Bitch, bitch, bitch!

Kim: That's it! That's it! That's what I hear in my head all the time! That's what she used to say to me everytime I turned around! I'd try to please her—there was no pleasing her! I couldn't do anything right! I couldn't even find a man who would want to stay at home with me! (Sobs.)

At this point the therapist indicated that the positive maternal figure should move closer to Kim but not touch her; Kim was huddled over, turned slightly away from the positive figure, covering her head with her arms. After a couple of moments her sobbing subsided.

Therapist: What would you like to hear from your Positive Mother?

Kim: Say, "You're OK and I love you."

Positive Mother: You're OK and I love you.

Although this was a positive comment, it did not balance the forceful negative voice that Kim had been hearing for years inside her head and, on this occasion, coming from outside as well. The therapist therefore encouraged Kim either to respond to the negative voice or to elicit a more forceful support from the positive voice. She did some of both, engaging in a dialogue with the negative figure while eliciting support from the positive figure, with very little additional prompting from the therapist.

The outcome of the interchange was Kim's positive voice giving her permission to feel angry with Ernie, and her realization that she did not have to be grateful for unsolicited material goods to which she was basically indifferent. Kim said she would talk with Ernie about her dissatisfaction, and she commented that having permission to feel angry made her feel less angry and more determined to change the situation.

The entire episode took about twenty-five minutes of group time. It is possible for these plays to take a great deal of time—easily, an hour or more. But there are two ways to guard against that. One is to contract with the client, prior to the start of the play, for a certain amount of time. It is difficult to get through one of these plays in less than about twenty minutes, and they tend to drag if they go on longer than forty to forty-five minutes. I suspect that everyone except the client gets tired of a play that goes on that long. So contracting for up to thirty minutes should allow enough time for most plays, while keeping the longer ones from getting interminable. The other way to handle the time issue, if the play begins to seem endless, is to indicate to the client that he or she has five more minutes, and, at the end of that, to indicate that time is up. Most people will conclude well within the five minute limit. When they do not, you can offer to resume the play during the next group session. The occasions when it is necessary to make such an offer are rare, and being taken up on it is even rarer.

In this example, the outcome was successful in two ways. First, Kim was able to give herself permission to talk with Ernie, and she felt unblocked about it. Second, she was able to deal with the internal critical voice that had its origins in her past and that had linked to a present situation in such a way as to inhibit effective action. If the play she constructed had ended in defeat, with the prohibition against talking with Ernie still in place, the therapist would have intervened, and asked, more or less directly, for a happier ending. It is important not to let the client lose in his or her own play; if the original ending comes out negative, change it.

Ending the Role Play

A ritual similar to the enrolling ritual must be performed when the play is ended. The therapist asks each character to say, "I am no longer role-playing X; my name is Y." In our example, George said, "I am no longer role-playing Ernie; I'm George." Some minor variation in the wording is permissible, but the message that the role play is over and that the group member has resumed his or her real name must be unambiguous.

The characters should be de-roled in a particular order: the most negative character first, the most positive character last. Otherwise, you could end up with all of the positive characters de-roled but the negative characters still there. It may sound foolish, but such a situation can frighten a client who has just concluded a very intense emotional experience having symbolic meaning and irrational components.

After the Role Play

When the last character has been de-roled, the other group members, who have been the audience up to this point, should be invited to comment. However, the client whose play it was should be left alone. If group members have questions or comments, they should be directed to the therapist, not to the client. Although the client might choose to participate in the discussion, he or she should not have to handle any direct questions or comments. This procedure is a protective measure for someone who has just been through an intense cognitive and emotional experience.

There usually are not many questions. If the play has been intense and poignant, there may be no questions at all, and the remainder of the group session may be subdued. Those comments that are made are most often empathic or supportive.

One task remains. At the start of the next group session, you should ask the client how he or she is feeling, how things are going, or something of the sort. If you do an opening survey, this inquiry should precede it. On rare occasions, a client may report distress as a result of the preceding week's play. When that happens, the client should be given the opportunity to do whatever additional work needs to be done in the group before anything else happens. Almost always, however, the client will either be noncommittal or report improvement. In our example, Kim reported, in response to the therapist's opening query, that she had in fact talked with Ernie, and that he had been surprised at how she felt. He promised to make some changes in his schedule that would permit him to be at home more frequently.

Concluding Comment

The technique described in this chapter for working with internalized parental voices works best with bright, articulate, imaginative individuals who are comfortable with intimate self-disclosure in group. While it may be attempted with less psychologically sophisticated groups, it should not be introduced until the group has established its atmosphere of warmth and supportiveness. Role playing is a powerful technique. Its main disadvantages include the intense focus on the individual and the tendency to disrupt the group process. Its advantages include the ability to facilitate a group member's working on ambivalent feelings and relationships, the ability to bring there-and-then issues into the here-and-now of the group, and the ability to bring intrapsychic issues into the interpersonal realm.

Notes

1. As any parent knows, there is sometimes a discrepancy between what is said and what is heard, between what is taught and what is learned. These discrepancies are greater during early childhood and adolescence, though they are not unknown even in communications between adults. While it is generally more helpful to assume that what was learned from the parents is different from what was taught or intended, it is also true that occasionally parents will instruct children not to feel the way they do. It is possible that such messages are pathogenic.

2. The reference is to a character played by comedian Bill Cosby on television during the mid-1980s. The obstetrician father of five children, the character is infinitely and unrealistically wise, patient, and understanding.

12

Working with Dreams

In this chapter we will consider three group therapy techniques for working with dreams. The first of these retains the interpersonal orientation with which the reader is already familiar. The second is derived from psychoanalytic dream interpretation. The third is derived from Gestalt therapy.

In the following discussion, I have assumed that neither you nor your coleader have solicited dreams from the group members. Rather, I am assuming a situation in which a group member volunteers a dream, without prompting. The dynamics of dream work and dream interpretation are slightly different if dreams are solicited by the therapists rather than volunteered by clients. By soliciting dreams, you imply to the group that an important focus of group therapy will be the intrapsychic and idiosyncratic rather than the interpersonal. Such a focus facilitates one-to-one client-therapist interactions, but it slows the development of group interactions. Unless you are working within the framework of a theory of group therapy in which dreams play a central role, it will be simpler not to solicit them.

The beginning of dream work is similar for the three techniques described in this chapter, and the following guidelines pertain to all three:

1. Do not start working on the dream without a clear contract with the client describing what you and the group will do with the dreams, and, if possible, describing the end point of the work. Most clients want interpretation at some level. You should avoid a contract stipulating that the client just wants to talk, with no response expected from you or from the group.

2. Ascertain when the client had the dream. The more recent a dream is, the easier it will be to work with. It is best to work with dreams that were dreamed the night before the group session. If several dreams are offered, always focus on the most recent. Dreams that were dreamed prior to the previous week's group meeting (when the client could have reported the dream) should be interpreted using the interpersonal technique to be discussed below. The same is true of dreams that the client describes as recurring but not recently dreamed. In these latter instances, the interpersonal situation in which they choose to report the dreams is likely to be more important than the dream content.

3. Let the client tell the entire dream, from beginning to end, with absolutely no interruption from anyone. This is easy in a group with low verbal activity. But in more verbal groups, it is common for other group members to try to offer interpretations of the dream, or to question the dreamer about it. Occasionally, other group members will try to share their own dreams that have similar components or similar outcomes. At this point, it is essential that you intervene to make it clear that you will not allow interruptions. And you have to refrain from asking questions as well. Even if the client begins speaking too softly to be audible, or says something that seems contradictory or nonsensical or something you do not understand, you should wait until you have a complete runthrough of the story. Then you may ask questions. If you had trouble hearing or understanding major portions of the dream, you might ask the client to repeat the whole dream from the beginning, and this time you can ask him or her to

speak more loudly or to explain as the story is told. Frequently you will get more details if you hear the description a second time. Listen carefully for change in any of the major components of the dream from first telling to second. Usually, but not always, the second and subsequent tellings are more accurate than the initial one. Once the client has described the dream (or, perhaps, is in the process of describing it), you can decide which of the three available techniques will best fit the dream.

Interpersonal Technique

The interpersonal technique is the simplest one, and, as noted above, should be used when the dream is more than a week old. In this approach, the content of the dream is regarded in the same way as any other verbal communication from the client is regarded. The client has a purpose in telling the dream in the context of a therapy group session, that is, some particular interpersonal outcome is sought. For instance, a recovering alcoholic may report a dream in which he found himself surrounded by empty beer cans, feeling both drunk and guilty. The most common response to the reporting of such a dream is sympathetic reassurance, particularly if the entire group is composed of recovering alcoholics. The therapist does not attend to the content of the dream. Its reporting, however, should be understood as an effort to elicit sympathetic reassurance. In this example, it would be important (1) to ensure the client got the reassurance he sought, if the group did not volunteer it, and (2) to point out the client's interpersonal maneuver and encourage him to seek such reassurance more directly in the future.

Usually, by reporting a dream, the client is seeking some kind of positive interpersonal reinforcement from the group and from the therapist. In the above example, the reinforcement was empathic reassurance. Additional types of positive interpersonal reinforcement include attentiveness and interest, the proffering of interpretive explanations, the sharing of dreams with similar components or outcomes, and any other of the wide range of interpersonal reinforcements typically available in a group. The therapeutic factors involved here are self-disclosure, acceptance, universality, and perhaps guidance.

In the above example, it was appropriate and desirable to ensure that the client received the reinforcement he was seeking. However, there are times when it is important that a client not receive that reinforcement. Look at the sequence as an exchange: the client seeks positive reinforcement from the group, and pays for it with the dream, which is a very personal self-disclosure. The nature of the reinforcement the client appears to be seeking may be unhealthy: the information the client is offering may produce a group response different from the one he or she is seeking; the level or magnitude of self-disclosure may be disproportionate to the level of reinforcement the client is seeking by reporting the dream; or the magnitude of self-disclosure may be too great if group cohesiveness is low. In these instances, therapist intervention is prudent.

Suppose, for instance, that a client has staked out an interpersonal position, both within the group and outside the group, as a clown: a person to be laughed at and not to be taken seriously. This person might report a dream designed to elicit hostile laughter from the group. The dreamer would experience the hostile laughter as reinforcing his pathological self-image; it is evidence of his ability to produce a specified response and it is evidence of group attentiveness. The therapist can treat the dream that evokes such a response in the same way he or she would treat any other interpersonal communication from that client designed to evoke a similar response. Another example is the borderline client who might report a dream intended to evoke an intensely hostile negative response from the group or from the therapist. The client's experiencing such a response as reinforcing is itself a central factor in his or her pathology. Usually in these situations, you should try to head off hostile responses from the group so they can discuss the dream rather than exhibit the anger or revulsion the client is trying to generate.

By reporting a dream, a client may be seeking the approval of the therapist, of the group, or of both. (The probability of this kind of interpersonal move, on the client's part, is higher if you have solicited dreams than it is if you are relying on spontaneous reports.) But sometimes, the content of a dream or the timing of its reporting will make it highly unlikely that the group's response will be positive or empathic. In these cases, reporting the dream is self-defeating behavior for the client, and therapist intervention may be required. Timing is important; you have to comment before anyone in the group has begun to respond. Regardless of the content, you must focus on the interpersonal situation, on what the client is trying to do, and on the most probable consequences of that effort. The group members will want to discuss the content of the dream, especially if the content is evocative of strong emotional response. But your work is to keep them focused on the interpersonal situation—on the difference between the desired and actual responses of the group.

Sometimes a client will report a dream, the interpretation of which will involve considerably more self-disclosure than he or she had anticipated. An example of this situation is a dream, reported at a client's second group session, which had an underlying homosexual theme. Desperate for approval and inclusion, the client was willing to reveal highly sensitive aspects of his own psyche, but the group, which had not yet granted him psychological inclusion, was not likely to offer either the kind or the magnitude of positive social reinforcement the client sought. In this instance, it would be particularly important to remain on the interpersonal level and not to get into dream content at all. The issue to focus on might be the discrepancy between the magnitude of self-disclosure of the dreamer and the magnitude of support from group members—support they found difficult to give to someone they did not know well.

Note that in the interpersonal approach, you do not negotiate a contract with the client to interpret the dream. If the client requests interpretation, it might be appropriate to ask what he or she would do with it. Again, your focus is on process and specifically not on content. Since dream interpretation necessarily deals with content, it would be inconsistent with this approach for you to get involved with the content of the dream or with any interpretation offered by the client or by the other group members.

The telling of the dream, and the subsequent discussion of the effect of its telling on the here-and-now interpersonal situation in the group, constitute the interpretive work. The interpretation is of process, not of content. It is not unusual, however, for the client or the group to perceive relationships between the manifest content of the dream and some interpersonal situation here-and-now in the group. Such perceptions reflect the therapeutic factor of insight, which may benefit other group members as well as the dreamer.

Psychoanalytic Orientation

This approach to dream interpretation is derived from Freud's theory ([1900] 1955). I have not seen this particular technique described in print; I learned it from Bingham Dai during my internship at Duke University Medical Center nearly a quarter of a century ago. Dai is one of a small group of nonmedical scholars who were trained in psychoanalysis at Yale during the mid 1930s. His technique of dream interpretation falls, I think, into the general category of ego psychology.

In the following discussion, I will assume that you have some familiarity with psychoanalytic theory and with psychoanalytic concepts of dream interpretation. I will, therefore, touch on those topics only lightly here. If you have not read *The Interpretation of Dreams* (Freud, [1900] 1955), you probably should do so before attempting this approach to dream work in groups. In addition, you will find Freud's little book on groups, *Group Psychology and the Analysis of the Ego* ([1922] 1949) helpful as well.

In this approach to dream interpretation, a dream is assumed to consist of two parts. The part you see, the visual experience remembered and reported, is the *manifest content* of the dream. The underlying thoughts make up the *latent content* of the dream. The latter contains the real meaning. An unconscious part of your mind translates the underlying thoughts into visual experiences and modifies the more uncivilized and primitive instinctual components of the dream so they are acceptable to the waking ego. The translation of latent thoughts into manifest content is necessary because of the visual nature of the dream. Modification occurs because our instincts, which are in some natural state unmodified by eons of civilization, generate thoughts or impulses of such unbridled savagery and lust that we could not bear to know that we are capable of even thinking them. However, the underlying dream-thoughts[1] are not changed; only their visual representation is modified, rendering interpretation more difficult. The process is somewhat like taking an X-rated movie script and disguising the steamy scenes to the point that the movie would qualify for PG or even G.

It is a characteristic of dreams that the emotions felt by the dreamer and the visual experience frequently do not match. This mismatch occurs because the dream-work—the translating of the underlying dream-thoughts into a visual representation and the modifying of the picture to avoid the metaphorical X rating—does not usually affect the underlying emotions. Thus, the emotions the dreamer reports are closer to the true meaning of the dream than is the manifest content.

In this approach to dream interpretation, it is assumed that the dreamer knows what the dream means; however, that knowledge may not be immediately accessible to consciousness. The task of the therapist is to help the dreamer discover the dream's meaning. Usually, a dream is a fulfillment of a wish; occasionally, it represents the dreamer's effort at mastery over a frightening or life-threatening situation.

In order to help the client interpret the dream, the therapist has to be familiar with how the dream-work translates latent thoughts into manifest content. There are a finite number of principles to apply, and these principles are described in Chapter VI of *The Interpretation of Dreams*. No one has described them better than their originator. Briefly, the dream-work makes use of pun, metaphor, simile, and analogy. Freud

gives an example of the dream element of falling as representing a fall from virtue, that is, becoming a fallen woman (or,
nowadays, man). It is a figure of speech that used to be considerably more common than it is now. The dream-work,
faced with the problem of representing the underlying dream
component that involves (in this instance) premarital sexual
desire, solves it by translating this desire into the visual representation of falling.

The dream-work also makes copious use of symbols.
Freud said that each person has his or her own set of symbols,
and he cautioned analysts against interpreting dream-symbols
automatically. In addition to differences among people, the
same dream-element or symbol might have different meanings
for the same dreamer at different times. In *The Interpretation
of Dreams,* Freud was scornful of the dream-interpretation
books of his time, which had lists of symbols supposedly
applicable to everyone. Similar books are still available at
your local shopping center bookstore. This universality of
symbols is an important component of Jung's theory, but not
of Freud's.

It is true that Freud listed some commonly encountered
symbols, and their interpretations, in *The Interpretation of
Dreams.* Snakes, umbrellas, and trees frequently are phallic
symbols in dreams and in the unconscious, according to
Freud. That part of his book, and of his theory, was picked
up by the popular press, and much has been made of it.
However, Freud's cautionary note, that symbols are not universal and are not constant even within the same individual,
did not receive the same attention. In later life, he is reported
to have commented that "sometimes a cigar is just a cigar."

In dream interpretation, as in any other therapeutic
work, it is important that the client does the actual work, and
that you take care to keep your own material and your own
assumptions out of the way. In addition, in group work, it is
sometimes necessary to ask the other group members to hold
back their own associations to the dream. Until the dream is
interpreted, at the relatively superficial level of interpretation
that is possible in group, it is important to keep the focus

narrowly on the dreamer and on his or her own psyche. Once
the dream is interpreted, the reactions, thoughts and feelings,
of other group members can be solicited.

Now let us return to the situation in which a group
member volunteers to report a dream to the group. First, you
should determine when the dream was dreamed; if it was
prior to the last group session, make sure you know why it
was not brought up at that time. Establish a contract to work
on the dream and to help the group member toward interpretation. Make sure that the dreamer has a chance to tell the
dream from beginning to end, without interruption. If there
is an interruption during the telling of the dream, such as
a physician coming into the room to pull out a client for
individual therapy, or a secretary bringing you an urgent
message—anything that breaks the client's train of thought—
ask the dreamer to start again from the beginning.

In this mode of dream interpretation, your assumption
is that the dreamer knows what the dream means. Therefore,
the first thing you do when the complete dream has been told
is to ask the dreamer what he or she thinks it means. With
surprising frequency, the dreamer will offer a perfectly good
interpretation, one that integrates both manifest and probable
latent content. When that happens, you can tell the dreamer
you agree with the interpretation and ask if he or she would
like to have comments from the rest of the group. If there is
anything other than silence, it is likely to be sharing of similar experiences or dreams. You can go on to offer further
dream work to other group members, but you do not have to.
Group acceptance of the dream and of its interpretation and,
particularly, the sharing of similar experiences are probably
therapeutic for the dreamer. Given the intrinsically idiosyncratic nature of dreams, the knowledge that anything at all
about them is shared by others is reassuring to the client—
reassuring that his or her deviance is neither as great nor as
repugnant as he or she had feared.

Now let us suppose that you ask the question, what do
you think the dream means? and the group member replies
that he or she does not have any idea. Then you begin the

work of dream interpretation. The origin of a dream is usually in something that happened during the day preceding the dream. Each day there are thoughts, feelings, and actions left unfinished or unresolved. When you undertake a task or start a train of thought, you allocate a certain amount of mental energy to it. If the task is completed, the energy is freed for the next task. Very few tasks take all of your mental energy, although even when they do, the same principles apply. If the task is not completed or the train of thought interrupted before coming to its logical or emotional conclusions, it retains some energy. During the day, you may be able to channel some of that energy elsewhere, into whatever new task is at hand; or perhaps, as is the more usual situation, you simply do not need it. You have enough mental energy to meet ongoing situations, and you do so. At night, however, the incomplete task or thought has relatively more energy, because you are not attending to anything else, and it is this undischarged energy that provides the motive power for the dream.

Empirical support for this notion of Freud's was provided by the Gestalt psychologists in the late 1920s and early 1930s. Two students of Kurt Lewin, Olga Zeigarnik and Maria Ovsiankina, showed that interrupted tasks were recalled more readily than completed tasks (the Zeigarnik effect) and the corollary, that interrupted tasks were more likely to be taken up and completed (*wiederaufnehmen*) when participants were given the option to complete a task or to begin a new similar task. These two research results provide clear evidence that uncompleted tasks retain mental energy or tension sufficient to provide the core around which dreams may be built.

There are usually many such uncompleted tasks left over each day, but not all of them give rise to dreams. Something more is required, and that is the presence of an unconscious group of thoughts or feelings that has (1) some small energy of its own, but not enough to overcome the forces of repression or to gain access to consciousness, and (2) some similarity, however slight, to the uncompleted thoughts or tasks in the day's residue. The principle is similar to that of sympathetic vibration, noted in Chapter Eleven. When there is some correspondence between the uncompleted day's residue and some unconscious complex, there is a symbiotic resonance between them. Through some complicated mechanisms, they bring together enough energy to build the dream, sometimes incorporating other elements of the day's residue as well.

The relationships are complex among all these feelings, thoughts, and tasks from the day's residue and those from the unconscious, which have their own relationships with other unconscious memories and associations. In individual psychoanalysis or psychoanalytically oriented therapy, the interpretation of a single dream may take many months of daily sessions. Group psychotherapy cannot (and should not attempt to) delve so deeply into the psyche of an individual group member. Interpretation will be relatively superficial, and it will usually be fruitful to stop with the first level at which the group member feels the task of interpretation has been completed.

After you have asked the dreamer for the meaning of the dream, and have gotten a negative response, the second step is to ask for a recounting of the events on the day of the dream. If the dream happened on, say, a Wednesday night, it is usually sufficient to ask, "What happened on Wednesday?" Probably about half the time, the client will reply, "Nothing," so you have to prompt him or her. Start with something like "Well, you got up, . . ." and ask the dreamer to go through the day at that level of detail. One reason why it is easier to interpret more recent dreams is that the dreamer has much greater recall of the day's events than he or she does of dreams that occurred in the remote past. Bear in mind that, in this modality of dream interpretation, the client knows what the dream means. Frequently, while going through the day's events, the dreamer will perceive a correspondence between something that occurred and the manifest content of the dream. It is then fairly easy to get from there to the latent dream thoughts.

For example, a client dreamed that he had missed the plane by first taking the wrong bus and then, once he got to the airport, going to the wrong terminal. Just as he arrived, he saw a plane pulling away from a different terminal and realized that it was his plane. In reporting the events of the day before, he said, almost in passing, that his wife had gone off in the family car without following her usual custom of telling him or leaving him a note. At the time he had shrugged it off because there was nowhere he wanted to go, and he was sure she would be back before the football game he was watching was over. And she was.

In recounting the events of the day before, the client identified the similarity between the dream and the day's events in terms of being left behind. This traced easily to his fear of abandonment, which was one of his major life themes, though he had denied consciously feeling abandoned when he discovered his wife's absence.

It would be possible to stop the interpretive process at this point. A link has been established between the day's residue and the manifest content of the dream. The latent content, however, has not yet been dealt with at all, nor is it apparent how this dream is a fulfillment of a wish, as nearly all dreams must be, within this theoretical framework for dream interpretation. Therefore, it is important to press on.

The dreamer's wife's failure to communicate with him before she left was, he had indicated, unusual, and the therapist asked why she had not done so. The dreamer replied that there had been some strain in their relationship over the past several days, although his wife had not gone off in a huff. The incident that had caused the strain was minor in itself, but it had touched off strong anger in the dreamer. His anger was related to some of his dissatisfactions with the marriage, which he felt unable to express because of his fear of driving his wife away (his words). Further exploration revealed the wish component of the dream: that his wife would have been on the plane that the dreamer missed. The dreamer offered that interpretation and the therapist accepted it. With the dreamer's consent, the therapist then invited comment from the other group members.

Further interpretation is possible, as are alternative interpretations. The therapist chose to stop at that level because he felt the dreamer's passivity and fear of expressing anger could be effectively dealt with in the group; fear of expressing anger, in particular, is likely to be common among group members.

But now let us suppose that the dreamer has gone through the day's events and nothing has suggested itself as relevant to the dream. The day was, in terms of the dream, unremarkable. The next possibility is the anticipated events of the following day. So if the client has told you about the events of Wednesday and than looks expectantly at you, and you feel a puzzlement that is probably shared by everyone else, you should say something like, "On Wednesday, what were you looking forward to on Thursday?" Or, simply, "What happened on Thursday?" In this instance, the kernel that gave rise to the dream still belongs to Wednesday because it was some anticipatory thought that occurred on that day. But the only way you can get to it is to ask about the following day.

Occasionally, the cause of the client's anticipation or worry is several days or weeks in the future. Rarely, the kernel of the dream will be an event that took place a day or two before the dream—an event the dreamer thought about on the day of the dream. Almost always, the major clue to the first-level interpretation of the dream will be found either in the events of the day or in the anticipated events of the following day.

Usually the client will make the connection between the day's events and the dream, but not always. The next place to look is in the affect. Ask the client, "What were your feelings during the dream?" As with other requests for affect, you may have to coach the client a bit. He or she may say something similar to, "I felt like I . . ." which is almost always a judgment rather than a feeling. Get a description of the feelings during the dream as detailed as you can. Then, explaining to the client that feelings during a dream are a reflection of something that was felt during the day preceding the dream, ask the client what he or she felt during that day that was at all similar to feelings he or she had in the dream.

may be necessary to track the process yourself: if the client mentions having felt fear in the dream, ask when during the day he or she felt even the slightest twinge of fear; or what he or she might be looking forward to on the following day, with some anxiety; and so on.

By this point, if the client has not acknowledged any relationship between thoughts, feelings, or actions during the day and the experiences during the dream, you may consider the possibility that he or she is being less than candid with you. If you suggest this possibility to the client, it will almost certainly be heard as an accusation, not only by the client (who may, nonetheless, know quite well what is going on) but also by the other group members. The issue is seldom worth risking a confrontation, and discretion may be preferable to disclosure here.

Another possibility is that, for some reason, the client is having more difficulty than usual gaining access to that part of his or her mind that knows the meaning of the dream. This possibility can be pursued in group. The client may be having difficulty with the interpretive process for several reasons.

- Having gotten a clearer picture of the dream through its telling and through the recounting of the day's events, the client is not yet ready to allow the underlying meaning of the dream into consciousness.
- The client may consciously see where the train of thought is leading and consciously choose not to go there, but may feel unable to put a more direct halt to the interpretive process.
- The client may fear the reactions or evaluations of the other group members if the dream interpretation is allowed to go on to completion.

All of these possibilities fall into the general category of *resistance*. In the psychoanalytic framework, resistance has to be analyzed and interpreted. In general, resistance should be treated as though it were a symptom, and, like symptoms, resistance is functional. Overcoming resistance should not be attempted unless its utility to the client is well understood and unless the client has something equally functional and healthier with which to replace it.

The three possible reasons for client difficulty with the interpretive process, as described above, are manifestations of resistance. You can talk about any or all of the three in group without having to use the term *resistance* and without trying to explain it to the group or even to convince them that there is such a thing that is causing the difficulty with dream interpretation. Such a move might work in a fairly sophisticated group, but it is not advisable otherwise unless you have been running a psychoanalytic group from the outset. In that case, you will have taught them the theoretical language already.

Gestalt Orientation

Gestalt therapy comprises a considerable range of therapeutic techniques based on a theory originated by Perls (1969; Perls, Hefferline, and Goodman, 1951) and elaborated, to some extent, by Erving and Miriam Polster (1973) and, beautifully, by Joseph Zinker (1977). The popularity of Gestalt therapy has waned from its heyday in the 1960s and early 1970s. But it has always had a core of dedicated practitioners who were, and are, superb therapists. It is this core group, now split into two or three schools, that is keeping a more conservative Gestalt orientation alive.

Gestalt therapy is usually practiced in a group format, that is, with several people and a therapist in the same room at the same time. However, it is not a group technique, but one-to-one in public. The therapist works intensely with one individual at a time, with the rest of the group looking on. Frequently a Gestalt therapist will ask the rest of the group to remain silent until he or she has completed working with the individual on the "hot seat," the focus of attention and energy. Some Gestalt techniques involve the group, but only as ancillary to the therapist as he or she works with the individual client. Harman (1984) has recently suggested that it is possible to retain a group orientation while practicing Gestalt therapy.

We will discuss here one Gestalt approach to dream interpretation. In this technique, there is a basic assumption that each component or element of the dream represents some aspect of the dreamer's own experience that has not been fully integrated into his or her own psyche. Such integration is highly desirable. The work of dream interpretation involves getting the dreamer to accept the various parts of the dream as integral to his or her psyche.

After you have contracted with the dreamer and he or she has told the dream once, uninterrupted, you should ask what the most vivid part of the dream was. Gestalters place a great deal of importance on the concept of *energy*, by which they mean mental or emotional energy or, sometimes, the amount of interest or importance placed on something. The most vivid part of the dream probably has the most energy. Gestalters follow a principle of "going with the energy," which is a way of saying that they focus on those aspects of a dream, or of a person's experience, that are most important to that person. Following the energy is a good and straight-forward way of doing so.

Here is an example of a dream and the beginning of Gestalt interpretation:

I was in an airliner, a big plane. I was sitting on the aisle, about three rows back. There were three seats on each side of the aisle, and all the seats were full—the plane was full. The stewardess was in the galley, which was at the front of the plane. All of a sudden, this man who had been sitting in the first row got up and turned around, facing backward. He had a gun, and he yelled that this was a hijacking and for everybody to put their heads down. There was a shout from the back of the plane, too, and I knew without looking that there was another hijacker back there. The one in front grabbed the stewardess and he kind of pointed the gun toward her, toward her head. As he did so, I came out of my seat, feeling a great

wave of enormous anger. I dove at him, roaring.
He wasn't sure whether to point the gun at the
stewardess or at me. As I was flying through the
air at him—this all happened in a split second—
he began to turn the gun toward me, and I
thought, My God, he's going to shoot me, and I
thought, No, no, no. But he didn't shoot, and I
knocked the gun away. As we started wrestling, I
tried to throw him over my shoulder. I got just a
glimpse of the hijacker in back, and there were
two people struggling with him. I was relieved
about that. But none of the other passengers
came forward to help me. "Come on, you bas-
tards," I screamed, "I need some help here!" But
nobody moved, and I subdued the hijacker
myself. I started to tell the other passengers what
I thought of them but then I remembered who I
was working for and didn't say anything. Then I
woke up.

Therapist: What was the most vivid part of the dream for
you?

Client: There were three parts that were really vivid. One was
right at first, just before the hijacker got up. It was the stewardess up front there, fixing coffee. She was beautiful. The
second part was as I was leaping at him and the gun was
turning from her head toward me. The third was when I was
wrestling him down and nobody moved.

Therapist: Of these three parts, which was most vivid or most
important? [Note that the therapist stays with the process of
getting the dreamer to identify the most vivid part, rather
than taking the three important elements one at a time.]

Client: The last part, wrestling with this guy in the aisle,
realizing that nobody else was moving.

Therapist: Of the wrestling and the realization that nobody
was moving, which was more important?

Client: Oh, the people not moving.

The essence of the technique is to ask the dreamer to take the part of, or become, each of the elements in the most vivid part of the dream. Here, the dreamer has identified the immobility of the other passengers as the most important component of this complex and highly polished dream.

Therapist: Would you imagine for a moment that you are one of those passengers, watching Don wrestle the hijacker to the floor?

Client: OK.

Therapist: What do you see?

Client: I see this man all of a sudden jump up out of his seat at this hijacker. The man has a look of, just, rage on his face. He knocks the hijacker's gun away and wrestles him to the floor.

Therapist: Don calls for help somewhere along in there.

Client: Yes, but he doesn't look like he needs help. He's doing just fine. Besides, if I went in there, I'd just be in the way.

Therapist: Well, now be Don again. How does that sound to you?

Client: Story of my life. I never look like I need help even when I need it the worst.

The therapist continued to work with Don, asking him alternately to be himself in the dream and then to be one of the passengers. The therapist considered asking Don to be either the stewardess or the hijacker, depending on which of those was more important to him. But it turned out, in this particular dream, that the part of himself that Don was having most difficulty with was his desire to be a passive onlooker—to let someone else tackle the problems that seemed to be taking his life in a direction he did not want it to go. (The latter concept of Don's life going in an unwanted direction was represented by the hijacker.) Don's aggressiveness, both in the dream and in group, was seen as an overreaction against his desire for passivity and as part of his struggle against his dependency needs.

The turning point in the interpretive process came when Don realized that it felt good to be a passenger looking at the struggle rather than being a participant. He was then able to put the interpretation together himself; thus he integrated the most salient components of the dream, and that was as far as he, and the therapist, wanted to go on this particular dream.

After that, the therapist invited comments from the other group members. They told Don that the conflict represented in the dream, and his reactions to it, were similar to the ways in which he related to them. Thus the dream served as a springboard for a group discussion of interpersonal behavior in group.

There are, of course, many other interpretations of this dream. It could, for example, be interpreted as a group dream, with the focal conflict going on between Don and one of the other group members while the rest of the group did nothing to give Don the support he wanted. The pilot might represent the therapist, or perhaps the two hijackers represent the coleaders. Such interpretations are consistent with the manifest content of the dream, but the actual interpretation did not unfold along those lines. In dream work, it is tempting to offer your own interpretations of the dream, especially when the meaning seems obvious to you.

Concluding Comments

The group therapist is constantly confronted with the dilemma of whether to focus on intrapsychic or on interpersonal events. Ideally, the focus will shift between intrapsychic and interpersonal, elucidating the relationship and interactions between the two. The problem is knowing how far into the intrapsychic to go, in the interpersonal context of group, and how much to focus on interpersonal here-and-now interactions that are strongly influenced, if not determined, by the intrapsychic dynamics of each group member.

Dreams are about as intrapsychic as you can get. If you solicit dreams, you may give the group the impression that you are going to focus on intrapsychic material at the expense of the interpersonal. But interpretation leads readily back to the here-and-now interpersonal situation in the group. Even in the more content-oriented approaches, the dream may be understood and explained, in part, in terms of current group dynamics.

In the interpersonal approach described in this chapter, the therapist responds to the dream in the same way that he or she would respond to any significant self-disclosure—in terms of its relevance to the interpersonal context of the group at the time the disclosure is offered. Yalom's interpersonal method (1985) is more content oriented, but it too relates the manifest content to current group issues.

With the psychoanalytic mode of dream interpretation described above, retaining the interpersonal orientation is more difficult. Once you have contracted with a client to work on a dream, the other group members must remain silent observers. Only when the work is done and an interpretation reached is it sometimes permissible for other group members to comment. As the other group members share their experiences or describe their own reactions to the dream or its interpretation, the focus may shift back to being more here-and-now interpersonal. But sometimes you may have to intervene actively to bring the group's attention back to the interpersonal context.

It is possible to understand or to interpret the dream as a manifestation of an underlying group theme or issue. Unless the relationship of the manifest dream to the group theme is clear, however, considerable care must be taken if you try to relate the dream to what has been going on in the group. Unless it is done quite carefully, the dreamer may feel that you are exploiting him or her for your own purposes, a feeling that may be shared by the other group members. Sensitivity of the dreamer and of the group to your using the dream in this way will depend in part on the extent to which they are accustomed to your following a psychoanalytic group orientation. If that is your usual method, the members should be prepared for a group-level dream interpretation. But if you are doing interpersonally oriented group therapy, and you use the psychoanalytically oriented technique only for dream interpretation, you will almost certainly have to exert some effort to refocus the group on the interpersonal when your dream interpretations are finished. The effort is well worth making.

The Gestalt technique is less intrapsychically oriented. It offers the opportunity for other group members to be involved in role play situations or, at times, to function as auxiliary therapists. But usually the roles are peripheral and there is little direct involvement by the other group members. Since the stage on which the interpretation is played out is in the group room rather than in the dreamer's head (contrary to the case with the psychoanalytic orientation), the experience of the dream is more accessible to the other group members, and they may report significant vicarious experiencing. As the group members report their vicarious reactions, the focus returns to here-and-now.

So, with all three of these techniques, you can effect a desirable end point by bringing the fact of dream interpretation, but not the dream itself, back into the unfolding process of the entire group. Telling the dream and interpreting it will have made some difference to the group as a whole, and it is important for you, as therapist, to describe what that difference is, as explicitly as possible. By doing this, you bring the intrapsychic explicitly into the interpersonal. The focus is once again on the group rather than on the individual, and it is easier to go on to the next topic.

Notes

1. In the discussion of Freud's theory of dreams, I have retained the hyphen in phrases such as dream-work, dream-thoughts, and dream-symbols, following his translator's usage.

Final Thoughts

In conclusion, I will pick up some loose ends that were left by the wayside in earlier chapters, and I will offer some concluding comments on the group therapy enterprise in general.

Open-Ended and Time-Limited Groups

The emphasis throughout the book is on open-ended groups, which continue indefinitely, with clients entering and leaving at various points. Because this is the most common model for groups in most clinics, I did not devote much attention to time-limited groups. The dynamics of time-limited groups are different from the dynamics of open-ended groups. Time-limited groups go through developmental stages, unlike most open-ended groups that go through such stages only if turnover is slow and membership stable over some period of time. However, in many clinics, the turnover rate is such that open-ended groups seldom get beyond the first or second developmental stage.

The reader will not, at this point, be surprised to learn that the number of developmental stages depends on the theorist rather than on the group. Bion (1961) and Whitaker and Lieberman (1964) describe three stages; Kellerman (1979) four; Beck (1981), writing from a systems theory perspective, nine;

MacKenzie and Livesley (1983), six. The MacKenzie and Livesley stages are: (1) engagement, (2) differentiation, (3) individuation, (4) intimacy, (5) mutuality, and (6) termination. Their thoughtful and concise paper is a good introduction for the reader who wishes to pursue developmental stage theory.

My own preference is for a three-stage concept: beginning, middle, and end. The beginning stage is characterized by introductory moves, the setting of the stage, as it were, and the gradual development of an atmosphere of warmth and supportiveness. The middle phase is the working phase in which people come to know and trust each other and to seek change in the problems that brought them into group therapy. The end phase involves assessment of the changes achieved, in terms of the initial agreement between therapist and group and in terms of new agreements which arose during the course of the group sessions. If turnover is slow, with changes in group membership occurring no more frequently than twice a year, an open-ended group will usually stay in the middle phase. If turnover is more rapid, the group may move between the first two phases. Most of the writers on developmental stages make similar observations, though they differ in terminology and degree of differentiation between one stage and another.

On Trusting One's Own Judgment

One theme running through the book is that there are many situations, from referral and screening through termination, in which ambiguity is high, in which there are no clear guidelines to indicate what to do, or in which there are many possible courses of action that appear equally good. In such situations I have encouraged the reader to use common sense and to trust his or her own instincts. Alternatives include attempting to extrapolate from what the book says or what your supervisor might say, looking to your cotherapist to deal with the situation, or remaining silent. When you feel great uncertainty, any of these three, and especially the last, may be entirely appropriate.

However, at some point you begin to formulate your own responses. My experience in training and supervising group therapists, over the years, has been that therapists new to group therapy formulate good responses and good decisions far more frequently than poor ones. In these instances, therapist reticence stems more from lack of confidence than it does from uncertainty about what to do. The sooner you begin to act on your intuitions or clinical judgments, the sooner you will be able to sharpen them and to have confidence in them. As you do that, you will begin to build your own sense of identity as a group therapist, different from your supervisor's. The process is similar to the process you went through in forming your sense of identity as an individual therapist, and it has similar benefits in terms of the immediacy and genuineness with which you are able to apply therapeutic principles and techniques.

On Tolerance

Another theme in the preceding chapters is that of tolerance for techniques and theories that differ from one's own. My own position, described in Chapter Three, is that growth and change are more likely to occur when needs are met than when needs are frustrated, and I emphasize contemporary, here-and-now interpersonal issues in the microcosm of the group session, and an orientation toward interpersonal change. But I have seen very powerful therapeutic work done in groups across a wide range of theoretical and technical approaches. Theories are used and techniques applied by therapists who differ widely in style, charisma, and other personality characteristics. Some data suggest that outcome, at least in very short-term groups, may be more closely related to such therapist characteristics than to the therapist's theoretical orientation (Lieberman, Yalom, and Miles, 1973).

The quest for truth is admirable; its attainment, dangerous. People who are certain they possess the truth are capable of considerable cruelty in the process of inflicting their truths upon others. This point has been eloquently made by

Jacob Bronowski (1973). Uncertainty leads readily to tolerance (what if the other fellow is right?), tolerance leads to multiplicity in viewpoint and theory, and multiplicity leads to an appreciation of the complexity, ambiguity, and transience that characterize reality.

The clinician or student who begins the study of group therapy (or, to some extent, of individual therapy) may receive indoctrination in a single theory or training in a single set of techniques. Too frequently, intolerance and belittling of rival theories accompanies the instruction. Tolerance of and respect for diversity is more likely to advance knowledge, technique, and effectiveness in group therapy (and in other fields) than is the comfortable, if implicit, assumption that one's own favorite theory has cornered the market on truth and beauty.

It is difficult to heed a plea for tolerance if you believe that harm is being done. Tolerance unhampered by prudent judgment may sanction the excesses generated by certainty. The belief of rival factions that the other people are hurting clients probably contributes to both the vehemence and the persistence of controversy. The precise limits of tolerance are difficult to define, but there is a consensus in the field represented by the codes of ethics of the various professional associations. These codes, however, pertain to individual actions, not to the tenets of theory.

Those theories of group therapy that have empirical support or are amenable to empirical investigation should be entitled to both tolerance and inquiry. Theories advocating in-group behavior that is far from the norms of everyday social interactions—of which Lowen's (1958) and Janov's (1970) are two examples—are deserving of our concern because, unhindered by any empirical support or social norms, their potential for doing harm is great. The excesses of the encounter movement, carefully documented by Yalom and his associates (Lieberman, Yalom, and Miles, 1973) are exemplary in this regard. When inquiries like Yalom's fail to demonstrate the safety of innovative group techniques, the limits of tolerance are defined.

The Politics of Group Therapy

The political aspects of a group therapy service comprise issues of power, status, and influence among the people who work in the clinic's or inpatient unit's health care delivery system. In outpatient clinics, there are usually at least five political entities: the administration, the medical staff, the nonmedical therapist staff, the ancillary staff, and the clerical support staff. In inpatient facilities, the nursing staff forms a sixth entity. Each of these entities can help or hinder the group therapy program. The more that key personnel in each of these entities understand and support what you are trying to do in the group therapy program, the greater will be the referral flow and the allocation of clinic resources necessary to support the delivery of group therapy services.

I did not find much in the literature pertaining to the politics of group therapy. There is a brief discussion in Mullan and Rosenbaum (1978). Yalom (1985) does not address the issue at all. Kadis and others (1974) devote a chapter to the development of an inpatient group therapy program in which they offer some helpful suggestions for program support.

The group therapy program often can be a barometer for staff relations in the clinic. If there is tension between the medical and nonmedical therapist staffs, the group therapy program can become a battleground on which issues of power and prestige are fought, but competent administrators can usually help by moving to address and reduce staff tensions and conflicts. Because the group therapy program is sensitive to stress and tension among the clinic staff or on the hospital ward, you will find it prudent to attend carefully to such tensions and to the ebb and flow of underlying staff conflicts. These conflicts are likely to influence the group interaction; knowing what they are and how intense they are helps you distinguish between tensions that arise within the group and those that represent a group response to external reality.

A Final Note

Some clinicians lead therapy groups because they have to; it is in their job descriptions. Others do it because they like to, whether it is in the job description or not. Usually, there is a lot going on in a group therapy session; the interactions are complex, there is an abundance of interpersonal stimuli, and things may happen so fast that there is no time for careful reflection before you have to say something. Some people like the high stimulus intensity, the challenges posed by the group situation, and the therapeutic work with several people simultaneously. Others do not, and those with a strong antipathy to group work probably do not do it very well. But if you like working with groups, the interpersonal context, the cohesiveness, the rich texture, and the complexity of the group experience, leading a therapy group can be one of the most rewarding experiences of your career.

References

American Group Psychotherapy Association. *Guidelines for the Training of Group Psychotherapists.* New York: American Group Psychotherapy Association, 1978.

American Psychiatric Association. *Diagnostic and Statistical Manual of Mental Disorders.* (3rd ed., rev.) Washington, D.C.: American Psychiatric Association, 1987.

Arieti, S. *The Narcissistic and Borderline Disorders: An Integrated Developmental Approach.* New York: Wiley-Interscience, 1981.

Arieti, S., and Rinsley, D. B. "The Borderline Syndrome: The Role of the Mother in the Genesis and Psychic Structure of the Borderline Personality." *International Journal of Psycho-Analysis,* 1975, *56,* 163–177.

Battegay, R., and von Marschall, R. "Results of Long-Term Group Psychotherapy with Schizophrenics." *Comprehensive Psychiatry,* 1978, *4,* 349–353.

Beck, A. P. "Developmental Characteristics of the System Forming Process." In J. E. Durkin (ed.), *Living Groups: Group Psychotherapy and General System Theory.* New York: Brunner/Mazel, 1981.

Beck, A. P. "The Participation of Leaders in the Structural Development of Therapy Groups." In R. Dies and K. R. MacKenzie (eds.), *Advances in Group Therapy: Integrating*

Research and Practice. American Group Psychotherapy Association Monograph Series, Monograph 1. New York: International Universities Press, 1983.

Beck, A. T. *Cognitive Therapy and the Emotional Disorders.* New York: International Universities Press, 1976.

Bednar, R. L., Melnick, J., and Kaul, T. J. "Risk, Responsibility, and Structure: A Conceptual Framework for Initiating Group Counseling and Psychotherapy." *Journal of Counseling Psychology,* 1974, *21,* 31–37.

Berzins, J. I., Friedman, W. H., and Ross, W. "Toward Patient-Therapist Matching." Unpublished manuscript, Indiana University at Bloomington, 1972.

Berzon, B., Pious, C., and Farson, R. "The Therapeutic Event in Group Psychotherapy: A Study of Subjective Reports by Group Members." *Journal of Individual Psychology,* 1963, *19,* 204–212.

Bion, W. *Experiences in Groups.* New York: Basic Books, 1961.

Bloch, B., and Crouch, E. *Therapeutic Factors in Group Psychotherapy.* Oxford, England: Oxford University Press, 1985.

Bond, G. R., and Lieberman, M. A. "Selection Criteria for Group Therapy." In J. P. Brady and H. K. H. Brodie (eds.), *Controversy in Psychiatry.* Philadelphia: Saunders, 1978.

Bowers, W., and Gauron, E. "Potential Hazards of the Co-Therapy Relationship." *Psychotherapy: Theory, Research, and Practice,* 1981, *18,* 225–228.

Bronowski, J. *The Ascent of Man.* Little, Brown, 1973.

Brook, D. "The Selection of Patients for Group Psychotherapy." *Issues in Ego Psychology,* 1980, *3,* 32–36.

Buda, B. "Das Borderline-Syndrom in Theorie und Praxis der Anstaltpsychiatrie" [The Borderline Syndrome in the Theory and Practice of Institutional Psychiatry]. *Dynamische Psychiatrie,* 1977, *10,* 144–153.

Cartwright, D. "The Nature of Group Cohesiveness." In D. Cartwright and A. Zander (eds.), *Group Dynamics: Research and Theory.* London: Tavistock, 1968.

Corsini, R., and Rosenberg, B. "Mechanisms of Group Psychotherapy: Processes and Dynamics." *Journal of Abnormal and Social Psychology,* 1955, *51,* 406–411.

Di Minicis, C., and Ranzato, F. P. "The Borderline as the Disrupting Element in Group Psychotherapy." *Rivista di Psichiatria*, 1969, *4*, 366–368.

Dies, R. "Group Therapist Self-Disclosure: An Evaluation by Clients." *Journal of Counseling Psychology*, 1973, *20*, 344–348.

Dies, R. "Group Psychotherapy: Training and Supervision." In A. Hess (ed.), *Psychotherapy Supervision: Theory, Research, and Practice*. New York: Wiley, 1980.

Dies, R. "Clinical Implications of Research on Leadership in Short-Term Groups." In R. Dies and K. MacKenzie (eds.), *Advances in Group Psychotherapy: Integrating Research and Practice*. American Group Psychotherapy Association Monograph Series, Monograph 1. New York: International Universities Press, 1983.

Dollard, J., and others. *Frustration and Aggression*. New Haven, Conn.: Yale University Press, 1939.

Durkin, J. E. (ed.). *Living Groups: Group Psychotherapy and General System Theory*. New York: Brunner/Mazel, 1981.

Ebersole, G., Leiderman, P., and Yalom, I. "Training the Nonprofessional Group Therapist." *Journal of Nervous and Mental Disease*, 1969, *149*, 294–302.

Ellis, A. *Reason and Emotion in Psychotherapy*. New York: Lyle Stuart, 1962.

Erickson, R. *Inpatient Small Group Psychotherapy*. Springfield, Ill.: Thomas, 1984.

Ezriel, H. "Psychoanalytic Group Therapy." In L. R. Wolberg and E. K. Schwartz (eds.), *Group Therapy*. New York: Intercontinental Medical Book Corporation, 1973.

Fielding, J. "Verbal Participation and Group Therapy Outcome." *British Journal of Psychiatry*, 1983, *142*, 524–528.

Filippi, L. "Psicoterapia Psycoanalitica 'Combinata' di Gruppo e Individuale, Consoggetti Borderline" [Combined Group and Individual Psychoanalytic Psychotherapy with Borderline Individuals: Results of 15 Years of Treatments]. *Archivio di Psicologia, Neurologia e Psichiatria*, 1983, *44*, 289–298.

Flapan, D. "The Borderline Patient in Group Psychotherapy." *Issues in Ego Psychology*, 1983, *6*, 52–57.

Flapan, D., and Fenchel, G. H. "Group Member Contacts Without the Group Therapist." *Group*, 1983, 7, 3–16.

Flowers, J. "The Differential Outcome Effects of Simple Advice, Alternatives, and Instructions in Group Psychotherapy." *International Journal of Group Psychotherapy*, 1979, *29*, 305–316.

Foulkes, S. A., and Anthony, E. J. *Group Psychotherapy: The Psychoanalytic Approach*. (2nd ed.) Baltimore: Penguin Books, 1965.

Freud, S. *Group Psychology and the Analysis of the Ego*. New York: Hogarth, 1949. (Originally published 1922.)

Freud, S. *The Interpretation of Dreams*. New York: Basic Books, 1955. (Originally published 1900.)

Friedman, W. H. *How to Do Groups: A Brief Introduction to Group Psychotherapy*. New York: Jason Aronson, 1979.

Friedman, W. H. "Group Cognitive Therapy for Older Adults." *Contemporary Psychiatry*, 1987, *6*, 97–99.

Friedman, W. H., Jelly, E., and Jelly, P. "Group Therapy in Family Medicine: II. Establishing the Group." *Journal of Family Practice*, 1978, *6*, 1243–1247.

Glatzer, H. "The Working Alliance in Analytic Group Psychotherapy." *International Journal of Group Psychotherapy*, 1978, *28*, 147–161.

Goodpastor, W. A. "A Social Learning Approach to Group Psychotherapy for Hospitalized DSM-III Borderline Patients." *Journal of Psychiatric Treatment and Evaluation*, 1983, *5*, 331–335.

Grinker, R. R. "The Borderline Syndrome: A Phenomenological View." In P. Hartocollis (ed.), *Borderline Personality Disorders*. New York: International Universities Press, 1977.

Grotjahn, M. "Basic Guidelines for the Conduct of Hospital Groups." In M. Grotjahn, F. M. Kline, and C. T. H. Friedmann, *Handbook of Group Therapy*. New York: Van Nostrand Reinhold, 1983.

Gurman, A. S., and Razin, A. M. (eds.). *Effective Psychotherapy: A Handbook of Research*. Elmsford, N.Y.: Pergamon Press, 1977.

Hall, C., and Lindzey, G. *Theories of Personality.* New York: Wiley, 1957.

Harman, R. "Gestalt Therapy Research." *Gestalt Journal,* 1984, *7,* 61–69.

Hartocollis, P. (ed.). *Borderline Personality Disorders.* New York: International Universities Press, 1977.

Hawkins, D. M., and White, E. M. "Indications for Group Psychotherapy." In J. P. Brady and H. K. H. Brodie (eds.), *Controversy in Psychiatry.* Philadelphia: Saunders, 1978.

Heckel, R. V., and Salzberg, H. C. *Group Psychotherapy: A Behavioral Approach.* Columbia: University of South Carolina Press, 1976.

Hill, W. F. "Analysis of Interviews of Group Therapists." *Provo Papers,* 1957, *1,* 1.

Horwitz, L. "Group Psychotherapy of the Borderline Patient." In P. Hartocollis (ed.), *Borderline Personality Disorders.* New York: International Universities Press, 1977.

Horwitz, L. "Group Psychotherapy for Borderline and Narcissistic Patients." *Bulletin of the Menninger Clinic,* 1980, *44,* 181–200.

Hurst, A. "Leadership Style Determinants of Cohesiveness in Adolescent Groups." *International Journal of Group Psychotherapy,* 1978, *28,* 263–279.

Janov, A. *The Primal Scream.* New York: Putnam, 1970.

Kadis, A. L., and others. *Practicum of Group Psychotherapy.* (2nd ed.) Hagerstown, Md.: Medical Division, Harper & Row, 1974.

Kadis, A. L., and Winick, C. "Fees in Group Therapy." *American Journal of Psychotherapy,* 1968, *22,* 60–67.

Kaplan, H. I., and Sadock, B. J. (eds.). *Comprehensive Group Psychotherapy.* Baltimore: Williams & Wilkins, 1972.

Kellerman, H. *Group Psychotherapy and Personality: Intersecting Structures.* Orlando, Fla.: Grune & Stratton, 1979.

Kernberg, O. F. *Borderline Conditions and Pathological Narcissism.* New York: Jason Aronson, 1975.

Kinder, B. N., and Kilman, P. R. "The Impact of Differential Shifts in Leader Structure on the Outcome of Internal and

External Group Participants." *Journal of Clinical Psychology*, 1976, *32*, 848–856.

Kissen, M. *From Group Dynamics to Group Psychoanalysis: Therapeutic Applications of Group Dynamic Understanding.* Washington, D.C.: Hemisphere, 1976.

Klett, W. "The Effect of Historically Based Inferences on the Behavior of Withdrawn Psychiatric Patients." *Journal of Clinical Psychology*, 1966, *22*, 427–429.

Kohut, H. *The Analysis of the Self.* New York: International Universities Press, 1971.

Kohut, H. *The Restoration of the Self.* New York: International Universities Press, 1977.

Kolb, G. E. "Group Therapy in an Outpatient Setting with Borderline and Narcissistic Delinquents on Probation." *Group*, 1983, *7*, 38–47.

Kosch, G., and Reiner, C. "The Co-Therapy Relationship: Mutuality, Agreement, and Client Outcome." *Journal of Contemporary Psychotherapy*, 1984, *14*, 145–157.

Krumboltz, J., and Potter B. "Behavioral Techniques for Developing Trust, Cohesiveness and Goal Accomplishment." *Educational Technology*, 1973, *13*, 26–30.

Lakin, M. *Interpersonal Encounter: Theory and Practice in Sensitivity Training.* New York: McGraw-Hill, 1972.

Lakin, M. *The Helping Group: Therapeutic Principles and Issues.* Reading, Mass.: Addison-Wesley, 1985.

Lewin, K. *A Dynamic Theory of Personality.* New York: McGraw-Hill, 1935.

Liberman, R. "A Behavioral Approach to Group Dynamics: I. Reinforcement and Prompting of Cohesiveness in Group Therapy." *Behavior Therapy*, 1970a, *1*, 141–175.

Liberman, R. "A Behavioral Approach to Group Dynamics: II. Reinforcing and Prompting Hostility to the Therapist in Group Therapy." *Behavior Therapy*, 1970b, *1*, 312–327.

Lieberman, M. "Comparative Analysis of Change Mechanisms in Groups." In R. Dies and K. R. MacKenzie (eds.), *Advances in Group Therapy: Integrating Research and Practice.* American Group Psychological Association Monograph Series, Monograph 1. New York: International Universities Press, 1983.

Lieberman, M., Yalom, I., and Miles, M. *Encounter Groups: First Facts.* New York: Basic Books, 1973.

Low, P., and Low, M. "Treatment of Married Couples in a Group Run by a Husband and Wife." *International Journal of Group Psychotherapy*, 1975, *25*, 54–66.

Lowen, A. *The Language of the Body.* New York: MacMillan, 1958.

Macaskill, N. D. "Therapeutic Factors in Group Therapy with Borderline Patients." *International Journal of Group Psychotherapy*, 1982, *32*, 61–73.

MacKenzie, K. R., and Livesley, W. J. "A Developmental Model for Brief Group Therapy." In R. Dies and K. R. MacKenzie (eds.), *Advances in Group Therapy: Integrating Research and Practice.* American Group Psychological Association Monograph Series, Monograph 1. New York: International Universities Press, 1983.

McMahon, N., and Links, P. S. "Cotherapy: The Need for Positive Pairing." *Canadian Journal of Psychiatry*, 1984, *29*, 385–389.

Maslow, A. *Toward a Psychology of Being.* New York: D. Van Nostrand, 1968.

Masterson, J. F. *Treatment of the Borderline Adolescent: A Developmental Approach.* New York: Wiley-Interscience, 1972.

Masterson, J. F. "Intensive Psychotherapy of the Adolescent with a Borderline Syndrome." In S. Arieti and others (eds.), *American Handbook of Psychiatry, rev. ed.* Vol. 2. New York: Basic Books, 1974.

Masterson, J. F. *The Narcissistic and Borderline Personality Disorders: An Integrated Developmental Approach.* New York: Brunner/Mazel, 1981.

Masterson, J. F., and Rinsley, D. B. "The Borderline Syndrome: The Role of the Mother in the Genesis and Psychic Structure of the Borderline Personality." *International Journal of Psycho-Analysis*, 1975, *56*, 163–177.

Maxmen, J. "Group Therapy as Viewed by Hospitalized Patients." *Archives of General Psychiatry*, 1973, *28*, 404-408.

Maxmen, J. "An Educative Model for Inpatient Group Therapy." *International Journal of Group Psychotherapy*, 1978, *29*, 321-338.

Meichenbaum, D. *Cognitive-Behavior Modification: An Integrative Approach.* New York: Plenum, 1977.

Moreno, J. L. *Psychodrama.* New York: Beacon House, 1946.

Mullan, H., and Rosenbaum, M. *Group Psychotherapy: Theory and Practice.* (2nd ed.) New York: Free Press, 1978.

O'Brien, C. "Group Theory for Schizophrenia: A Practical Approach." *Schizophrenia Bulletin*, 1975, *13*, 119-130.

Ondaraza Linares, J. "Some Group Phenomena in Borderline Patients: Introductory Considerations." *Rivista di Psichiatria*, 1969, *4*, 381-388.

Paulson, I., Burroughs, J., and Gelb, C. "Cotherapy: What Is the Crux of the Relationship?" *International Journal of Group Psychotherapy*, 1976, *26*, 213-224.

Perls, F. *Gestalt Therapy Verbatim.* Lafayette, Calif.: Real People Press, 1969.

Perls, F., Hefferline, R., and Goodman, P. *Gestalt Therapy: Excitement and Growth in the Human Personality,* New York: Dell, 1951.

Persic-Brida, M. "Institucionalna Grupna Psyhoterapija Granicnih Slucajeva." *Socijalna Psihijatrija*, 1984, *12*, 315-321.

Pesso, A. *Experience in Action.* New York: New York University Press, 1973.

Pines, M. "Group Analytic Psychotherapy and the Borderline Patient." *Analytic Psychotherapy and Psychopathology*, 1984, *1*, 57-70.

Piper, W. E., and McCallum, M. "Short-Term Analytic Groups for Patients with Person Losses." Paper presented at 45th annual conference of the American Group Psychotherapy Association, New York, February, 1988.

Polster, E., and Polster, M. *Gestalt Therapy Integrated.* New York: Brunner/Mazel, 1973.

Power, M. "The Selection of Patients for Group Therapy." *International Journal of Social Psychiatry*, 1985, *18*, 290-297.

Rinsley, D. B. "An Object Relations View of Borderline Personality." In P. Hartocollis (ed.), *Borderline Personality Disorders*. New York: International Universities Press, 1977.

Rioch, M. "The Work of Wilfred Bion on Groups." *Psychiatry*, 1970, *33*, 56–66.

Robinson, D. *Systems of Modern Psychology*. New York: Columbia University Press, 1979.

Rogers, C. *Client-Centered Therapy*. Boston: Houghton Mifflin, 1951.

Rose, S. D. *Group Therapy: A Behavioral Approach*. Englewood Cliffs, N.J.: Prentice-Hall, 1977.

Rosenbaum, M. "The Co-Therapeutic Method in the Psychoanalytic Group." In H. Mullen and M. Rosenbaum (eds.), *Group Psychotherapy: Theory and Practice*. (2nd ed.) New York: Free Press, 1978.

Rosenthal, L. "Resistance in Group Therapy: The Interrelationship of Individual and Group Resistance." In L. R. Wolberg and M. L. Aronson (eds.), *Group and Family Therapy 1980*. New York: Brunner/Mazel, 1980.

Roth, B. E. "Six Types of Borderline and Narcissistic Patients: An Initial Typology." *International Journal of Group Psychotherapy*, 1982, *32*, 9–27.

Ruger, U. "Die Stationär-ambulante Gruppenpsychotherapie—Ergebnisse im Hinblick auf Änderungen im Bereich von Symptomatik und Persönlichkeitsstruktur" [The Outcome of Outpatient Group Psychotherapy with Regard to Change in the Domain of Symptoms and Personality Structure]. *Zeitschrift für Psychosomatische Medizin und Psychoanalyse*, 1982, *28*, 189–199.

Russell, A., and Russell, L. "The Uses and Abuses of Cotherapy." *Advances in Family Psychiatry*, 1980, *2*, 401–410.

Rutan, S., and Stone, W. *Psychodynamic Group Psychotherapy*. Lexington, Mass.: D. C. Heath, 1984.

Sank, L., and Shaffer, C. *A Therapist's Manual for Cognitive Behavioral Therapy in Groups*. New York: Plenum, 1984.

Shaffer, J. B., and Galinsky, M. D. *Models of Group Therapy and Sensitivity Training*. Englewood Cliffs, N.J.: Prentice-Hall, 1974.

Shaskan, D. A. "Successful Signs in Borderlines." *Group, A Journal of Group Dynamics and Psychotherapy,* 1974, *6,* 15–17.

Slavinska-Holy, N. "Combining Individual and Homogeneous Group Psychotherapies for Borderline Conditions." *International Journal of Group Psychotherapy,* 1983, *33,* 297–312.

Slavson, S. R. *Analytic Group Psychotherapy.* New York: Columbia University Press, 1950.

Spitz, H., Kass, F., and Charles, E. "Common Mistakes Made in Group Psychotherapy by Beginning Therapists." *American Journal of Psychiatry,* 1980, *137,* 1619–1621.

Stone, W. N., and Gustafson, J. P. "Technique in Group Psychotherapy of Narcissistic and Borderline Patients." *International Journal of Group Psychotherapy,* 1982, *32,* 29–47.

Szasz, T. *The Myth of Mental Illness.* New York: Hoeber/ Harper, 1956.

Tahacchetti, L. "Il Paziente Borderline in Psicoterapia di Gruppo" [The Borderline Patient in Group Psychotherapy]. *Rivista Sperimentale di Freniatria e Medicina Legale della Alienazioni Mentali,* 1984, *108,* 91–117.

Toseland, R., and Siporin, M. "When to Recommend Group Treatment: A Review of the Clinical and the Research Literature." *International Journal of Group Psychotherapy,* 1986, *36,* 171–201.

Truax, C. B. "Therapist Empathy, Warmth, and Genuineness and Patient Personality Change in Group Psychotherapy: A Comparison Between Interaction Unit Measures, Time Sample Measures, Patient Perception Measures." *Journal of Clinical Psychology,* 1966, *22,* 225–229.

Truax, C. B., and Carkhuff, R. *Toward Effective Counseling and Psychotherapy: Training and Practice.* Hawthorne, N.Y.: Aldine, 1967.

Truax, C. B., and Wargo, D. G. "Effects of Vicarious Therapy Pretraining and Alternate Sessions on Outcome in Group Psychotherapy with Outpatients." *Journal of Consulting and Clinical Psychology,* 1969, *33,* 440–447.

Tuttman, S. "Applications of Object Relations Theory and Self-Psychology in Current Group Therapy." *Group,* 1984, *8,* 41–48.

Weiner, M. "Genetic Versus Interpersonal Insight." *International Journal of Group Psychotherapy*, 1974, *24*, 230–237.

Weiner, M. *Techniques of Group Psychotherapy*. Washington, D.C.: American Psychiatric Press, 1984.

Weisselberger, D. "Sexual Acting Out in Group Psychotherapy: A Reassessment." *Groups: A Journal of Group Dynamics and Psychotherapy*, 1975, *7*, 35–37.

Whitaker, D., and Lieberman, M. *Psychotherapy Through the Group Process*. New York: Atherton, 1964.

Winick, C., and Weiner, M. F. "Professional Activities and Training of AGPA Members: A View over Two Decades." *International Journal of Group Psychotherapy*, 1986, *36*, 471–476.

Wolberg, A. R. "The Uncovering of Family Dynamics in Psychoanalytic, Individual, and Group Treatment of Borderline Patients Using a Dynamic-Danger-Stress-Defense Model." *Dynamic Psychotherapy*, 1985, *3*, 3–26.

Wolf, A., and Kutash, I. L. "Di-egophrenia and Its Treatment Through Psychoanalysis in Groups." *International Journal of Group Psychotherapy*, 1985, *35*, 519–530.

Wolf, A., and Schwartz, E. K. *Psychoanalysis in Groups*. Orlando, Fla.: Grune & Stratton, 1962.

Wolf, A., and Schwartz, E. K. "Psychoanalysis in Groups." In H. Kaplan and B. Sadock (eds.), *Comprehensive Group Psychotherapy*. Baltimore: Williams & Wilkins, 1971.

Yalom, I. *Inpatient Group Psychotherapy*. New York: Basic Books, 1983.

Yalom, I. *The Theory and Practice of Group Psychotherapy*. (3rd ed.) New York: Basic Books, 1985.

Yost, E., Beutler, L., Corbishley, M. A., and Allender, J. *Group Cognitive Therapy: A Treatment Approach for Depressed Older Adults*. Elmsford, N.Y.: Pergamon Press, 1986.

Zinker, J. *Creative Process in Gestalt Therapy*. New York: Brunner/Mazel, 1977.

Index